SHOW WINDOW

ELMER DAVIS

NEW YORK

THE JOHN DAY COMPANY

1927

PRINTED IN THE U. S. A.
FOR THE JOHN DAY COMPANY, INC.
BY THE QUINN & BODEN COMPANY, RAHWAY, N. J.

To

E. M. KINGSBURY

ABOUT THE AUTHOR

ELMER DAVIS was born at Aurora, Indiana, in 1890. He studied at Franklin College and at Queen's College, Oxford.

For ten years he was on the staff of *The New York Times,* first as a reporter, later as an editorial writer.

His novels include *Times Have Changed, I'll Show You the Town, Friends of Mr. Sweeney* and *Strange Woman.*

ACKNOWLEDGMENT

I extend my gratitude to the editors of *Harper's Magazine, The Saturday Review of Literature,* the *New York Times* Review of Books, *Collier's Weekly, Beach's Book Notes, The American Hebrew,* and *The New Yorker* for permission to republish various portions of this material.

ELMER DAVIS

Douglas Manor, New York
30 *June* 1927

CONTENTS

	PAGE
TO YOU, WHOEVER YOU ARE	3
THE AGE OF IMPOTENCE	6
THE PRIVATE LIFE OF PARIS OF TROY	58
THE COMSTOCK LOAD: Reflections on Censorship	71
THE GENTLEMAN FROM VERONA	94
THE PASSING OF THE GREAT RACE	105
BEDS OF IVORY: A Note on Contemporary Anti-Semitism	116
PROLEGOMENA TO A FUTURE CHRISTOLOGY	132
REMARKS ON THE PERFECT STATE	164
HAVE FAITH IN INDIANA	191
PORTRAIT OF AN ELECTED PERSON	218
PORTRAIT OF A CLERIC	257

SHOW WINDOW

TO YOU, WHOEVER YOU ARE

"THIS book lacks unity," complained a man who looked over the manuscript. "There may be good reasons for it, but you ought to give your readers some excuse."

But I shall not. Whoever asks two dollars and a half for a collection of his opinions has already committed an act of effrontery beyond any excuse but one —that the book is worth two dollars and a half; as I believe this one is. Yet, for the benefit of those cautious customers who prefer to look over the first page or two before laying down their money, it should be said in all candor that you probably won't like it.

For most of us incline to think a book is good if it inspires the reflection, "I have always felt that way myself"; and I am afraid these opinions are deplorably unorthodox. Deplorably, for I have passed the age when unorthodoxy seems praiseworthy in itself. It is expensive; it reduces one's reputation and limits one's income; and whether or not it is worth the cost depends on what one is unorthodox about.

Certainly for a little time, a few years ago, unorthodoxy was the surest road to fame and fortune; but that was only because it was becoming orthodoxy. Persons who spat in the face of accepted American tradition in the early years of this decade prospered as notably as people who bought land, about the same time, on the water front of Lake Worth or Biscayne

Bay, and for the same reason—they were lucky enough to arrive just ahead of the crowd. (Some of them appear to suspect now that their movement, like Florida, is going to suffer a slump, and they are unloading quietly before the market breaks.) But at this felicitous moment in time, when the most standardized of American institutions is the revolt against standardization, this great republic is doubly blessed with two competing brands of orthodoxy, differing in everything else but alike in the conviction of each that it is the sole authorized purveyor of revealed truth.

These following opinions must seem damnable heresies to both sides. I am so unfortunate as not to belong to a gang, in an age when gang thinking is pretty nearly all the thinking there is; I am as unable to believe in the divine commission and verbal inspiration of Henry Louis Mencken as in that of Calvin Coolidge. Which is not to claim that I have made any original discoveries, or offer a unique point of view; I suspect that if some taxonomist of opinion took the trouble to classify the writers of the United States I should be listed in a subspecies (probably tagged with the comment, *Rare and Obsolescent*) whose other members would be Mr. Simeon Strunsky and Mr. Lee Wilson Dodd. There are, it may be hoped, some people who agree with us. But if you are convinced that eternal truth, still wrapped up in the original package, can be found in the editorials in the *Nation,* or in the remarks of the White House Spokesman, go down to the other end of the counter and buy a copy of *Elmer Gantry* or *The Plutocrat,* according to taste.

If any excuse is needed for assembling in one volume

commentaries on literature, religion, and politics, it may be found in the fact that truly devout persons, in the Christian Era at least, have commonly regarded politics as a subdivision of religion; and now that we are perhaps passing into an Anti-Christian Era, religion has annexed art and letters as well. To the new orthodoxy not only what you say, but the very language in which you say it, has become a matter of dogma. It would not surprise me very much if within a few decades men and women were being burned at the stake for writing "police" instead of "Polizei," and leaving the "o" out of "Americanos." If the idea startles you, consider that a third-century Roman Senator would have been equally amazed by the news that his grandson would be butchered for entertaining incorrect opinions as to the divine and human natures in Christ.

Meanwhile, thanks to the temporary happy balance between Right Wing and Left, Babbitts and Rabbits, we live in a moment of equilibrium in which neither faction, at least in the larger cities, controls the secular arm. *Rara temporum felicitas, ubi quæ velis sentire et quæ sentis dicere liceat.* In this brief interlude between consecrated man hunts, I venture to emit these opinions, in the hope that they may find favor with such scattered persons as have not bowed the knee to Baal, whether that deity be locally worshiped in the form of an acid Vermont Yankee or a chubby Baltimore German.

But if you don't like the book, don't say you were not warned.

THE AGE OF IMPOTENCE

THE accord of Locarno was saluted as marking the end of that famous and deplorable war psychology, which was responsible for so much evil, and bore the odium of so much more that sprang from nothing but the ordinary cussedness of human nature. After the lapse of a little time, one perceives that some of this jubilation was premature; despite Locarno, a number of persons remain unreconstructed, among them Raymond Poincaré and Harry Elmer Barnes. I would not be unjust to either of these talented and hard-working gentlemen, but they have both acquired their present standing by the championship of issues which are part of the war psychology. To adjust themselves to the new interests of a changing time would require an effort, and perhaps the admission that some of the old issues were no longer so all-important as they used to be; so naturally these publicists, and numerous others of their kind, can be depended on to wave the bloody shirt so long as their strength holds out.

So is it with the equally famous and deplorable post-war psychology in literature.[1] Just as much so-called war psychology was only normal envy or

[1] Recent literature is here dealt with from the standpoint of contemporary controversy. A later chapter, "The Passing of the Great Race," treats more briefly of the same period as it may conceivably appear to a more enlightened posterity. I hope I shall not be damned as a Victorian optimist for admitting the hope that posterity will be somewhat more enlightened.

cupidity, to which the war and its consequences gave
abnormal scope, so much of this post-war disillusionment was no more than a perfectly natural gutless
laziness, into which the average member of the human
race is inclined to lapse whenever circumstances permit
him to get away with it; and which in the curious dis-
tortion of values, or denial òf all values, obtaining of
late years, was accounted to its victims for merit.
That too is drawing to an end; the domination of literature in America and Europe by the Invertebrate
school is passing, so visibly that some of these following observations may seem like broadsides fired after
an enemy in full retreat.

But here again too much jubilation would be premature. For as the war-time politician clings to his old
issues as long as he can, so a good many writers who
found fame and fortune in the days of easy pickings,
when a man had only to write the history of his own
amours in verbless sentences to be acclaimed a genius,
will not consent to work for a living until they are
driven to it. I do not suppose that the life of the writer
was ever so easy in all history as it has been in the past
decade—not even in the days of Pliny the Younger,
when every Roman gentleman wrote poetry, and spent
all his spare time reading it to his friends or listening
politely while his friends read to him. For while the
content of those poems was probably pretty poor, their
authors at least regarded themselves as constrained to
observe the laws of prosody; whereas in the late happy
days the breaking of all the rules of syntax was as
absolute a prerequisite to renown as the breaking of
the Seventh Commandment.

Never was it easier to write, and never was writing more opulently rewarded, in credit if not always in cash. It is only a year or two since a critic of high standing, concluding a two-thousand-word review of some book or other already forgotten, observed with perceptible uneasiness, "For some reason, it is impossible to call this novel great." Evidently he felt that if it isn't great it isn't a novel. Nor was he by any means alone in this way of thinking. Just as the traditional Southerner was never taught to distinguish between adjective and substantive elements in "damnyankee," young people who have grown up since the war must think that "greatnovel" is one word.

Well, those days are drawing to an end; and some writers who flourished in the fat years, reading the signs of the times, are trying to reëducate themselves into a new trade like any other disabled war veterans. But there are enough of them who are determined to fight it out on the same old line to make it worth while spending a little space on examination of this literature of post-war disillusionment. There seems more danger that the evil the Invertebrate writers have done will live after them than that the good will be interred with their bones.

For there was plenty of good in them. It could hardly be denied that American literature, at least, in the decade after the war, was immensely better than in the decade before the war. There was a release from old restraints; there was unlimited freedom for experiment and innovation. But in literature as in politics few people seemed to know just what to do with the new freedom. There were many brave beginnings, but few enterprises carried through to any sort of conclusion. Writers who experimented in a new technique seemed to think they need waste no time learning even the most thoroughly tested fundamentals of the old technique; as if, to employ the customary illustration, a mathematician should feel that the theory of relativity dispensed with the necessity of mastering the multiplication table.

And, with all the new values that the new writers brought into literature, certain old values were conspicuously lacking from the most approved exemplars of the new movement. That there was, on the whole, an increase in candor and clarity no one could deny; but there was a depressing lack of suavity, of humor, of courage—the last the most fundamental of human virtues, the first two the virtues which ought to be the peculiar flower and distinction of civilized man. The characteristic gestures of post-war literature are the acid snarl, the despairing groan, and the shrug of a possibly premature resignation.

HERE a little relativity would have done some of our authors a great deal of good. Their faults sprang from a too great concentration on Things As They Are, or, perhaps more exactly, Things As They Seem to Be. The business of an artist, however, is not with either appearance or reality, but with the reconstruction of phenomena into a more sightly pattern, a rebuilding nearer to his (and, quite as important, to his public's) heart's desire. The post-war writers were often reminded of this, notably by Mr. Cabell, who might be supposed to have some authority; yet his excellent esthetic doctrines seem to have had no more effect on most of his contemporaries than water on a duck.

If you believe the textbook on geology prescribed for the schools of Tennessee, the earth, prior to nine o'clock in the morning of September 21, 4004 B.C., was *tohu* and *bohu*, without form and void. If you believe T. S. Eliot, William Gerhardi, Rose Macaulay, Aldous Huxley, John dos Passos, Ernest Hemingway, John Gunther and the rest of their school, it is that even now. Life is meaningless, effort is futile, the perceptible phenomena of existence have no interrelation.

I am far from denying it. I do not pretend to discern any unifying or arranging principle in the data of human affairs, and while in my quality of member of the human race I am depressed by the thought that after all this time we have got nowhere (if these authors are right about it) but back to the starting point, I would not allow the local patriotism of a resident of this planet to blind me to the facts. But even if life is without form and void, it does not follow that the novels dealing with life must also be without form and void. Suppose life is chaos—full of sound and fury, as Miss Macaulay assures us, signifying nothing. Whatever life may be, two dollars is two dollars; and two dollars will buy a current novel or a quart of kitchen-stove gin. Persons who live by selling the books they write are obviously interested in persuading the customers to spend their money for the novel.

The manufacturing novelist goes into this commercial competition with one great advantage over the bootlegger; he knows, as a rule, the charms of the rival attraction; the novelist usually drinks gin, whereas the bootlegger rarely reads novels. The novelist knows exactly what gin gives the consumer; how, then, is he to persuade him to buy a novel instead? Obviously by meeting the needs of the trade; and by failing to do this, novelists of the Chaotic, Invertebrate, or Futilitarian school have worked considerable harm to the interest of the industry at large.

What are the needs of the trade? Well, what does the average citizen want, when he has perceived that life is meaningless and that nothing can be done about it? If he has any sense at all, he wants to forget it. He wants something that will give him a sense of order, even fictitious order; a meaning that he can enjoy, even though he knows (or will know when he sobers up) that the meaning is wholly artificial. He wants to see life as an arrangement of some symmetry and significance, in which he himself occupies a position not without dignity.

He can get exactly this gratification, if he spends his two dollars for gin; but of late years it has been extremely difficult to get it out of the contemporary novel. Gin veils life with a roseate mist and endows its phenomena with unnatural magnitude and factitious importance; which is exactly what art ought to do, and must do, if artists expect to make a living out of it. Whatever its merits, a book such as Mr. Gerhardi's *Polyglots*, or Miss Macaulay's *Told by an Idiot*, or Mr. dos Passos' *Manhattan Transfer*, is treason to the working class, a deadly blow at the goose that lays the golden eggs. For if the customers on whom novelists depend for their bread and butter find in fiction only the futility and chaos they have already found, and are likely to keep on finding, in life, they will go to gin, quite sensibly, for the illusion that art ought to furnish.

Whatever you may think of the Futilitarian novelists as artists, biologically they are degenerates. They have gone shamelessly back to the Stone Age. For so life must have appeared to the first man who speculated about it at all—futility and chaos, without form and void. And the reason we are not living in the Stone Age at present is that the tendency of most men, confronted with inexplicable chaos, is to try to explain it none the less—to read into it some sort of order, to cling to that order till it is plainly seen to be untenable, and then to invent some other order more nearly in accord with the evidence.

The first order, naturally, is a crude primitive animism. Every object of sense perception has in it some latent power of evil. Some of the Futilitarians have risen that far, which is at least one step above the primitive chaos, but none of them have gone any farther. And one cannot help feeling that there is more hope for the devil worshipers who see in the faults of our age the workings of certain Wicked Old Men at Versailles than for the reactionary Chaotics who cling to their dogma of the emptiness of everything as stubbornly (and, one suspects, as fearfully) as the late Mr. Bryan clung to Jonah and the Whale.

But, says your Futilitarian, we must Face the Facts. We must Tell the Truth. For an adequate answer to that one need go no farther than that much underrated gentleman, Pontius Pilate. "What is Truth?" he asked, and stayed not for an answer. If he had, he would be waiting yet. Personally, I am inclined to provisional

agreement with the metaphysics of the Futilitarians.
So far as I can see, all is vanity and vexation of spirit.
But I am not convinced that I have attained to intui-
tive perception of ultimate truth, even though Aldous
Huxley and T. S. Eliot happen to agree with me.

Granted that what we see is chaotic and inexplicable,
it is possible that we do not see all of it. The freaks of
lightning were chaotic and inexplicable for a long time,
and the human race, which is normally addicted to
provisional explanation, ascribed them to the caprices
of a god. So even otherwise enlightened persons were
till lately inclined to ascribe the freaks of sexual attraction, yet it seems possible that before long the laws
of sexual attraction will be at least as well known as
the laws of electro-magnetism are now (if indeed they
are not a subdivision of the same subject). Likewise in
other matters. Mr. Woodward in *Lottery* has suggested that what we call crazy luck is perhaps merely
the working of a natural law as yet undiscovered; that
an attraction for undeserved material good fortune
may be as much a part of a man's chemical constitution
as an attraction for undeserved women.

So possibly the gentlemen who urge us to Face the
Facts are not yet facing all the facts; which would
make a difference. Perhaps they are not even facing all
the facts that are perceptible now. The ancient meta-
physicians held that the universe is not a chaos but an
arrangement, even if unsatisfactory and incomplete, of
indiscriminate matter; and the modern physicists have
returned to a very similar point of view. For a little
while, in ancient times, philosophy and science and
art and religion (the religion of intelligent men, if not

that of the general public) were at one in this opinion.

Perhaps there was more in this than our disgusted young spiritual nihilists would admit. Greek philosophy failed on its political side, because it was keyed to the city state which was washed off the map by the Macedonian conquests; and political failure shattered the whole system and diverted philosophy into the channel of personal ethics where it dried into the ground. But the cosmology of the later Greeks bears an amazing resemblance to the cosmology of the physicists of to-day, and the religion of such intelligent men of our time as happen to be inclined to religion at all is not so very different from the religion of Plato. Somebody or Something (take your choice according to taste) has started the business of arranging; the God of the Modernists is arranging still, even though he is apt to find his material a little too much for him. And the artist, seeing that arrangement is in fashion, thinks it no robbery to be equal with God to this extent. If the scientists are right a drop of water, a puff of smoke, a lump of lead, and Edward Bok are alike made out of electrons; the only difference is in the arrangement. Here is encouragement for the artist. His arrangement of the common material need not be as heavy as a lump of lead; it might even be an improvement on Edward Bok.

But this is treason, to the Futilitarians. Science and philosophy and religion may be coming to agreement once more; but if they have their way art must stand off in splendid isolation, clinging with fanatical zeal to the dogma of the meaningless life. In plain language, that is intellectual suicide; a deliberate rejection of

all human progress, a deliberate return to the cave, if
not to the treetops.

POSSIBLY the chaos is not so much external as internal.
For the typical author of our time is more interested
in himself than in anything else; the external universe
is apt to be little more than a background; sometimes,
indeed, it looks suspiciously like a mere reflection. The
confession magazines are abhorrent to our heavy
thinkers, yet perhaps their chief offense is only that
they have reduced the doings of the heavy thinkers to
the absurd; they are the natural flowering of an age
which has been copious in autobiography but rather
weak in creation.

Well, the introspectives have high authority for
their omphaloscopic practices; the very highest, if you
believe Aristotle, who argued that God must obviously
lead the perfect life, which is that of contemplation,
and that just as obviously the only object worthy of
His attention is Himself. H. G. Wells, yearning some
time ago for men like gods, sees his ideal realized a
couple of thousand years sooner than he expected in
our novelists who contemplate themselves with unend-
ing naïve delight. This is all very well, but the novelist
has a responsibility to the man who pays two dollars
for his product. Mr. Cabell argues that the literary
artist plays for his own amusement; but when the artist
asks the price of a quart of gin for the toy he has
manufactured, he may reasonably be expected to provide something that will amuse the purchaser, as Mr.
Cabell indeed generally does.

But there is not much nourishment for the customer

in the average introspective novel of these times. A disgruntled and inadequate age produces disgruntled and inadequate heroes who are accurate reflections, in most cases, of their authors. It would be absurd to condemn the autobiographical novel as such; but it must be judged pragmatically, like any other book. Not, Does it satisfy the author? but, Does it satisfy the reader? Of course it satisfies the author; it deals with the subject in which he is most keenly interested, and it is easier than anything else to write. But for the reader its value, in so far as it is autobiographical, depends on what the author has to remember.

This may be clarified a little by going back to the very beginnings of European literature. When Homer smote his blooming lyre he'd heard men sing by land and sea—but not about themselves; if the literary artist of those days played for his own amusement, he did it after office hours, and in some lonely spot between the shadowy mountains and the sounding sea, where no passer-by would be disturbed by his caterwaulings about his sex life and his spiritual frustrations. The simple and turbulent lords and ladies who were Homer's public did not care whether he had a sex life and frustrations or not. They had a perfectly satisfactory sex life of their own and needed no compensations in literature; and such frustrations as occurred in the Heroic Age came by the sword and spear.

So you will find nothing about Homer in Homer's writings; not even indirectly. He wrote about kings who fought and the ladies they fought over, not about persons of letters. The nearest approach to a personal allusion you will find in his complete works is a single line somewhere in the Odyssey to the effect (the exact phrasing escapes me) that a prudent king will be kind to the poet and feed him well. In return for which the poet will handle the king's publicity, celebrating his deeds and those of his ancestors with whatever editing and embellishment may be necessary to give his customers that satisfied feeling when the song is ended. Which proves that Homer was not only an honest man but an intelligent man, who discerned quite accurately the proper function of an artist.

Well, times will change; the Heroic Age degenerated and its view of life wore out, as views of life have a way of doing. With decadence came introspection, and, for the time being, a public for introspective literature. Archilochus of Paros, first of men of whom we have knowledge, put his personal grievances into a book intended for the market. (First of European men, that is; Hosea had already done it in Palestine.) Some scholar or other has observed that Archilochus is the first flesh-and-blood man whom we can actually discern and catch hold of through the mists of Hellenic antiquity. Therein lies his strength, and his weakness, as a literary artist. Archilochus wrote about himself and his name is still familiar to students of the history of prosody; Homer wrote about persons more interesting than himself, and in the ages since ten thousand people have heard of Helen and Odysseus for every one who has heard of Archilochus. Archilochus survives in fragments; what Homer wrote survives intact and even expanded, by the infiltration of later writings which crept under the shelter of his great name. Archilochus wrote to gratify his grouch and Homer

wrote to gratify the customers; and when, three thousand years later, a retired merchant came halfway
round the world, braved the ridicule of the experts, and
devoted his life and his fortune to the search for the
remains of men and places celebrated by a literary
artist, it was not the walls of Paros that he sought,
and the tomb of Archilochus, but the tomb of Agamemnon and the walls of Troy.

And while we are appealing to the example of first-
rank artists, some mention might be made of William
Shakespeare, who is sometimes cited as an exhibit on
the other side. Shakespeare's whole body of writings,
say some of the experts, is his spiritual autobiography;
you can read his history in his plays. So you can; in
fact you can read it in several different ways, according
to your preconceived idea of it. But you can read more
than that in Shakespeare's plays, and with somewhat
greater confidence. Beatrice may be a sketch of Mary
Fitton as Shakespeare saw her in the first illusion when
their love was fresh, or she may not. What is certain
is that with her wise cracks and her hot temper and her
sex appeal, she is an excellent box-office heroine for a
romantic melodrama that Shakespeare wrote to make
money.

Shakespeare played for his own amusement—when
he could afford it, and when he could be sure that other
people would be amused too. There is no doubt a good
deal in "The Merchant of Venice" that amused Shakespeare; but that was all buried underneath some very
competent hokum, designed to hit the anti-Semitism
of the audience. Shakespeare, the experts assure us,
believed that he would live in history, if at all, as the

author of "Venus and Adonis" and "The Rape of Lucrece." Here the literary artist played for his own amusement and that of the cultivated minority; meanwhile, to pay the rent, he wrote a play called "Hamlet."

Quite possibly some of Shakespeare's spiritual autobiography has trickled into "Hamlet," but when you see "Hamlet" properly played you never think of it; and it could safely be asserted that Shakespeare would never have let it trickle in if he had not been perfectly sure that people who saw the play would be thinking about something else. What would be done to his plays after he became a classic he fortunately could not foresee. If "Hamlet" is treated as an excuse for some aging actor to put on tights and mouth archaic orotundities, the spectator may be justified for reading anything he pleases into it to mitigate his boredom. But dress the actors like the audience—as they dressed when Burbage played Hamlet and Shakespeare played the Ghost—give them such a stage setting as the audience (or at least the more opulent members of it) has at home, and the spectator is not going to waste any reflection on the author's opinions about morals and the art of acting, still less about the relation of these opinions to Shakespeare's life history. He will be absorbed, and utterly absorbed, in a story about a neurotic boy who has just learned that there was a Snyder-Gray case in his own family, and what he does about it.

Shakespeare, according to all accounts, was a man of extraordinarily engaging personality; his friends knew he was a good working playwright, but they do not seem to have thought of him as an artist of enduring fame; they thought of him as a merry com-

panion at the gin mill after the day's work was over.
But the average autobiographical novelist has less in
himself to put into his books. It stands to reason that
in most cases an author is less interesting than his
books; for in his books he can (if he has so much
fortitude) select and eliminate and suppress, and
shape into proportion; whereas his personality is
all there, with all the warts on. Recently the reading public has been passionately interested in personality, warts and all; it has insisted on paying money
not only to read spiritual autobiographies but to see
the author face to face. In so far as this has enabled
novelists to make enough money out of lecturing before
women's clubs to spend more laborious care on the
writing of novels, it is excellent—for the novelists. One
cannot help wondering, however, just what advantages
it brought to the reading public. And surely the prudent author would rather be judged by the invented
product which is the work of the best that is in him
than by the shameless display of everything that is in
him.

It depends on the author. Dr. Maugham's spiritual
autobiography is one of the great books of our time,
considerably better than anything else he has written,
before or since. But in ordinary hands the spiritual
autobiography is a delicate matter. I intended for some
years to write one myself, but gave it up eventually
on the principle that *de minimis non curat lector*.
Even such very modest self-abnegation, I am pained
to observe, is rare.

Especially since of late years we have had such a
swarm of amateur novelists. Even fifteen years ago

the writing of novels was usually approached as a trade that needed learning, that called on its practitioners to scorn delights and live laborious days, that was too onerous to be ordinarily taken up except by someone who meant to make it the chief business of life. Now all the bright boys and girls seem to feel it incumbent on them to write a novel when they leave college, just as they have an affair; not for the pleasure it gives them so much as by way of an announcement of having attained maturity. Naturally these first-and-last novels are autobiographical. Now and then one of these Great Announcers has something to say; Mr. Scott Fitzgerald is an example; but he straightway sat down with unflagging diligence and learned how to say it. But most first novels nowadays are a gesture, and a gesture never repeated. In my not so very remote youth we felt the same impulse, but we usually took it out by going to Europe on a cattle boat. This was easier on the reading public, hard as it may have been on the cattle.

WELL, there is not much point in indicting a whole nation, which is pretty nearly what a condemnation of the autobiographical novel amounts to in these all-too-literate days. The tendency was a natural consequence of the inability, above-mentioned, to see anything intelligible, important, or worthy in the external universe. Aristotle's God contemplated himself. Not so the gods of Homer, who were far too much interested in what was going on around them. But by Aristotle's time men and their gods alike were bored by the unsatisfactory world they saw outside, and turned inward for a change. The Greeks invented psychology and moral philosophy only after they had lost hope of realizing their aspirations in action; but after a little experience of trying to find whatever it is that one wants by looking inward, the more energetic of them turned back to the outer world, went east on the trail of Alexander, and got a new kick out of life. So it may be with our introspective writers.

They turned inward because the outer world was displeasing; but the inner world is no better, if correctly reported by the average autobiographical novel. The best survey of the introspective realism of the nineteen twenties was written sixty years ago by Walt Whitman in *A Hand Mirror:*

Hold it up sternly—see this it sends back, (who is it? is it you?)
Outside fair costume, within ashes and filth
A drunkard's breath, unwholesome eater's face, venerealee's flesh,
Lungs rotting away piecemeal . . .
No brain, no heart left, no magnetism of sex:
Such from one look in this looking-glass ere you go hence—

One suppresses the more loathsome details, from a sense of decency which must appear old-fashioned. Some of us, after studying specimens like this, are about ready to turn back for a good long look at the world outside. We cannot open up a new world, as did the Greeks with Alexander; this unsatisfactory world we live in seems to be all the world there is. External phenomena may be distressing, but apparently they are no worse than internal phenomena. And, as

Mr. Santayana observes, the world is not respectable, but it is exciting.

Luckily there is reputable precedent for a return to the old familiar spectacle, with a somewhat more resolute eye and a stronger stomach. No writer of this age is more highly sophisticated than was Gaius Petronius. Petronius, one supposes, had looked within long enough to disgust his somewhat fastidious taste with what he saw there. So, then, he looked out; from the surviving fragments of his writings one learns practically nothing about Petronius (except his views on education and the art of literary composition) but a great deal about the world he lived in. Now that world, the Roman Empire under Nero, was quite as painful to the discerning eye as Europe and America in the nineteen twenties. Petronius was able to endure it, and get a laugh out of it, and pass that laugh along to posterity, precisely because his eye was penetrating and his stomach strong; because he not only could report what he saw, but saw more keenly and with a better sense of proportion than his predecessors.

This, perhaps, is the function of introspection—to send us back to the world of phenomena with a shade more of balance and tough-mindedness, to enable us to confront the unpleasant outer world with some equanimity because we have learned that the inner world is no better. Petronius took the wind out of fiction and reduced it from poetry to prose. His successors found plenty of material in the world around them; they rearranged it to suit the demand of their public and wrote stories full of action and romance and humor, the sort of stories that will always be written and will always be sold because they will always meet a biological need.

There are other biological needs, of course. Objectivity and subjectivity are as complementary as high and low, odd and even, concave and convex. But we have been overdosed with one and are about due for a turn at the other. We have seen what our generation is; we have seen it in novels and we have seen it in ourselves. We know what it is, all too well. In a world so full of pity and terror and excitement there are surely things better worth writing about than the futile and dissatisfied young men and women who have the habit of writing.

BUT this, after all, is matter for the metaphysician rather than the artist. The question which concerns the novelist more directly, both as artist and as business man, is what is to be gained by facing the facts, external or internal, even if they are as stated. Here the artist may learn not only from the bootlegger but from the garment trade. A great many facts, both physical and metaphysical, have been faced of late years; but from some of them our eyes have turned away. Even in this age of confusion one lesson has been thoroughly and generally learned—that the average human knee is less sightly in its factual nudity than when it is sheathed in the illusory artifice of a silk stocking. Our realists may presently learn that the principle has a wider extension. Out of joint the times may be; but few of us are so perverse as to take any pleasure in prolonged contemplation of chaos; and in fact it rarely

seems to amuse even the people who write about it. To
the three qualities mentioned above, as absent from the
characteristic literature of the post-war period, might
be added a fourth—enjoyment of life and art; what is
commonly called gusto.

You can be as pessimistic as you like and still get
excitement out of existence (see for an example the
spiritual education of the hero in *Of Human Bondage*).
And if the Futilitarian argues that gusto is a matter of
good digestion and healthy nerves, one might counter
with the suggestion that perhaps Futilitarianism, the
philosophy of Impotence, is dependent on bad digestion
and unhealthy nerves rather than on a searching perception of the faults of the universe.

Argue if you like that Futilitarianism is sound metaphysics, but you cannot very well maintain that it gives
pleasure, even to its devotees. From the merely he-
donist point of view, Mr. Stribling's Tennessee moun-
taineers are better off than Mr. Aldous Huxley's truf-
flers of the arts; for they please other people quite
as much and please themselves a good deal better.
The Russians, of course, derive a keen pleasure from
contemplation of their own worthlessness; which has
the further advantage of being objectively comic to
non-Russians. But our authors cannot quite be Russian, no matter how hard they try; their asplanchnous
heroes and half-wit heroines do not even delight their
creators.

Regard, for example, the recent enthusiasm about
Sex. I do not suppose there has been a period in the
history of literature when sex was so copiously reported
and so little enjoyed. Our novelists may have felt that

as unflinching truthful reporters they should announce
the fact that there is not much in sex after all; but
if that is so, why waste so much space on it?

Doris in John Gunther's *Red Pavilion* is a fair
specimen of recent heroines. She went from one man
to another as she went from one restaurant to another,
without finding anything very savory in any of them.
After taking three lovers (to use a conventional term
which is quite too flattering) in one week, she walked
out with her golden head held high, or words to that
effect; and Mr. Gunther appears to admire her as a
gallant young person. One may grant that she was, and
that gallantry is all well enough as far as it goes; but
it is equally obvious that this Doris was a good deal
of a sap. And some of us are crabbed enough not to
be amused by saps, however gallant.

The leather medal in this field of competition must
be awarded, without any argument, to Mr. Maxwell
Bodenheim, whose well replenished heroine Jessica indulged in 259 amours, if I remember correctly, without getting the emotional wallop out of any of them,
or out of all of them together, that the lady of Victorian literature would have derived from a single
competently conducted seduction. For sex was a serious matter to the Victorians; a lady who let herself be
seduced in those days usually felt that she was imperil-
ing her immortal soul. Between the listless complais-
ance of the modern heroine, and the Victorian girl's
abandon, there was the difference between betting a
white chip and pushing in a whole stack of blues.

It may be contended with some plausibility that the
Victorians took sex more seriously than it deserves.

But here again our Impotents show their basic confusion between reality and representation, between the true nature (if any) of the Universe, and the view of the Universe that is worth two dollars to the customer. Even if sex is of minor importance (and I should be more convinced of this if I knew of any large number of novelists, male or female, who personally indulged in a rigid chastity) a topic that occupies most of the pages of most modern novels ought to be treated as if it were of some importance. I do not and probably could not write sex novels, but I read a good many of them, as anyone must who reads contemporary fiction at all; and as a reader I become infinitely bored with these monotonous half-hearted affairs that apparently give as little amusement to their participants, and their inventor, as they do to the reader. To adapt the excellent maxim of the old copy book, if sex is worth doing at all it is worth doing well; worth endowing with a certain glamor and excitement which in practice some people seem to get out of it, even yet, and which the reader who gives up his two dollars for a novel, instead of a quart of gin, would like to believe that the hero and heroine are getting out of it.

Herein our art authors might learn a useful lesson from two novelists otherwise not particularly notable, Miss E. M. Hull and the Reverend Robert Keable.

The Sheik was literature of escape. Escape from what? From the art authors, I suspect; from the dullness of this alleged realism. You may say that people who read *The Sheik* would not read artistic or so-called artistic novels, at all; which is true of some of Miss Hull's immense public, but not of all of it. For there

are, or were a few years ago before the sex novel became so common, plenty of people who will read any
novel that is what they like to call risqué, who will
wade through any amount of art to get one or two good
seduction scenes. (Consider much of the early public
of *Jurgen,* people who were not interested in Mr.
Cabell's philosophy but were violently enthusiastic
about Jurgen's experiences with various ladies.) It can
be conjectured with confidence that thousands of readers of *The Sheik* had already tried the sex novels
of well ballyhooed artists, and seized upon Miss Hull's
book with a feeling that at last they were getting their
money's worth. *The Sheik* was an absurd book; but it
was absurd in the right direction, for a sex novel.

Then there was the Reverend Mr. Keable, who
seems to have discovered at the age of thirty-odd that
members of the human race are either male or female,
and that relationships between persons of opposite sexes
are sometimes productive of a pleasurable excitement.
He discovered this, and instantly with a glad hurrah he
ran out into the street, shouting to all the passers-by:
"Stop! Listen! I will tell you about what I have
found!" Heartened by this enthusiasm, several hundred
thousand people stopped and listened. What they heard
was no news, of course; but Mr. Keable's exhilaration
must have been news, at least to those who had been
reading our art authors. This was not art, no doubt;
but it was gusto. And gusto is a commodity for which
the customer is usually glad to lay down his money.

I may appear to be insulting the art artists by
implying that they are interested in the monetary return from their productions. Certainly, with nineteen

authors out of twenty, the very worst as much as the very best (or perhaps even more), the money is secondary; most fiction writers would go on writing so long as they could get published, even if their books never brought in a nickel. But, the literature business being organized as it is, they do get money for their writings; nor can I recall, at the moment, a novelist who refuses royalties, or requests that they be turned over to the poor. And whether or not the money means much to the author, it means something to the customer. It is not only good morals but good sense to try to give him his money's worth.

There was lately published, without much fanfare of trumpets, a modest novel which I suspect is a sign of better times—Mr. C. S. Forester's *Love Lies Dreaming*. This was a sex novel pure and simple—pure and simple in the literal meaning of those words; its theme was a quarrel, and a reconciliation, between a young married couple. Whether Mr. Forester personally takes sex seriously I do not know, but he has the sense to realize that he must seem to take it seriously when he writes a sex novel. He has managed the rather difficult technical task of combining Georgian candor with Victorian delicacy, with the gratifying result of demonstrating that delicacy of sentiment gives a redoubled value to physical candor. This material was perhaps a little tenuous to spread over a full-length book, but Mr. Forester had the astuteness to attach a time-fuse to his climax; he built up a mounting impatience in his hero that communicated itself to the reader, until you could not help feeling, however unreasonably, that it was a matter of immense importance to get this man restored to his wife's arms. Sentimental absurdity, perhaps, to our modernist authors; very different, this heightening tension, from the slap-dash go-on-and-get-it-over-with method now current. But when the delayed detonation came at last it had an enhanced significance; Mr. Forester had demonstrated, for the time being and to the satisfaction of his readers, that the synthetic intoxicants of casual illicit amour had nothing like the kick, or the flavor, of the old pre-war aged-in-the-wood connubial bliss.

Artificial? Perhaps. What else is all art? The difference between good art and bad art (if I may descend once more to the obvious which is not yet obvious to the art authors) is that in good art the artificiality is plausible and pleasing. All this is an old story; it has been reiterated by Cabell and others; yet despite their labors, it would appear that the cardinal fault of the novelists of the last decade is their bigoted conviction that realism means being "true to life." That sort of realism is only petty larceny. The ingenious gentlemen who a few years ago took their stand at the entrance to the naval aviation field at Lakehurst, where a newly arrived Zeppelin drew crowds of sightseers, and charged admission until belatedly detected by the police, are in exactly the same case with the realist who sets down life as it is, and sells it for two dollars to people who are already living life as it is, and can go on living it and seeing it all around them without contributing to the gate receipts.

OUR true-to-lifers will have to strike a little deeper, in any case, before they find anything that may even provisionally be called reality. Some of them are trying to dig down to the subsoil, but they have hardly got beneath the sod. What is under the American surface, if you believe contemporary realism, is repressed sexual desire. Now there has never been a time within my recollection—if what one hears is true, there never has been a time since the landing of Columbus—when the sexual desires of the male American needed to be repressed for more than twenty minutes. The ladies were not so felicitously situated in earlier times, but the automobile has changed all that.

What is actually under the surface is no mystery. Millions of dollars are being spent every year in advertising aimed at the true subconscious desires of the American people, advertising which would not continue unless it paid a profit. No social philosopher has discussed its implications yet because it appears chiefly in magazines which are not read by social philosophers —*True Stories* and its imitators, which get closer to the throbbing heart of this great nation than any other form of literature except the movies. Two classes of commodities above all others are advertised in these truly popular or vulgar magazines—using the adjectives in their strict and interchangeable senses—and the continued success of this advertising lays bare the American soul as all the Freudian researchers have failed to expose it.

Then what are the cravings of the American people? Take it from the advertisers, who wouldn't go on spending their money if they hadn't guessed right. The dominant desire of the American woman is to be thin without exercise or dieting. The dominant desire of the

American man is to learn to play the saxophone or the Hawaiian guitar in six easy lessons by mail.

Secondary aspirations, still deserving of some notice, come rather nearer to the picture of the Great American Subconscious which we get from literature. The ladies would like to be successfully amorous without the wide and all-inclusive practice that usually brings success in any endeavor; the gentlemen would like to be well read and good conversationalists on ten minutes a day. But these after all are subsidiary ambitions, as measurement of the advertising space will prove. All women would like to be both thin and amorous, but compelled to choose, most of them would rather be thin. Most men doubtless have some inclination to a rounded culture which shall include both music and letters; but compelled to select one accomplishment and stick to it, the greater majority would rather be demons on the saxophone than authoritative commentators on the history of human thought.

Here, then, is a job for the realists. Let them treat all of life instead of selected fragments of its surface. Let them really dig down into that enormous subconscious area which we are assured is so much larger and so much more important than what we keep in the show window above the threshold of consciousness. Let the realists go after something real.

A lot of American literature would have to be revised if it were realistic as advertised. Some of us who could never quite believe in the irresistible impulse that compelled John Webster to take off his clothes and tell his daughter the story of his life may begin to understand him, if we can grasp the idea that

John would have stayed at home, kept his clothes on and been happy if he had only taken a correspondence course in the pure and applied saxophone. Trivial romancers have given us hundreds of books about women who were starved for love. Where is the Great Pathfinder who will explain that his heroine's craving to be well besheiked was only incidental, and that what she really wanted was to keep her figure without having to stay away from the soda fountain? That man will remodel American literature, but he will have to fight a terrifically powerful vested interest of men and women who think they are realists now, and who will be as hopelessly outdistanced, when realism gets beneath the surface, as buggy manufacturers after the invention of automobiles.

Meanwhile, if they must write sex novels, let them try to write good sex novels. If sex is not interesting in fact, all the more reason why it should be interesting in fiction. American literature, to be truly national (an objective dear to Mr. Mencken and other patriot esthetes), should have a slogan. I venture to suggest one, which for the next decade or so may be salutary: "Fewer and better seductions."

THE philosophy of impotence is nothing new, in art or life; and in the past it has sometimes had a certain grace and beauty. There was decadence in the nineties, but the men of that Jonquil Decade at least tried to be beautifully useless, to give their worthlessness (which, like most literary worthlessness, was mostly pretense) a decorative value. Our current brand of futility is about as unappetizing as any that has ever been offered; it seems to be regarded as its own excuse and justification; graceful living is as much beneath the dignity of a man of feeling as work. To be sure nothing has been done of late with any notable suavity; but it does not appear that impotence gains in value by being flung in one's face with a snarl.

Against this unlovely tendency the first protest, at least in a book that was taken seriously by the heavy thinkers, must be credited to Mr. Carl Van Vechten.

How was it possible to read an author who never laughed? For it was only below laughter that true tragedy could lie concealed, only the ironic author who could awaken the deeper emotions.

When these reflections of Mrs. Campaspe Lorillard were confided to the public some three or four years ago, they were as the voice of one crying in the wilderness. In those days solemnity was a categorical imperative; to take one's self and everything else seriously was the first and great commandment. Indeed, it was almost necessary to read authors who never laughed if one read at all, for laughter was one of the stigmata of inferiority, and any prudent writer of that period shied away from it.

But one ventures to hope that the reading public is growing up. The season of 1925-26 was a vintage year in American letters, producing more good American novels than any other three or four in recent memory. Some of them were gloom books, but some were joy books; and two of the joy books were the best sellers of that season. Most amazingly, these best sellers—*Gentlemen Prefer Blondes* and *The Private*

Life of Helen of Troy—were also highly regarded by the heavy thinkers.

I do not suppose that most book buyers, or most heavy thinkers, share the distilled taste of Mrs. Lorillard; probably most readers of *Gentlemen Prefer Blondes* regarded it merely as a scream. But it is something to have the appetite for an occasional scream legitimized. Even the earnest Mencken, whose ordinary taste in fiction (if indeed, properly speaking, he has any taste in fiction, as will appear doubtful from some considerations to be urged in a subsequent article) runs to such worthy but not very entertaining products as the constatations of Miss Ruth Suckow, gave Miss Loos's book his *nihil obstat*. This must have released thousands of his votaries from the horrendous suspicion that they had committed a mortal sin in liking it.

But perhaps it was more than a scream. The head of one of the great educational foundations told me, at the time of its currency, that he had picked it up for an evening of diversion and found it a profound social study. As to that I can offer no opinion; I move in humbler social circles and do not know the sweethearts of the members of the Racquet Club. But I rather hope the gentleman is right; for if Miss Loos has established the fact that a profound social study need not be embodied in a book of deadly solemnity, she has performed a service to society as great as Mr. Lewis's, when he exploded the myth of the superior merit of the small town.

The amazing popularity of Dr. Erskine's reinterpretation of Helen is harder to explain. A story went the rounds at the time that the publishers enclosed in each

copy a return postcard, asking readers who liked the
book to write in and tell them why; and that the overwhelming majority of answers set forth as its chief
merit the demonstration that even a woman who had
sinned could be redeemed by a pure home life. But this
explanation turned out, on investigation, to be a pure
myth.

There is a suspicion that a good many people bought
that book to keep in display on the living room table,
rather than to read; and certainly much of its fame,
and its sale, can be credited to the amazingly lucky
accident that a copy found its way into the hands of
Mr. James A. Stillman, with results subsequently
chronicled at length in the newspapers. But I suspect
more of it is due to the illiteracy of this generation.
The family affairs of the Atridæ are not the most
hilarious topic in history. A tradition fortified by some
of the greatest names in literature dictates that they
must be treated with proper solemnity. To a classically
educated generation, even a cautiously humorous account of these famous tragic figures would seem as
sacrilegious as Mr. Rea Irvin's play about Moses at
Pharaoh's court would seem to a congregation of
Fundamentalists.

But it was Dr. Erskine's luck to be born into a generation in which not more than one reader in a thousand would ever have heard of the classic writers who
had handled his material before him, or indeed of any
of his characters except Helen. And this illiteracy
opens up new prospects for the enterprising historical
novelist. It is not only the classic literature that is
forgotten; people have quit reading the Bible too.

There are some good stories in the Bible, and some of them might profitably be excavated and retold.

But after all the most sacred history, to this generation, is current history. Probably that has been true of most generations; but in times past people addicted to reading had records of the past available for comparison. They were aware that history had not begun yesterday, that they and their problems were not unique; and this perception gave them some sense of proportion. But with the universal extension of the rudiments of literacy we have built up a reading public which is ninety per cent illiterate, in the sense that it knows nothing of what has been done, and thought, in the past. A good deal of the solemnity of recent literature, like a good deal of the embittered zealotry of recent political radicalism, is obviously the work of earnest young people who are unaware that they are not the first earnest young people in history.

It does not take the earnest young person very long to perceive that the Universe is unsatisfactory, in a number of respects. This is not exactly a novel discovery, but it is news to most of the earnest young people. Quite naturally they feel that something ought to be done, or at least said, about it; and it follows that whoever fails to realize the urgent and immediate duty of taking everything seriously is not merely a light-minded and negligible person, but a traitor to society.

Without in any way defending the Universe, I am unable to perceive that it becomes any more appetizing merely because somebody has written a gloomy book about it. More appetizing, certainly, to the author who proceeds to live in opulence on his royalties; and since authors have to eat they can hardly be blamed for taking advantage of a half-baked public which is willing to pay for earnestness and gloom. What the public gets out of it is another matter. Doubtless one of the most depressing of human experiences is to attain all one's desires, and find this fruition wholly unsatisfactory. This unhappy situation has rarely been set forth more clearly than in "The Gold Rush." It seems to me that "The Gold Rush" as art is worth all that Eugene O'Neill ever wrote. Is its artistic value impaired by the fact that the customers are doubled up with laughter?

The Athenians, in a famous instance, fined one of their authors for reminding them of their misfortunes. When an author does that to us, we make him rich and call him a prophet. Why did the Athenians display such criminal levity? Well, there is a suspicion that Themistocles had put Phrynichus up to remind them of their misfortunes for partisan reasons; but leaving aside the political complications of the case, I suspect they fined him because they were perfectly well aware of their misfortunes already, because they could see no easy and immediate solution, and accordingly saw no point in shouting about something that could not be cured by mere noise.

They were not averse to heavy literature, in itself; there is the notable case of Æschylus. But it is a matter of record that Æschylus usually embellished his plays with striking spectacles—the retinue of Okeanos, the irruption of the Erinyes—and I suspect he did this precisely to hold the customers who were unable to probe his profundities. He had a high reputation in Athens, but apparently the Athenians admired him as our parents admired Browning and Meredith, without quite knowing what it was all about. However, if an author can handle gloom as well as Æschylus—or as Dreiser, descending to our own time—well and good; he earns his reputation, and his money.[2] That is a very different matter from the lately current theory that gloom was meritorious in itself and that reluctance to get excited about the state of the universe was criminal negligence.

WELL, says your Chaotic novelist (and he has been saying it more and more industriously since the beginning of the reaction against his domination), why should I care what people think of me? I am faithful to my Vision; I paint the thing as I see it. Impotence and futility may be neither pleasurable nor beautiful, but they are what is.

Even so, the faults of the Universe may be admitted without groaning about it. Granted that the face of Nature is dark, I know of no cosmic law which forbids a grin on the face of man. Who is the most bitterly misanthropic of living American writers? Why, that distinguished popular humorist, Mr. Ring Lardner. Jonathan Swift never wrote anything more uncomplimentary about the human race than *A Caddy's Diary*. Lardner merely happens to be more mature than most of our current gloom spreaders; he sees no reason to cry over incurably spilt milk; and he has learned that

[2] Or, on the other hand, if he handles gloom and solemnity as comically as Mr. Sherwood Anderson, from whose *Dark Laughter* and *Many Marriages* I have derived some healthy merriment.

your argument is apt to be more effective if you thrust
it in with some little subtlety, that *suaviter in modo* is
not necessarily incompatible with *fortiter in re*.

Outside of Lardner's stories, I suppose the bitterest
books in American letters are *The High Place* and *The
Man That Corrupted Hadleyburg*, and in each of them
the reader, whether or not he sees the underlying trend,
gets a laugh on every page. In sixteen books, Mr. Cabell
has restated with much ingenuity the same old argument—that all is vanity but there is no point in
getting steamed up about it. And probably Cabell,
since he has long been a favorite with the *illuminati*,
deserves much of the credit for this sudden maturity
of the reading public which has flowered in the fabulous
profits of Dr. Erskine and Miss Loos. Certainly a
reader who has soaked in the doctrine set forth—most
recently and most persuasively, though Cabell has been
preaching it for years—in Dom Manuel's post-mortem
interview with Coth, is pretty well vaccinated against
any subsequent attack of earnestness.

But I think the Futilitarians can be convicted out
of their own mouths; from internal evidence in their
own books, it can be proved that they do not even set
down the thing as they see it. Futility is not a faithful
report, but the result of a process of selection and suppression.

The not very subtle symbolism of the hero and
heroine of *The Sun Also Rises* is, I suppose, the simplest statement of the philosophy now current among
our most admired art authors. Before a world of un-
precedented complexity and fascination Man stands
helpless, paralyzed by consciousness of his own in-

curable incapacity; what is the use of trying to live with Life since she would only deceive us with everybody? The argument would be more convincing if it were practiced by the author who sets it forth. I do not know whether Mr. Ernest Hemingway gives himself to Life, but he has certainly given a good deal of himself to Work. Not by resignation to insuperable difficulties did he evolve that style, so bare, yet so lucid and suggestive, that it makes any sentence containing ten words, or one semicolon, seem as superfluously ornate as the Ritz Tower. It was his ill fortune, after he had learned to write with economy and effect, that he knew no one worth writing about; but he would never have acquired that disciplined and compact style if he himself were as worthless as his acquaintances. The most that can be proved from *The Sun Also Rises* is that in the world as known to Mr. Ernest Hemingway all, perhaps, is vanity—except Mr. Ernest Hemingway himself, who is a person of serious and substantial importance, or at any rate will be as soon as he has discovered subjects worthy of the exercise of his undeniable talent.

The characters of Mr. John dos Passos find existence a quite irretrievable disaster; in one way or another they give it up, or eventually wish they had. But it was not by giving up that Mr. dos Passos erected the complex structure of *Manhattan Transfer*. Jimmy Herf, disgusted with New York and Life, starts off across country toward no known destination; John dos Passos, with apparently the same views, stays in town and goes to work, and gets himself called a realist.

Some men, of course, are so made that in the face

of difficulties they curl up and quit; their novels never
get into print, though they may diffuse in conversation.
But others, faced with difficulties, set their teeth and
dig in. And so, perhaps, these novels about impotence
are only a specialized form of literature of escape.
Their authors are lazy, like all human beings; they
would like to acquire the art of what Miss Cather calls
"yielding gracefully to the inevitable or the almost inevitable"; it would be a good deal more comfortable.
But inside them is something (is it a hormone?—I am
no biologist) which makes them work anyway, and
work hard; hence the paradox of industrious novelists
writing exacting books about the delights of utter
worthlessness.

Not, of course, that industry and determination and
success have been neglected by recent novelists. We
have had plenty of novels about the successful man,
but they are concerned with showing that the sweets of
triumph turn to ashes in his mouth. Naturally this engaging doctrine, though several thousand years old, is
still good for a big sale; we all like to be assured that
the grapes were sour. I should be a little more con-
fident of their acidity, however, if the novelists who
write about the emptiness of fame and fortune shunned
the public view and turned all their royalties into the
Authors' League Fund. Read these devastating exposures of the hollowness of Success, and then go out
to Long Island or Westchester and look at the country
estates of their authors, and you will be driven to conclude that the only wealth and fame that brings satisfaction is the wealth and fame earned by writing dev-

astating exposures of the hollowness of wealth and fame.

I do not object to fairy stories, but I am not persuaded that it does any good to call them realism. No doubt between surtaxes and alimony and arteriosclerosis many rich men lead a hard life, or what looks to them like a hard life. There are probably certain satisfactions which the industrial magnate can never get, but they happen to be satisfactions that he cannot understand, and would not want if he did understand them. I believe that more truth about our plutocrats will be found in their autobiographies written by Mr. Burton J. Hendrick than in these penetrating psychological analyses by our alleged realists. These moralizers on the vanity of riches earn their money, or come nearer earning it than the ordinary Futilitarian; Lazarus can always get two dollars' worth out of the picture of Dives with his tongue hanging out. Their fairy stories have a pleasing artificiality which makes them, to that extent, good art; and if they are done with sufficient dexterity to escape affronting common observation, they may be very good art indeed.[3] But whatever they may be, they are not realism.

Well, is this not what I have argued the artist must do—select and suppress, shape and alter? Why blame the Futilitarians for selecting according to their own

[3] I hesitate to mention, in this connection, the name of Mr. William Dean Howells, which must be abhorrent to the current generation, unless it is already forgotten. Mr. Howells was a timorous writer, who built a fence around himself and would not climb over it; but it must be observed that the things he tried to do he usually did better than anything has ever been done by most of those who now scoff at him.

taste rather than mine? One reason is mentioned above —because they pretend it is not selection, but complete and unalterable truth to which adherence must be given by everybody, under pain of losing civic rights in the republic of letters. But there is a further reason lying in the fact that every writer has, or wants to have, a public. If the Futilitarian hammered off his views on the hopelessness of things, and then locked up the typescript in his desk for his subsequent private perusal when he felt so inclined, that would be nobody's business but his own. But when he offers his unsavory mess for sale the purchaser may reasonably complain that he has been defrauded; and the practicing novelist who disagrees with the Futilitarian philosophy is not beyond his rights in offering protest—a sort of minority stockholder's suit, to prevent what has of late years been the majority interest from wasting the assets and dissipating the good will of the fiction industry at large. Futilitarianism is not a selection from the available evidence, for the purpose of building a structure worth the customer's money; it is a selection made to the end of proving that no structure is possible. Disagreeable as the phenomena of life may be, better things can be done with them than that.

Returning to Mr. William Gerhardi, from whose various books I have gone away sorrowing, for he has great possessions if he would only invest them in productive industry. He owes his reputation, I believe, chiefly to Mrs. Edith Wharton, who found in his first novel, *Futility*, the first account of Russians which was comprehensible to her. She explained this intelligibility on the ground that Mr. Gerhardi, being half Russian

and half European, was able to function as a Mediator
between two worlds, a sort of Logos arranging the in-
effable mysteries of the Russian soul into a pattern
which Europeans could understand. But his later books
suggest that he must be explained by the heretical doctrines of the Monophysites, if not even of the Gnostics;
there is only one nature in him, and that is Russian.

So Mr. Gerhardi, having found that in the life of
Eastern Siberia in 1919 all was vanity and vexation of
spirit, sets it down exactly as he saw it. Now one may
grant that this was a peculiarly aggravated form of
chaos, though ultimately it did work out into a sort of
order. But even if Mr. Gerhardi saw no patterns in it,
if his Russian soul derived an unnatural pleasure from
its pointlessness, it was hardly fair to assume that this
pleasure would be shared by non-Russian readers. The
Russian literature that is read abroad has some sort
of pattern. It may be a loose pattern as in Tolstoy,
or a close pattern as in Turgenieff, even an accidental
pattern as in Artzibasheff's *Breaking Point,* where that
endless succession of suicides made a magnificent farce
for Western readers out of something that probably
seemed tragic to the Russians. But a pattern there
must be.

There are Russians, after all, who protest that Russia
is not the Great Incomprehensible. Whether they are
right or not, there is or has been something in Russia
besides formless laxity. The organized aggressive Russia of Nicholas I and Skobelieff and the Treaty of San
Stefano, which had all Europe shivering with fear, was
as real in its day as the chaotic Russia of Artzibasheff
and Kerensky. And even in the chaos of revolutionary

Russia a creative artist was able to impose his own order.

It is no doubt too late to call the attention of the American public to a book called *The Red Garden*, which was issued as long ago as 1920, and of which Mr. Knopf managed to sell some 600 copies before giving up in despair. But this little collection of sketches, dealing with the same sort of material that Gerhardi contemplated with a helpless Russian shrug, seems to me altogether the best book that has been written about Russia since Turgenieff died and Tolstoy became afflicted with what he called religion. The Russian soul, it may be, is without form and void; but a creative mind can impose order on even Russian phenomena. So Henning Kehler who wrote *The Red Garden*—it is a very grave misfortune that his subsequent works, if he has written any, have not been translated into English—regarded Russia with a critical Danish eye, a European eye, the eye of an artist; and from that chaotic welter he made excerpts which produce in the reader a sense of pity, and of terror, and of beauty; and beneath it all an impulse to overwhelming laughter. Read *The Red Garden* and *The Polyglots*, and you will see not only the difference between the Russian and the European, but the difference between the reporter, however faithful and observant he may be, and the creative artist.

It has been suggested that the metaphysics of the Futilitarians is perhaps not quite so final and unassailable as they think; that perhaps the physicists may be right in seeing signs of order in the Universe, even

though they cannot yet guess what that order is.
But whether or not the Chaotics are right about this
sorry scheme of things entire, they are visibly and
egregiously wrong about one portion of the Universe—
an insignificant portion, to be sure, one that may well
be trivial and negligible in the larger view; but one
which is of some importance to the fiction writer. I
refer to the human race.

Whatever God may have done or failed to do in the
last few thousand years, the accomplishment of Man
is spread before our eyes. Certainly it is nothing of
which one can be inordinately proud; but no one can
deny that in the comparatively brief time he has had
to work in, Man has succeeded in effecting a perceptible
improvement. What is still more important for the
novelist to remember, he keeps on trying—everywhere
except in the pages of the Invertebrate novelists.

His endeavors may be doomed, ultimately, to ludi-
crous failure. He may be able to depend on no help outside himself; he may even be struggling against an in-
soluble problem, playing with a deck that is hopelessly
and irremediably stacked against him. Still, he keeps
on trying. A novelist who will not acknowledge that is
not only falsifying the record which he pretends to be
reproducing in all fidelity, but he is offering no palatable
or nourishing food to his readers. One need not maintain
that a novelist should whistle to keep up his customers'
courage; let him see things as black as he chooses.
But if he says that because the prospects are gloomy
one might as well quit trying he says what is neither
true nor amusing. For, however distasteful the fact
may be to the Invertebrate novelist, the average bio-

logical organism is so made that it is going to keep on trying anyway, however thin its hopes of success. And people who are doomed to keep on trying, regardless of the probable outcome, will not be pleased for very long with the cult of quitting before you have got started.

Here, I believe, lies the chief explanation of the visible waning of the glory of the Futilitarian school; as may be inferred from the success of Mr. Warwick Deeping. The epiphany of a new novelist is never so amazing as the belated arrival at the top of the hill of a veteran, who had to make the grade under the burden of a name for years familiar and unimportant. So it might be profitable to inquire why Mr. Deeping, after a dozen novels which got nowhere in particular, got so notably somewhere with *Sorrell and Son*.

You may say that this was only a commercial success, that Mr. Deeping is not an art author. Well, as remarked at the beginning, the world teems and overflows with art authors of late years. Mr. Deeping is something rarer and possibly more significant—the producer of a book to which several hundred thousand people turned with grateful relief, after sampling the product of the art authors. (Like *The Sheik?* Not exactly; Mr. Deeping's public was not Miss Hull's; *Sorrell and Son* was read and enjoyed, with reservations, by a large number of highly intelligent people.) And if he should happen to be the forerunner of a new movement in fiction even the art authors, so long as they draw royalties and try to live on them, may profitably give him some attention.

How did he do it? Well, the trick of the mixture

is his own secret, but it is not very hard to identify the principal ingredients. *Sorrell and Son* began with a story—the oldest and simplest story in the world, but one that will be popular till the stars are old and the sun grows cold; the story of the man facing starvation, who hustles out and gets himself enough to eat. Add to that the history of a parental relation which was not a curse to both parent and child (here alone was sufficient novelty, in modern letters, to entitle the book to be called "daring"); and a sexual philosophy which seems a sensible middle-of-the-road adjustment, resting on no supernatural sanctions, allowing the reasonable measure of liberty which we all permit ourselves while condemning the excess we deplore in others.

But these explanations hardly explain. The story, engrossing as it is, peters out when Captain Sorrell is relieved from danger of actual want, less than half way through the book. The sexual philosophy, however attractive, turns out on closer inspection to be of little practical use; "do what you like so long as you don't hurt other people" is a rather irrelevant precept in a world where it is impossible to exist without hurting other people. I believe the popularity of *Sorrell and Son* was chiefly due to its pervasive tone. The book has guts.

Whatever the intrinsic value of this quality, it has been so absent from recent literature as to have acquired a scarcity value, and when Mr. Deeping served it up, readers rushed for it like wild beasts for a salt lick. Twenty years ago we were overfed with visceral literature; the recent cult of impotence is no doubt partly a reaction from that. But now the pendulum has begun

to swing the other way and Mr. Deeping was fortunate
enough to catch hold of it at the right moment. When
Captain Sorrell, so buffeted about by unjust Fate that
he had a perfect right to sit down and whine about it,
elected to get up and go to work instead, the thump-
thump of the first trunk he carried upstairs resounded
as loudly, and may echo as long, as the slam of Nora
Helmer's door.

Mr. Deeping must have realized this, though perhaps unconsciously; for the echo of that thump is responsible for most that is good in his next offering,
Doomsday. There is nothing very novel in the history
of Mary Viner's unwillingness to work for her living
as the wife of Arnold Furze, the farmer, and her
disillusionment, and her ultimate return. All this is too
carefully arranged, like one of those bridge hands which
Mr. Foster lays out in *Vanity Fair* to show how Y and
Z take five of the last six tricks against perfect defense.
As an argument in the case of the Old-Fashioned Virtues vs. Sin and Sophistication, it is pretty feeble.
  Mr. Deeping is not quite so bad as Booth Tarkington and Freeman Tilden, who seem afraid that the Old-
Fashioned Virtues cannot take the rubber unless they
hold all the face cards every hand, while Sin and
Sophistication are dealt nothing but a succession of
Yarboroughs. But he allows Mary, in her flight, to get
nothing but money; the husband and the friends she
got with it were pretty sad sticks. One cannot help feeling that Sin and Sophistication have more to offer than
that. Mr. Deeping knows better, when he is not
cramped by the exigencies of a plot. He appears to

think poorly of money, in *Doomsday;* but Stephen Sorrell made money, and enjoyed it, and was proud of it. He was less interesting to read about after he had it than while he was getting it, but neither he nor his creator pretended that the sweets of achievement were sour.

But on the other side of the argument of *Doomsday,* Arnold Furze echoes something of the spirit of Stephen Sorrell. The story of his wrestle with a stubborn soil has the same interest as the history of the pioneers who chopped this country out of the wilderness. For this Furze was spiritually a frontiersman, and it is a fact of some significance that he found England frontier enough for him. He had no illusions; he knew that "all work is dull, unless you have got the spirit in you." He had an immense amount of hard luck, but he stood up under it; he saw his farm as "a battlefield upon which to fight the god of all cussedness and inter-ference, Man's eternal fight." So he would seem signifi-cant, also, in the spiritual history of the human race, which has not got even this far by graceful gestures of resignation. Hard luck is plentiful in post-war England, and facing it the people of Mr. Aldous Huxley, for ex-ample, curl up and quit. Unless all biology is a lie, their fossil remains will some day be collected and catalogued and preserved in museums, by the descend-ants of the people of Mr. Warwick Deeping.

Mere survival is of course no conclusive proof of merit; yet even the Futilitarians elect to survive, in their own persons, though they rarely desire continua-tion in children. And nobody can survive, nobody would have survived this long, unless somebody had had guts.

Without that quality—the spirit that makes a man stand up against hard work and hard luck—the machinery of what we call civilization could not be kept going at even its present low degree of efficiency; and however poorly the Futilitarians think of civilization as a whole, they are apt to be rather tenderly addicted to the comforts and suavities which the machinery creates. A certain amount of work has to be done to keep the furnaces stoked and the engines going, and it is not quite certain that "What's the use?" will forever be accepted as an excuse for ducking out of it.

All literature, as Aristotle, Cabell, and others have reminded us, is literature of escape—escape for the artist, and for his readers too if he is competent. But our Futilitarians seem to have no desire to escape from the sticky chaos around them; they love to wallow in it, and paleontology suggests that this is a very perilous occupation for any of the larger mammals. The species that wallowed are the species whose bones are now on display in the Museum on Central Park West; the species that still survive, notably the species known as *Homo Sapiens* which contemplates the evidence of paleontology (none too sapiently in the case of the Chaotic novelists) are the species which had energy enough to try to bring order out of chaos, or sense enough, failing that, to pick out the nearest exit. This illustration from biology, I believe, has a valid application to esthetics.

It is customary to call this Invertebrate philosophy a consequence, or a distinguishing feature, of post-war disillusionment. So far as America goes, I suspect it is quite as much due to post-war prosperity. For

Futilitarianism is a luxury, which must be paid for by somebody. It can be afforded only in societies which are either beneath hope or above fear. There were plenty of societies in Europe after the war which seemed momentarily too far sunken for hope, but after the shock had passed they all set to work to try to pull themselves out, and they have met with some modest success. Even the most thoroughly wrecked of them all, the Russian emigrés, have usually managed to stitch some sort of scheme of life together by now. Only America, for the moment lolling in prosperity, with neither danger nor discomfort in immediate prospect, can afford to support a whole school of thinkers who conclude that all is sound and fury, signifying nothing. Futilitarians who remain in European letters are apt to be rich men, aristocrats, who in the present quiescence of subversive political movements have no reason to fear danger or discomfort for themselves, and accordingly have leisure to spare for gloomy contemplation.

One must go down, to savor properly the pleasure of climbing up, which probably explains why the reaction against Futilitarianism is most visible in England. England lost the war, even if the British Empire won it; but England straightway set to work to get back as much as possible of what was gone, and has visibly recovered a good deal of it already. (The people Mr. Aldous Huxley writes about have not helped much in that recovery, and unless human nature has greatly changed they will not enjoy much of the profit.) America used to like success stories, while the country was being built up. Now, for us as a people, the thrill of the hard ascent is gone; we ride at the moment on the top of the wave, and can afford to play with the discovery that all is vanity. A collapse of our uneasy prosperity might hasten the change in taste which is already on the way.

So, at any rate, it has happened before. We live in an age of disintegration, but only inexcusable ignorance of history can account for the impression that it is the first of its kind. It is the sixth major period of disintegration in recorded Occidental history; and the record of the five preceding ages teaches that the chaos succeeding the breakup of old patterns is inevitably followed by the formation of new patterns. That the artist can occasionally help in that process is suggested by one of the classic instances of the literature of escape, St. Augustine's *City of God*.

The age which Augustine contemplated was quite as appallingly chaotic as that which has come under the observation of Miss Rose Macaulay or Mr. Aldous Huxley. Rome had fallen, the world was breaking up; even as Augustine wrote the Vandals were at the gate. In that situation Augustine reacted instinctively as the true artist will always react; he sought a pattern, and finding none in the mass of external phenomena, he rolled his own. He evolved an order out of his own consciousness, and his pattern, a work of the creative imagination begotten by the need to escape from unendurable reality, served very largely as the model on which Europe was ultimately reorganized in a new order which endured for centuries. It can be argued that Augustine did more lasting harm to the human race than all the Goths and Vandals who ever looted a palace or stormed a wall; but that is beside the point. Augustine is an instance of man fighting instead of surrendering, fighting his way upward. Not very far up as yet? Perhaps not; but do our Futilitarians really wish that *Homo Sapiens* had gone the way of *Eoanthropus?*

Suppose they do, others disagree with them; which others, according to all the prospects, will presently include the majority of book buyers. Just as the overdoing of success stories at the beginning of the century promoted the reaction to the all-is-vanity school, so the normal reader, speaking psychiatrically as well as statistically, feels that a little impotence goes a long way. The Chaotics have had things their own way for a decade and it begins to appear that most readers are becoming weary of them. For there is no nourishment in their bill of fare. A good deal of the world's great literature has dealt with unsuccessful men, but very little of it with men who quit trying. Consider Roland, who had enough grievances to satisfy even Mr. dos Passos. He was betrayed by a scoundrel, he was overwhelmed by irresistible numbers; he was even allowed the gloomy perception that his own strategical mistakes were partly to blame for his misfortunes. None the less he kept on until he could no longer stand up; when he fell, he managed to expire with grace and dignity; and even as he lay beaten and dying, he made the triumphant Saracens shake in their boots with one blast on his ivory horn.

Mr. Warwick Deeping has ventured a toot on that celebrated trumpet. Unless all signs fail, it will presently be picked up and blown by somebody of greater lung power, and when that happens recruits for the cause will come running. For the Impotents are flying in the face of Nature, a Nature which created the majority of organisms with a tendency to fight rather than quit.

Call this a hopeless and foredoomed adventure, if you like; you may be right. So far as I can see, the human race is only playing out the schedule for the short end. But we are still a long way from the end of the season (barring some unexpected explosion of the solar system), and even if we are not going to finish anywhere in particular we may reasonably hope to win a few games on the way. Any intelligent man who did not believe this would commit suicide; and our Futilitarians have never given this crowning proof of their sincerity. We're here, quite possibly, for no better reason than because we're here, but here we are at all events, and the artist, like anybody else, must regard himself and his work in their relation to this community enterprise.

What he chooses to think and do for his own amusement is his own affair; but when he asks the world to feed him in consideration for the services he renders, he obligates himself to give his money's worth like anybody else. The artist is an entertainer, whether he calls himself a realist or a romancer; in one way or another he must amuse, or at least divert, his public. He sings for his supper. You may hold with Mr. Kipling that he sings to encourage the workers of the community in their labors, or with Mr. Cabell that his song distracts them from the perception that their labors are in vain; but at any rate he sings for their entertainment, and by virtue of satisfying his public he is enabled to live by his trade instead of by selling gents' furnishings. Some of our earnest interpreters of life may not relish this emphasis on the economic aspect of their labors; but the very greatest artists have always most clearly recognized that they sang for their supper, however they chose to select their public, and whatever time they may have taken off after supper to warble another song or two for their private amusement. I cannot see that a commercial integrity which was not unworthy of William Shakespeare is beneath the dignity of our average young spiritual autobiographer.

Nobody will pay another man to entertain him if he can entertain himself as well; the author must live by giving the customer something better. Anyone can observe his own chaos, perceive his own futility. The novelist must provide something more amusing. If he can find no unifying principle in perceptible phenomena he must invent one. It may be as mistaken as the cosmologies of Thales or Heraclitus, but like them it will serve its purpose by giving satisfaction, however impermanent, to its inventor; and to the persons who would rather pay money for his entertaining inventions than contemplate the void and formless chaos which anybody can see for himself.

So it matters not at all, so far as the novelist's peculiar problem is concerned, whether the chaos is in the material or in the soul of the artist. The point is that order, if there be any, lies, and has always lain, and must always lie, in the soul of the artist; whether that soul belong to a Great Architect of the Universe or a practicing fictioneer.

THE PRIVATE LIFE OF PARIS OF TROY

By courtesy of Dr. Egidius Kuemmelspalter of Heidelberg I am able to present excerpts from a cuneiform tablet lately discovered in the excavations at Boghaz-Keui, which that distinguished savant has identified as nothing less than the diary of Princess Cassandra of Troy. Publication of the full text is unavoidably deferred; but as recent volumes by John Erskine and Edward Lucas White have reinterpreted the history of Helen purely from the standpoint of Achœan propaganda, Dr. Kuemmelspalter feels that materials for a Trojan view of the question of war guilt should no longer be withheld.

WELL, Paris has gone abroad at last and left that woman behind on Mount Ida, so now perhaps we can have some peace in the family. I must say I think this whole affair has been mishandled from start to finish, but of course they never pay any attention to me.

Father thinks that when the boy has seen the world, and other women, he'll be willing to talk about an annulment, and that Œnone will accept any reasonable offer. But I'm not so sure.

"Besides," I said to father, "why annul it? He'll only marry somebody else, probably just as undesirable. If the boy can't even spend a summer in the mountains without getting married you might as well let him stay married. Give Œnone an allowance—it needn't be much to look big to a country girl up state —and she'll stay on Mount Ida, where she belongs. Then Paris can't get into that kind of trouble again."

"I agree with your conclusions," said Hector, "though not with your reasoning. Marriage is a sacrament. The abuse of the privilege of parole and commutation is wrecking our entire system of penology. . . . I mean—" (Hector makes so many public speeches that he doesn't always remember what subject is under discussion.) "I mean the divorce evil is gnawing like a canker at the heart of our civilization." (He gets that sort of thing from Andromache, of course.) "Whither are we drifting? Something ought to be done about it. We families of the old stock should uphold the sanctity of the home. Shall we go the way of Greece? Shall we get a reputation like that of the Pelops family?"

"People of no breeding," said father. "What can you expect?"

"Precisely—but it's that sort of people that are coming to the front in Greece. It's all due," Hector went on in his best statesmanlike manner, "to this influx of alien races that can't understand our institutions and our ideals. Unless something is done to stop this Nordic immigration—"

"Now don't get on that again," said Deiphobus irritably. "This girl Paris married isn't a Nord. I hear she's rather suspiciously brunette. She told him her father was an Achæan with jaundice; but how she explained herself—"

"Sunburn," said Hector. "A tanned healthy daughter

of Zeus's own country. You remember the stories Uncle Anchises used to tell us about that girl he picked up on Mount Ida—"

"You'd think she was Aphrodite," Deiphobus admitted. "But all these old gentlemen become romantic when they recall the vanished days of youth."

"Come, come!" said father. "No use raking over these old scandals. Whatever your Uncle Anchises may have done when he was a young man, he's long ago lived it down. As for Paris, we can trust the boy to come to his senses."

"His what?" I asked. "Anybody who'd serve as judge at a beauty contest—"

But of course they don't pay any attention to me.

But such a place to send him! That was mother's doing, of course.

"Off to Salamis," I asked her, "to visit Aunt Hesione? Why, he'll be bored to death in that poky little town! He ought to have taken this chance to see Cnossus."

"They say Cnossus isn't what it used to be," mother explained. "Since the war in Crete prices have gone up so terribly that you don't see anybody but Achæan war profiteers taking advantage of the exchange rate."

"Just the same," I reminded her, "Cnossus is still Cnossus."

"Well, that's the trouble," she admitted. "I'm afraid for Paris. A boy brought up in a Zeus-fearing home might meet with temptations—"

"Paris will find temptation in Salamis," I told her, "if Aunt Hesione has a pretty maid. Mother, you've kept him tied to your apron strings; no wonder he's easy for any clever woman. Those Cnossus girls might at least give him some experience." But of course that was going too far.

"Cassandra, I'm surprised at you! You girls have such advanced ideas; you talk about everything, you dress so immodestly— When I was a young girl no woman felt decently dressed without a corset; but you go around in your loose clothes and talk about experience—"

There's no use arguing with mother when she gets like that. The poor dear is so hopelessly Mid-Minoan.

WELL, at least Paris didn't get into trouble in Salamis; he didn't stay long enough. I don't like this idea of his going on to Lacedæmon, but father seems to think it's all right. He says it may ease our diplomatic relations with the Achæans—rather strained, just now. They're always writing notes about the tariffs on the Hellespont. Whose Hellespont is it, anyway? And Hector only makes things worse with his speeches to the Kappa Kappa Kappas about hundred per cent Trojanism and exclusion of Nordic immigration.

"But," I told father, "it may be all very well to know people like the Atridæ in a business way, but you wouldn't invite them to your house. And if Paris visits Menelaus—"

"Oh, the boys are well enough—Menelaus and his brother. Serious young men, who seem to be trying to live down the family reputation."

"Everyone has his pet Nord," I reminded him rather ungenerously.

"Certainly," said father, very stately, "I have no sympathy with Hector's race prejudice. Some of my best friends are Nords. . . . Besides, Helen belongs to the old Mediterranean stock."

"Yes," I said, "but her mother—!" He waved his hand impatiently.

"Cassandra, I don't understand where you young people get hold of these old scandals! Leda's dead— let's give her the benefit of the doubt. And at any rate Helen's father—I knew him well—was a gentleman of the old school. It will do the boy good to be the guest of a woman of his own class. May help him forget that taste for country girls."

WELL! I told them he ought to have gone to Cnossus. . . . Deiphobus had a letter from Paris yesterday.

"Σήματα λυγρά," he said (he does so love to flaunt his few phrases of Achæan). "In other words, bad news. Paris is coming home—with Helen."

"Helen!" I gasped. "Good Olympus! You don't mean—"

"But I do," said Deiphobus. "I mean exactly that."

"Well, what was Menelaus doing all this time?"

"Why," Deiphobus explained, "it seems he had to go to Cnossus a day or two after Paris arrived. Of course they couldn't both go, and leave a guest to his own devices—"

"So Helen stayed and Paris was left to her devices," I finished. "Oh, you know he wouldn't have had brains enough to do a thing like this of his own accord. That woman wound him round her finger. But Menelaus! I suppose it was his first chance to get over to Cnossus alone since he was married, but mere courtesy ought to have kept him at home. Still, what can you expect from these new rich?"

"It was a business trip," said Deiphobus. "You don't suppose anybody would voluntarily leave a woman like Helen, do you, even for a trip to Cnossus?"

"Nonsense. He was bored and so was she; and when a silly boy like Paris came along— But the idea of his doing such a thing just when the international situation was clearing up! Of course he'll have to send her back."

"Well, you know, I'm for letting him keep her," said Deiphobus. "This Achæan saber rattling has gone far enough. Must we always be the ones that have to make the concessions for the sake of peace?"

Did you ever hear of such a thing? Risk another crisis for the sake of a bored wife and a silly boy? Well, Hector won't hear of it, I know; he's so strong for the sanctity of marriage. And mother won't, either; when she puts her foot down father always lets her have her way, and of course she's furious at this woman.

WELL, they're here, and I must say Helen is behaving very well. (She'd better.) Beautiful? Well, hardly; but you never have time to think about that. Very chic, of course; and quite a manner. All these Tyndaridæ have a manner. Deiphobus thinks she's charming; but then he's such a helpless ignoramus about women.

I THINK they must all have gone crazy, except me. Father has annulled Paris's marriage and served Menelaus with divorce papers by publication. He charges desertion, on the strength of that trip to Cnossus; I saw the tablet myself. And it's mother's doing—mother who was so enraged at Œnone.

"After all," she explained to me, "Helen is one of the old stock, like ourselves." (Mother takes her Society of Argo Descendants so seriously, poor thing.) "It's too bad she made that unfortunate first marriage with a man so far beneath her, but why should one mistake ruin a whole life? Helen has quite opened her heart to me. Her manners are sophisticated, of course; she belongs to her generation. But she agrees with me about the importance of keeping up the old traditions. Just a sweet old-fashioned girl—"

I see plainly that this woman is going to get us all into trouble.

WELL, they're here, and I must say Helen is behaving and I don't understand yet just how it happened. Maybe it will all be clear when they've finished that White Tablet they're getting out to explain it for the neutrals. Anybody can see, of course, that this war has been forced upon us; but all this about ultimatums and the Achæan mobilization is too complicated for me.

But what it comes down to is that Hector—yes, Hector, the defender of the sanctity of marriage—was really to blame. Hector and his ethnology and his Anti-Immigration League. When he said that this demand for the return of Helen was foreign interference in a purely domestic issue, that was the end of watchful waiting. It would be unpatriotic to say so, but I can't help wondering if it doesn't look like a purely domestic issue to Menelaus too.

Oh, our whole diplomacy has been badly bungled!

The idea of Deiphobus asking the Achæan ambassador at their last interview if he was going to war just for a word, matrimony; just for a scrap of brick. I'm afraid they'll use that in their propaganda.

At this point there is a lacuna in the document, covering apparently a space of several years.

Who would ever have thought it would drag on like this? Hector talks about the trench war having reached a stalemate, and depending on attrition and waiting for the growth of war weariness in the Achæan people, but I don't know. They're tightening the blockade and everyone is beginning to feel it.

Everyone but Helen, that is; if she's ever had a meatless day yet nobody's heard of it. Not that I see much of her, of course; I'm busy with my war work. But I hear enough about her—always entertaining. "One must keep up the morale of our boys who are home on leave," she says.

Home on leave! Paris has never been away from home, and I'm afraid unless he goes to the front before long the prestige of the dynasty will be affected. Deiphobus would have sent him into the trenches with his regiment at the very start, but Hector stopped it. "Keep him at headquarters," he insisted. "We must use the boy's talents as liaison officer."

Imagine Hector joking about a thing like that! Troy hasn't been the same since Paris brought that woman home.

HECTOR's great spring drive has started off splendidly. The Achæans have lost their first line of trenches all along the front and they say Agamemnon has relieved Achilles of his command. Now's the time to end the war with a knockout blow. I don't think any of us could stand another winter of this deadlock in the trenches.

AND still it drags on. Since that counter-offensive when Hector was killed I've begun to wonder if we can really beat them after all. But of course I don't dare say so; there's enough defeatist propaganda about already.

One thing that helps is that Helen and I are becoming quite good friends, now that Paris is in the trenches at last. After all, the war does bring people together. I'm afraid I judged her too harshly in the old days; she's really had a hard life.

"You can't imagine," she told me, "how dull my girlhood was. Always reminding ourselves that we of the old stock must set an example to these pushing parvenus of the newer immigration—I hated it! I longed for a breath of clean air from the open spaces. I wanted to get away from it all. . . . And then I met Menelaus. Here, I thought, is a man unspoiled, red-blooded and virile—a fit mate for me. . . . And then to marry him and find that his one ambition was to make himself a synthetic gentleman, to live down his family and live up to me—!

"But I always affect men that way. When Theseus kidnaped me I expected to suffer the ultimate outrage. I tried to steel myself against it, to reflect that after all one grows by experience—that it makes a full life— And then to have this dreadful ruffian turn me over to his mother and treat me like a trust fund— Oh! The men I have known!"

"No wonder you were attracted to Paris," I observed. "He may not be clever but at least he's a gentleman."

"Yes," she said thoughtfully, "yet the war doesn't seem to have matured him as it has most people. See how wonderfully Deiphobus has come out since Hector was killed and he had to take over the High Command. . . . But perhaps now that Paris is in the trenches—"

"It wasn't fair of Deiphobus to send him to the front," I said hotly. "Poor Hector would never have torn your husband from your arms—"

"We mustn't blame Deiphobus," said Helen. "He's doing his best to mobilize the man-power of the nation. I gave Paris willingly to my adopted country. I am no hyphenated Trojan. I too must do my bit."

PARIS came to see me yesterday—home on leave—and I was amazed at the change in him. He's lean and hard and self-reliant—and the astounding thing is that he seems to like trench life.

"I was getting fat and lazy at the base camp," he said, "and I felt like a slacker. The minute Helen changed her mind and agreed to let me go to the front I jumped at the chance."

"She must be delighted to see you looking so well."

"I don't know," he said with an uneasy frown. "She seems to think I'm out of character. . . . By the way, do you ever hear anything about Œnone any more?"

"Œnone? Good heavens, no! Why should I?"

"I just wondered," said Paris. "Well, good-by. I'm going back."

"Back to the front?" I asked. "Why, you only came home yesterday. Do you mean to say Deiphobus gave you only twenty-four hours' leave?"

"Don't blame Deiphobus," he said as he went out. He added something I couldn't catch; it sounded like "worse places than the front."

I wonder what he could have meant.

Poor Helen! I suppose I ought to say poor Paris, but after all he's dead and she's left to bear her grief. And the worst of it was that there was a pacifist movement to send her back to Menelaus and end the war with a peace without victory. But Deiphobus stopped that. He explained the underlying causes of the war—Mycenæ-to-Mesopotamia and all the rest of it—and said that the only answer was force to the uttermost.

No, I can't pretend that the marriage wasn't as big a surprise to me as to everyone else; and I do think Helen might have told me. There's been rather malicious talk in certain circles; but while of course it is rather soon after Paris's death our petty proprieties seem trivial in times like these. Helen has been disappointed in all the men she's known, but Deiphobus is a better mate for her. . . . And how wonderful for him! He's always been grim and solitary but I know he's loved her for years. Now he has attained his heart's desire at last.

Poor Deiphobus is so devoted to his duty! He's only been home on leave once since the honeymoon. Of course, as he says, the Commander-in-Chief has to set an example, but he might think of Helen's side of it. It can't be so easy to be a war bride, especially when you're of enemy alien origin.

But thank goodness it can't last much longer. The last Achæan offensive was smothered in mud and blood. I think we've broken their will to victory.

AT last! . . . I don't believe I could live through another armistice celebration. We're all more or less crazy, I suppose, with the lifting of the long strain; but I'm really worried about Deiphobus. He looks terribly depressed.

"You need a long rest," I told him. "Now that it's all over you and Helen ought to go away somewhere for a second honeymoon." He looked at me very queerly.

"Cassandra," he said at last, "you remember how all this began? With Menelaus making a trip to Cnossus, alone. Well, now that the war is over we can afford to be fair to the enemy. Menelaus may have been a rather impervious person, but he had some sound ideas, I imagine. He certainly could appreciate Cnossus. . . . I'm thinking of running over to Cnossus myself as soon as we've demobilized."

"Oh, Helen will love that!" I told him. "The blockade hasn't given her a chance to get a Cnossus gown for ten years."

"Oh, I'm going alone," he said hurriedly. "Just a business trip."

What kind of business, I wonder? I'd have asked

him, but he went off to see about bringing in the Wooden Horse.

Personally I think it's a great mistake to be so hasty in putting up a war memorial, and I don't like the design of this one at all. But of course they never pay any attention to me—

At this point, for obvious reasons, the narrative abruptly ends.

THE COMSTOCK LOAD

Reflections on Censorship

AMONG the scientific researches that the Rockefeller Foundation might profitably finance is the beginning of a meteorology of opinion. Why do listless, almost imperceptible thought-currents suddenly become overheated and go straight upward at terrific speed, with much resultant damage to whoever happens to be in the vicinity? Let the foundations of this science be laid by those who are competent to do it; but it happens that the genesis of one recent tornado was visible to everybody, and from that episode some moral reflections may be drawn. To say that they will be drawn would be quite too visionary; for the lesson to which these happenings point was one that ought to have been evident long ago. Still there is some hope that the men responsible, thick though their heads appear to be, may have dimly grasped the obvious at last.

The agitation for a censorship of the arts recurs as irregularly but as inevitably as Florida hurricanes, and any prudent artist will build his house accordingly. 1927 was another year of the Big Wind, and this time the hurricane was the most destructive of a generation. Outwardly, indeed, it worked only moderate harm; its material result was the bestowal of long life and prosperity on a worthless play which was about to close

when the police raided it, and whose producers could
well afford the ten-day jail sentences and moderate
fines which they eventually incurred in consideration
of the extended run; and the suppression of an excellent play, "The Captive," without due process of law,
by a campaign of intimidation which reflects about
equal discredit on the District Attorney's office and on
the motion picture magnates who own the trade mark
of the late Charles Frohman.

But there were two other consequences which may
presently bring immense injury to all the arts. One
was a tightening of the New York obscenity laws,
which, though at first sight it may seem little more
than ridiculous, opens the way for about all that the
wildest fanatics have been howling for in recent years;
and the other was the bringing of a new and enormous
reënforcement to the champions of censorship. The
recent excitement resurrected all the old war cries on
both sides; among them, on the side which may be
provisionally if not quite accurately described as the
friends of the arts, much indignant protest against
"Comstockery." But this year's censorship wave, in
New York and Boston, was not Comstockery. It was
something much older and more formidable; it was the
result of the entry into the argument of a force which
had been rather quiescent of late years, and might have
remained quiescent still if it had not been provoked
by the criminal folly of a few theatrical producers. The
cardinal distinction of the censorship movement of
1927 was that for the first time in American history the
decisive forces behind it were not Protestant but
Catholic, even though in New York the Protestants

were still allowed to appear in their traditional posts of leadership. That is a much more serious matter than the sporadic and derisory activity of vice societies, as all the arts may presently discover.

IT happened that the biography of Anthony Comstock, by Heywood Broun and Margaret Leech, appeared, most felicitously for the authors, while this excitement was at its height. As the first publication of the Literary Guild, this book provoked so much excitement and debate over trade ethics, trade customs, and what not, that actually to read the *corpus delicti* in so notable a test case seemed as irrelevant as poking into the private life of Dred Scott. But a great many people read it none the less and found it instructive and amusing; I found it so, but found something else rather disquieting. This book came near converting me to the principle, so beloved of patriotic societies, that the business of biography is moral edification. A study which treats Anthony Comstock almost with admiration, which makes him out at worst as a human being, in whose defense extenuating circumstances might be urged, comes near deserving suppression by the Vice Society as pernicious to the morals of American youth.

For all of us may appeal to extenuating circumstances; the argument that in the course of justice none of us should see salvation has been perverted into the genial contention that in the course of charitable good-fellowship all of us might as well see salvation. But such salvation as there is or ever will be (one may in reason hope for at least some temporary amelioration for the race, however cheerless the prospects of the individual) must be achieved by hard work; and the criterion of a man's goodness or badness is whether he has helped or hindered. (If you don't believe this, read no farther; you won't believe the rest of it either.) Comstock, on the whole, seems to have hindered, even if you allow for the service he rendered by making his ideas ridiculous. He was unquestionably sincere, as the saying goes; but one would have supposed that after six thousand years of civilization the human race might have outgrown the practice of regarding sincerity as a virtue in itself.

Possibly Miss Leech and Mr. Broun would not go that far; but they appear to regard life from the standpoint of motive and intention, which is natural enough, for they are novelists. But it seems to some of us (and with the concurrence of so good a novelist as Samuel Butler) that life may more properly and usefully be regarded from the standpoint of results. Not what a man meant, but what he did—and if you say that what he did was not his own fault, but that of his environment or his ancestors, you are saying what may be true, but is irrevelant to the more urgent question of what all of us, together, are going to be able to do. Once begin making exculpatory allowances and you had better scamper back to the shelter of an atonement theory as quickly as you can, for that is the only place where you will find safety.

This biography, of course, must have been finished before the outburst of censorious zeal that marked the early months of 1927; and the authors may owe some of their excess of Christian charity to a conviction that the devil was already bound in the bottomless pit and that there was no use kicking a fiend who was down. If St. Michael, victorious, had sat down to write an obituary of the dragon, he might have felt a sportsmanlike impulse to deal generously with the record of that old serpent; which he would no doubt have regretted if the dragon had come out of his coma and started the fight all over again after the paper had gone to press. A year earlier it might have seemed safe to dance Comstock's scalp; but he is not dead so long as our statute books are weighted with the oppressive and unreasonable laws that he devised and lobbied through Congress and Legislature. There will probably never be another Comstock; he was a unique and peculiar embodiment of a spirit which existed before him, and still persists, and would persist if he had never lived at all. But thanks to him that spirit is armed with a weapon of unholy power; because of his fanatical singlemindedness, his irresistible energy, his genuine conviction of what most people, even in his time, believed only perfunctorily, that one with God is a majority, each of his successors is armed for offense and defense almost as invincibly as Siegfried and Perseus. This is the burden of Anthony, the Comstock load.

THE customary defense of Comstock is that all his blunders are nullified by his service in suppressing the smut pamphlets which seem to have been pretty generally on sale sixty years ago. How much harm this printed filth actually did may be open to question, but it does not appear that it ever did any good except to the people who got the money for it. Mr. Broun

indeed argues that such works as *Only a Boy* vaccinate impressionable youth against the undesirable
glamor of sex, which may be true. But they are quite
as likely to vaccinate against the desirable glamor, if
one admits that there may be such a thing. No tears
need be shed over this first stage of Comstock's activity, but it is going pretty far to treat it as complete
justification for the later Comstock, who attacked *Mrs.
Warren's Profession* and the wax figures in department
store show windows with equal zeal; or to treat it, as
some worthy persons did, as full justification for the
prosecution of *Jurgen* by Mr. Comstock's successor.

Indeed, one finishes the biography with the impression that there was a deeper irrelevance in Comstock's
crusades against pornography and what he thought was
pornography. His abnormal fear and hatred of sex or
anything that suggested it to his superheated mind
was, after all, not his dominant characteristic. Essentially he was a bully; if the human race were asexual,
reproducing by fission, Comstock would still have been
a nuisance. Courage he certainly had and plenty of it
—but he was a large and powerful man who could reasonably count on getting the best of any physical encounter; and behind him, after the first few years, he
had the Law, which in that less sophisticated day was
still some protection against the knife and the gun.

Possibly the most significant sentence in the book
is a quotation from Comstock's diary, occasioned by
no more flagitious an occurrence than a game of
croquet with his wife and a few friends: "I insisted on
fair play and some thought different." There, in a line,
is the biography of Anthony Comstock. What he in-

sisted on was fair play, and God help those who
"thought different."

His first feat was the famous killing of the saloon
keeper's mad dog, in his home town in Connecticut;
his next the destruction of the saloon keeper's stock.
During his Civil War service he seems to have spent
most of his time in trying to keep the army from swear-
ing and smoking. Not till he returned from the war, in
that state of mind of the returned soldier which has
been blamed for so much of late years, did he turn his
chief attention to the preservation of what he regarded
as purity.

From the beginning he had much success, but the
courts had an inconvenient habit of occasionally acquit-
ting people whose guilt was clear enough to Comstock.
More law was needed, then, and Comstock got it; got
it by a persistent and indefatigable effort which certainly compels admiration, whatever you think of his
creed and his methods. Not that there was any grave
danger that legislators of the early seventies would
offer open opposition to his demands; they agreed
with his doctrines in theory at least, even if few of
them cared enough about purity to give their time to
its preservation. But they were too busy to pay much
attention to Anthony's crusade until, like the unjust
judge in Holy Writ, they were wearied by his continual coming and gave in.

This was in the Gilded Age, the low water mark of
American public morals; lower even than the new bene-
diction of understanding between public officials and
private interests which took place in the golden prime
of Harding. Of the members of the Congress which

wrote Comstock's views on obscenity into the statutes
of the United States where they remain in force to
this day, it is hardly an exaggeration to say that half
of them had already been caught stealing, and the
others were wondering how soon they too would be detected. But of all this the holy Anthony was oblivious.
Not that bribery did not look like vice to him; he
was more than once approached with bribes himself,
and he always refused them. But bribery was a trivial
matter, if only the bribe takers would fall in with
Comstock's ideas and enable him to belt the *ceinture de
chasteté* on American youth. As presently they did.

There does not seem to be much evidence that the
sexual morality of the American people was materially
higher in the late seventies than in the earlier seventies;
but whatever the boys and girls might be doing, Comstock certainly purified the news stands. Armed with
the sword he himself had forged, he was irresistible.
In a decade or so his victory over his first enemy was
complete; the obscene pamphlets which had provoked
him into an activity that had made him famous had
been driven into a furtive obscurity from which they
have never since emerged. And here was Comstock, re-
nowned and powerful, with the laws of his own writing
behind him, his own hand-made fighting machine, the
Vice Society, at his command—and his occupation
gone. Not unnaturally he made himself more occupa-
tions, and some of them were grotesque enough.

Some of them were worse than that. He appointed
himself the champion of orthodoxy and found the
free-love doctrines of earnest atheists an excuse for
persecuting them less as free lovers than as atheists.

He drove to suicide an unbalanced woman guilty of writing a book which endeavored, however clumsily, to make marriage more decent and beautiful—but this was only one of fifteen suicides which he was proud of having inspired, and the last one. As time passed people stopped committing suicide to gratify him; sex appeared less of a peril, contributions to the Vice Society decreased, the world seemed moving away from Comstock. Desperately he tried to catch up with it, tried this and that. He spent much time attacking lotteries, and local gambling houses which were by-products of political corruption. But a short-sightedness that sprang inevitably from his temperament and upbringing confined him to accidentals; he was unable to diagnose the disease of which protected gambling and protected prostitution were symptoms, and so he missed the chance of his lifetime. The more intelligent Parkhurst grasped political corruption as a whole; on that issue he got the spotlight, and thrust Comstock into a shadow from which he never really emerged.

He descended to raiding art stores, trying to suppress the catalogue of the Art Students' League, turning "September Morn" from an unimportant painting into a valuable commercial property; he essayed to abolish Bernarr MacFadden and Bernard Shaw; but he seldom got anywhere. As Mr. Broun observes, he had finished the giants and there was no one left to fight but windmills. He became a joke. His last effort of consequence, in 1914, was a protest against a French comedy of delicate and wistful beauty (naturally it looked revolting and obscene to Comstock) which the District Attorney simply laughed off.

Yet still the soldier of the Lord went on fighting, and not the Lord's battles only. More quarrelsome and ill-tempered as the years went by, he kept getting into fights, not with agents of Satan selling implements of sin, but with lawyers who dared to cross-examine him, with pedestrians who resented being knocked down because they brushed against him on crowded sidewalks. He had pampered his overbearing and bellicose disposition because he had been big enough and strong enough to get away with it; when he grew too old to win his fights, he still could not help provoking them. Here, plainly, was the ruling passion of his life; his pathological sex phobia merely happened to give it a picturesque direction.

WELL, what did he accomplish? Comstock is gone but Shaw and MacFadden are still with us; and between Comstock and MacFadden it would be uncharitable to express a preference. Sex is still with us, for all Comstock's efforts; rather noticeably with us, one might say. But certainly the deliberate obscenity of our time —and without going into the question of what is and is not obscene, one may remark that obviously there is a good deal on the stage and the news stands to-day which at least tries to be obscene—is more suave, less repulsive than the obscenity which Comstock drove underground. Unless you hold with Comstock that sex is sin, that improvement in taste—much room as is left for further improvement—is something gained.

But not all of that credit can be given to Comstock; it is a change in the popular temper, the popular taste; it might have happened without him. Indeed, with the notable exceptions of his law-making and his stimulation of suicide, his biographers find it rather hard to see just what he did accomplish. Comstock had his virtues; he lived plainly and died poor though he could have enriched himself by giving up his crusades. Nor was he a hypocrite; despite what seems to have been an extraordinarily tepid marriage this "strong, virulent man" (to borrow the unforgettable phrase of a lady peace delegate on the Ford party) was never charged with sexual laxity. Though that would perhaps give no great surprise to the psychiatrist; his was the lust of the eye, which could be fed by the immense stock of obscene books and pictures which he had to retain as evidence.

His faults, to some extent, were those of his time; the decisions of various judges before whom he brought his complaints were even more savage than Comstock's own outbursts; some of them virtually decided that accusation was conviction, that no defense could be offered, that the book on which the complaint was based was too obscene to be offered to the jury. And in general, in the seventies and eighties, he had the support of public opinion; his principles were those professed by most respectable people, his only difference was that he was willing to act on those principles even at the cost of making himself ridiculous. His biographers appear to feel that it is creditable not to be afraid of looking ridiculous; and no doubt it is. But from the pragmatic point of view the fear of looking ridiculous has prevented an immense amount of harm to the innocent bystanders.

Times have changed; current opinion permits a

freedom of expression on sexual matters that would
have been unthinkable ten years ago; but for a few
enthusiasts—most of whom know as little about art as
the average reformer does about purity—that was not
enough. Hence the latest censorship wave, the blame
for which lies beyond any doubt upon the show business, or more exactly on the lunatic fringe of the show
business whom the sensible producers were unable to
control. They had more freedom than the stage in any
English-speaking country had known for the last two
hundred years, more freedom than it enjoys in many
Continental cities to-day; but that was too little. They
had all the traffic would bear, but they insisted on
reaching out for more. And when the explosion came,
some of the friends of art who rushed up all primed
for the battle wasted their ammunition by standing
out for free expression as a matter of principle.

This is not a matter of principle; it is a concrete,
not an abstract question, and regarded from any practical point of view the behavior of the producers who
set off the censorship movement of 1927 was no better
than suicidal lunacy. The acrobat in the circus who
piles tables one on top of the other and then sways
back and forth on this precarious pediment knows that
he can teeter just so far. One millimeter farther, and
over he goes. But he has a mattress to land on, which
is more than can be said for the theater.

That there was a point at which the stack of tables
would overbalance ought to have been obvious to every
showman, and no doubt was; but every man whose productions were in danger went on hoping, I suppose,
that he might get away before the crash. When the

crash came, it caught some of these fly-by-nights, though it did them no great injury; but it missed Mr. Belasco and Mr. Brady, who had accelerated the teetering of the stack of tables by producing a couple of pretty bad plays the year before (for the purest of moral purposes); it missed some other astute persons who were shrewd enough to take cover in time. But it worked far-reaching injury on interests considerably more important than these various showmen.

THE late eruption of righteous wrath in Boston had other origins, but it worked out to much the same conclusion as occurred in New York. For twenty-odd years the protection of Bostonian morals against impure books was in the sure and sinewy hands of the Reverend J. Frank Chase of the Watch and Ward Society, a Baptist; while simultaneously the Honorable John Michael Casey, whose religion is presumably that of the other Caseys, safeguarded the souls of theatergoers. Mr. Casey, it seemed, acquired his authority to bind and loose the ideas of Shaw and Ibsen by virtue of the fact that he had once been a trap drummer in theater orchestras, and accordingly knew all there was to know about the dramaturgic art. From the recent article by Mr. Karl Schriftgiesser in the Authors' League Bulletin one gathers that Mr. Casey is about as obtuse as most censors, yet in one respect one cannot help admiring him. The ideas by which he is guided in his decisions may be narrow enough and absurd enough, but at least, unlike other censors, he is willing to admit that they are Casey's ideas, and does not pretend that they are necessarily God's.

The Rev. J. Frank Chase was gathered to his reward some time ago, and since then the Boston Irish in public office have undertaken the control of published literature too. If Chase chastised the novelist with whips, the Irish chastise him with scorpions; Chase was willing to content himself with crucifying a novelist once in a while to encourage the others, but the Irish started off with a general St. Bartholomew massacre. This did no great harm to the novelists, all of whom can live without the Boston trade; indeed it furnished an easy criterion for division between the sheep and the goats. A man who has not had a novel prohibited in Boston can now be set down without further argument as a writer of no importance.[1] The Massachusetts statute dealing with obscene literature is provided with a clause which may damn a book on the strength of a single word, however blameless the rest of the volume; yet even so there are intelligent judges in Boston, and the courageous resistance of Mr. Mencken to the Watch and Ward Society a year or two ago showed that a man courageous enough to stand trial has some chance of laughing at the reformers. But thanks to the rabbit-like timidity of Boston booksellers there seems no great likelihood of any flood of test cases.

Boston, however, can be left out of account. The Irish own Boston and they might as well be left to control it in their own way. The beginnings of a distinct Boston-Irish culture are already visible; it owes

---

[1] I myself, at the moment of writing, am in that shameful category; but I suppose that the vigilance of the Sheehans and Flahertys will attend to my promotion before long.

as little to the defunct culture of historic Boston as
the Anglo-Saxons owed to the Romans of Britain, or
the Dorians to the dispossessed Minoans. (Though in
both these cases the ancient civilization did make its
mark on the newcomers, by a process of infiltration;
as the old New England culture will doubtless affect
the Irish, even against their will.) To those who observe the rise of that culture, without any particular
partisan preference for the old New England, it offers
much of interest, and it may be instructive to see what
it evolves out of its own materials, uncontaminated by
the nefarious doctrines of novelists from New York
and the Middle West. Let the tender shoots of the Neo-
Bostonian philosophy of life sprout and blossom, protected by the impenetrable fence of the Boston Irish
censorship; nobody but the Boston Irish themselves
can be greatly harmed.

But the provocation of the New York Irish is a much
more serious matter.

THE cultural average of the New York Irish, with
all allowance for exceptions on both sides, is about
two generations ahead of that of the Boston Irish.
Also, most of them are much more de-Hibernianized.
In Boston the Irish immigrants had to conquer and
possess the land over the opposition of an old stock
cohesive and well entrenched; but the Irish immigrants
came to New York at about the same time as another
swarm of immigrants from up-state and New England;
and to the making of the town by these two immigrant
streams the old New Yorkers, static and admirably de-
tached, offered no opposition, content to let who would

make the laws and manage the business of their city so long as they collected ground rent from the real estate. So, contributing each his separate talents, the Irishman and the up-stater and the New Englander made New York, built that structure to which later immigrants—Jews and Southerners and Italians—only added some few adornments; and in the process they all lost some of their racial consciousness. Your typical New York Irishman may be Irish for political and business purposes, but in his essential habits of thought he is a New Yorker.

Now of late years the New York Irish have been a pretty open-minded race, about such matters as absorb the interest of vice societies. Which may possibly be another indication that they are New Yorkers first, rather than Irishmen or even than Catholics; for certainly in the last decade Catholic bishops the world over have issued, on the whole, rather more, and more deplorable, pronouncements against short hair and short skirts and similar hellish devices than have the Protestant clergy. In 1922, indeed, an entirely legitimate meeting in New York, called to discuss the desirability of changes in the anti-birth-control laws, was broken up by the police, on what was, if not an order, certainly a pretty strong hint, from the archiepiscopal offices; but that was a mistake and to all appearance the local leaders of the Church promptly recognized that it had been a mistake. Nothing of the sort has occurred in the five years since.

How much of this liberalizing of the New York Catholic attitude in the past few years is due to the personal influence of the common-sense moderation of

Al Smith I do not know; but indirectly Al Smith is
certainly responsible. From the moment a New York
Catholic became a possible nominee for the presidency,
the other New York Catholics have carefully avoided
anything that might look like ecclesiastical interference
with secular affairs. (If Western and Southern Protestants were astute they would encourage this praiseworthy tendency, but apparently they would rather
have their grievance.) So, though a Catholic leader,
Monsignor Lavelle, was one of the little group of
earnest workers who used to go to Albany every year
and petition the legislature to put more teeth into
Comstock's laws for the preservation of aseptic literature, he was not the foremost of the band, nor did he
profess to command the authority of the church.

But why did Comstock's laws need more teeth?
Why, because the world had moved beyond Comstock;
because of late years judges and juries had shown an
inclination to common sense, and were no longer persuaded, as were the judges and juries of the seventies,
that accusation was conviction and defense was sheer
impertinence. For some years the Clean Books League,
whose ostensible leader (whatever forces may have
been behind it) was Justice John Ford, a jurist notable
for the frequency with which his own decisions are
reversed by higher courts, has been trying to get the
New York legislature to imitate the law of Massachusetts and provide that a single line may damn a
play or a book as "obscene, indecent, immoral or impure." These crusaders have always had some supporters at Albany, most of them rustic Republican
moralists from up-state; but year after year they have

been sent away empty-handed—and the decisive force in beating them was Tammany Hall.

Well, in 1927 they were beaten too; once more the novelists escaped. But at the same time the excesses of the show business provoked the legislature—specifically the Tammany members—into voting amendments to the laws covering indecency in the theater which apply to plays exactly what the Clean Books League wants to apply to published literature. Next winter Justice Ford and his colleagues may be expected to ask the Legislature, and with some reason, why a fable obscene on the stage is not equally obscene on the book-store counter.

IT was "The Captive" that started the trouble, and it is pretty hard for anybody to maintain that "The Captive" is obscene, indecent, immoral or impure. The District Attorney of New York (a Protestant) said that he so regarded it; but he never dared bring it to trial to see if a jury would agree with him. He bluffed it off the stage, thanks to the facts that Charles Frohman, Inc., is owned by the Famous Players and that the average motion-picture magnate is as timorous as a Boston bookseller; but he would not give it a chance for its life before twelve good men and true.

If "The Captive" had stood alone, however, it would have escaped. But on its trail came other plays dealing with sexual inversion, for which, according to the reports of those who saw them in the outlying regions, nothing at all could be said. That these plays were scared away from New York can certainly not be regarded as any loss; and it was when they had been scared away from New York, and before the legislature had acted, that Mr. Simeon Strunsky offered about the most intelligent comment that was made on this whole uproar. What the stage needs, he observed, is not censorship laws on the books, but censorship bills constantly awaiting the report of legislative committees —a censorship always *in posse,* always threatening, to keep the smutmongers scared into good behavior.

But that was too much to hope. The amendment to the obscenity laws which was enacted before the legislative session ended was introduced by a Republican up-state legislator; but it was prepared by the Tammany Protestant District Attorney and passed mainly by the votes of Tammany Catholic members. The best proof that Mr. Banton regarded his views on the obscenity of "The Captive" as eccentric is shown by the fact that he included in this bill an *ex post facto* clause condemning it—a provision that any play "depicting or dealing with the subject of sex degeneracy or sex perversion" is hereafter obscene, indecent, immoral and impure *per se.* By this principle of definition, any play (or any book) dealing with a love affair, whether consummated or not, outside of marriage, could be declared obscene by statute, however austere its plot or its language; and if some of the reformers get their way it soon will be.

Well, the bill was passed; and it was passed essentially because the show business had sinned away its day of grace. Tammany which in recent years had been open-minded and tolerant, Tammany which was content to allow more freedom of expression than the more fanatical of the Protestants would permit, or do

permit where they are in control—Tammany had been
wantonly provoked by the stupid excesses of the
theater. Whatever may be said in principle for the
late inclination of playwrights and producers to turn
over everything and see what is underneath it, it was
about as intelligent in practice as stepping off the
Woolworth Building to see how far you will fall. The
love of money was certainly the chief root of this evil;
but the love of principle helped too.

So far as the show business goes, this new law brings
us back to the days of Comstock; forty years' education of the public taste has been annulled by statute.
Yet it passed with singularly little opposition from
those whom it less obviously threatened. It was opposed, and diligently, by theater owners, because one
of its clauses provides that a theater where a play
subsequently found indecent is produced may be pad-
locked for a year. Naturally a business whose toes
were thus vigorously stepped on yowled to the skies;
but the general public regarded the prospective sufferings of theater owners with complete and admirable
indifference. Unfortunately this concentration on the
last clause of the bill distracted attention from the
other two.

The only protest, at the moment, against this inject-
ment of a new principle into the regulation of literary
morals came in an editorial in the New York *Times,*
which subjected the clause dealing with perversion
plays to an analysis whose logic can hardly be refuted.
Beneath all our indecency laws, state and national, lies
the general principle that what is indecent is what
seems indecent to any twelve men who happen to be

selected as a jury in any given case (or, allowing for local differences in procedure, to any judge or board of judges.) If, the *Times* argued, a play such as "The Captive" is found obscene by that process, that settles it, and would settle it, anyway, without this addition to the statute; whereas if it were found unobjectionable by a jury or bench of judges it is a pure play according to all the principles of American jurisprudence, though now made impure by statutory definition. If the play is in fact obscene this amendment is unnecessary; if it is in fact (as determined by a jury) not obscene the law which pronounces it so is arbitrary and oppressive.

All this is true enough, but it does not change the situation. And more serious still is the provision that any "scene, tableau, incident, part or portion" damns the whole play as indecent. Obviously this condemns everything Shakespeare ever wrote; just as obviously, neither police nor vice societies will prosecute Shakespeare. But the moderns will have to watch their step. And while this amendment will undoubtedly purge the theater of the needless and pointless foulness with which so many plays of the last year or two were disfigured, one need not be a professional writer to feel that the purifiers, in order to do a little right, have done a great wrong. Writers of printed fiction have been curiously insensitive to the great danger of this innovation. When it is extended, in a year or two, to their own works, they may perceive at last that something has happened.

So the beatified Comstock must be regarding the course of earthly events with entire satisfaction; he was a Protestant, but he was more interested in the suppression of vice than in Protestantism; he would be

willing to let the Catholics take over his duties,
now that he is no longer able to give them his personal
attention here below. For the Catholics are considerably better equipped for this enterprise. The Protestants, with no coherence and continuity, must depend
on the sporadic appearance of some inspired soldier of
the Lord like Comstock; but the Catholics have a
permanent organization, a permanent body of doctrine,
and a standing technique of procedure. Think what you
like of Catholic practice in such matters at other times
and in other places; you cannot deny that the New
York Catholics, in their political manifestations (whatever they may have felt in private theory) were willing
to let the theater alone until they were provoked beyond endurance. I am afraid before it is over we are
going to find that the men who rocked the boat have
drowned some innocent bystanders.

Comstock himself may seem to have been thrust into
obscurity by this new movement, but he has played his
part. We owe to him the laws which made dissemina-
tion of contraceptive information obscene by definition;
we owe to him the all-embracing phraseology of the
present statutes, which enables a judge to interpret
them according to his own taste. An indecent play, by
the New York law as it stood before amendment (and
this part of course still stands) is one which "would
tend to the corruption of the morals of youth, or
others." And so a judge before whom "The Captive"
was finally brought, indirectly, happened to be inclined
to follow the strict letter of the law (another judge
might as reasonably have given the opposite decision,

and with as sound recent precedent); he admitted that this play was not likely to harm an intelligent and normal adult, but he refused to authorize its production for fear it might do injury to those whom previous court decisions have described as "the young, the immature, the ignorant, or the sensually inclined." In other words, the diet of all of us must be that prescribed for the weakest stomach; for fear that the wicked may be still further depraved, the pervert still further perverted, the clean and intelligent must be treated as of no account.

We owe that to Comstock. He was a psychopathic case; and if you say that we all are, more or less, it must be observed that in his instance it was considerably more. In his chosen field, this foul-minded man ruled the nation for a couple of decades. It would be inexact to say that his soul goes marching on; it was a peculiar soul, hardly to be duplicated. But the weapons he invented and manufactured still arm the forces of repression; his laws are still on the books, and laws which profess to effect the moral improvement of the citizenry are rarely repealed in this virtuous nation. For a century to come, all the forces of obscurantism will have reason to be grateful to him.

THE GENTLEMAN FROM VERONA

CATULLUS, Mr. F. A. Wright reminds us in the preface to his recent translation, has had a narrow escape from oblivion. Most of his work has come down in a single manuscript discovered in the fourteenth century by a citizen of Verona, who seems to have published the news less from appreciation of the poems than from pride in the achievement of a home-town boy. And it may be doubted if any translation can save him from the oblivion that is descending on all classical authors in an America which is determined to forget the classical languages.

For no one has ever distinguished himself by translating Catullus, though scores of poets, amateur and professional, have tried. Even Byron, setting himself to translate "Ille mi par esse deo videtur," succeeded only in writing a similar poem on the same theme. (That ode itself, of course, is a translation of Sappho's φαίνεταί μοι κῆνος ἴσος θεοῖσιν, and persons who have a better feeling than I for the refinements of Greek rhythm and phraseology seem to think that Catullus translated Sappho not much more successfully than his translators translate him.) If you do not read Catullus in his own language you do not read him at all, for no man ever used the compact Latin speech with more magnificent economy than this young man from Verona who may quite possibly (though not so

94

certainly as some literary historians have argued) have had a good deal of Celtic blood.

The experts, for reasons unknown to me, seem to prefer the epigrams to the hendecasyllables. Some of Catullus's epigrams are certainly magnificent, but the elegiac meter with its mechanical metronomic beat is an almost incurable temptation to prolixity. Even "Odi et amo," which contains only fourteen words, has four words more than anything but the meter requires. The hendecasyllable is doubtless an easier instrument to handle, but no other Latin writer ever used it so well as Catullus. Mr. Wright argues that as it was the traditional meter for frivolous trifles, Catullus's abusive hendecasyllables were not meant, and not taken, seriously. Perhaps not; when he used fighting words to his friends Furius and Aurelius he may have accompanied them with the requisite smile. But one doubts if the Vibenni, father and son, appreciated any playful intent in "O furum optime balneariorum," nor does it seem likely that "Ameana puella defututa" was regarded as a compliment by the lady to whom it was addressed.

Grant all you like to the love poems, to "Phasellus ille" and "Pæninsularum Sirmio," to the first epithalamium and the bits of exquisite imagery scattered all through his work, and it remains true that the man's supreme virtuosity was in abuse. Sometimes he overshot himself and merely frothed at the mouth, but at his best he could distill more venom into a quatrain or two than you can find in a whole issue of the *Nation*. Marcus Tullius Cicero, a gentleman gifted with a fine capacity for hatred and a copious ability to say what he thought, devoted a large part of one of his orations

to the argument that Clodia was a bad woman who
exerted an evil influence on numbers of young men.
Yet when he had finished he had said no more than
Catullus packed into three lines:

> Quos simul complexa tenet trecentos,
> Nullum amans vere, sed identidem omnium
> Ilia rumpens.

The theory that Catullus had Celtic blood finds
plenty of color in the invective poems. Much of his
hatred seems to have had inadequate provocation; he
had a low flash point, he went off at half cock, Celtic
traits certainly; but whether or not the motive was
sufficient the execution was usually superb, which is
also a Celtic talent. Consider the attacks on Cæsar, his
father's friend. They seem to have been purely political; and Catullus apparently neither took any active
part in politics nor had any profound insight into the
reasons for the degeneration of public life in his time.
He was merely annoyed by it, as any uncritical good
citizen might have been, and adhered to the faction
that was trying to pump oxygen into the corpse of the
republic. He felt that the times were out of joint and
that Cæsar was the chief dislocator; from which not
very profound conclusion issued the neatest excoriations
ever flung at a politician.

This talent for working up a violent fury, whether
or not you are sure of your facts, is one to which our
age gives a wider scope than his. Had Rome enjoyed
that crowning glory of civilization, the newspaper,
Catullus, who thought that any man worth abusing at
all was worth abusing well, would have been the greatest editorial writer who ever lived.

YET it seems possible that the best of his work escaped oblivion even more narrowly than Mr. Wright suggests. It may have escaped only because Catullus died at the age of thirty. If he had lived, if he had survived civil wars and proscriptions, he might have spent his later years buying up and burning his early poems.

For his collected works could be entitled "The Journal of a Disappointed Man." From every personal aspect his life was a failure. He succeeded only as an artist, but in his own view and that of his contemporaries he was an artist because he had written "The Letter to Mallius" and "The Marriage of Peleus and Thetis," because he had translated "Atys" and the "Coma Berenices." Of the shorter poems, the only ones which are apt to attract a modern reader, most were apparently not works of art at all, in Catullus's eyes; they were slices of life, appeals, arguments, revenges; they were drops of blood.

The favorite epithet of his contemporaries were "doctus," the scholarly Catullus; if you want to know what that means read "The Marriage of Peleus and Thetis." He excelled in one of the pastimes of the age, the translation or imitation of Alexandrian poems whose merit was supposed to depend on obscurity and complexity; the worse they were the better they seemed to Catullus, if we can judge from his admiration for his friend Cinna's "Zmyrna," which seems from all accounts to have been a prototype of "The Waste Land." Catullus was too great a poet to be utterly spoiled by this passion for mystification, or to get hopelessly entangled in the morass of Greek mythology and classical allusion in which Latin poetry eventually bogged down and suffocated. Nevertheless, when he died he had set his feet firmly and hopefully on the wrong road. And, perhaps quite as important, he was getting Lesbia out of his system.

For Lesbia (I refuse to call her Clodia; only a German could think of her as Clodia) Lesbia undoubtedly made Catullus what he is to-day. He was of course practicing poetry before she came to Verona; it seems that the Po Valley wheat belt sprouted poets as copiously, in the seventh decade B.C., as the Mississippi Valley corn belt a dozen years ago. All the same, Catullus was the son of a local dignitary of Verona, no mean city in the estimation of its own inhabitants then and since; if he had never met the proconsul's lady he might very possibly have married a Veronese girl and settled down, to forget the lyric Muse, and become a leading figure, in due time, of whatever equivalents Verona had to offer for Rotary and Kiwanis.

But he did meet Lesbia, and he followed Lesbia to Rome; and the fantastic intensity and persistence of his passion for her shaped all the rest of his life. Probably he was never a model of sweetness and light, but the unmeasured bitterness of his later years we certainly owe to his experiences with Lesbia. For he not only failed as a lover; he failed in everything. Certainly he succeeded in using his failures as the material for brilliant poetry. But he regarded his personal poems less as Art than as arguments and exhibits in the case of Catullus vs. the Universe—in short, as editorials; and here he not only failed, but suffered that last refinement of the editorial writer's misery—nobody paid any attention to him.

He implored all his friends in turn not to take his Lesbia, and in turn they all took her. He maligned her with all the ingenuity of a supreme talent fired by supreme passion, and more often than not she was merely bored. When Cælius Rufus, after their quarrel, called her Quadrantaria—Old Two-Bits—she tried to send him to jail; but she never paid any such compliment to Catullus. Quadrantaria was a mild epithet beside his invectives, but what Catullus said didn't count.

Politically he was just as futile. He abused Mamurra and Mamurra prospered; he pelted Cæsar with the foulest epithets and Cæsar only asked him to dinner. What is more, Cæsar's dinner invitations seem to have had the effect of Coolidge's breakfast invitations; Catullus went to dinner and came back to write of "Cæsaris monimenta magni" with none of the sarcasm he had once put into his "unicus imperator."

So, at the age of thirty, Catullus was about ready to settle down. He had gotten over the hatred of Cæsar which had been the principal plank in his political platform; and he was getting over Lesbia. The scar still ached, but there was no more prospect of that "continuous excitement" which had made him a poet. Had he lived, he would probably have sided with Cæsar in the civil wars, and he would certainly have gone on turning the complexities of Alexandrian verse into Latin. He preserved his immortality by dying young.

For how would the mature Catullus have regarded the young Catullus's poems about Lesbia and Lesbia's lovers? Their distinction comes from their superhuman intensity; there is nothing novel in the emotion which makes up their raw material; it is the sort of thing that every man has felt in the twenties and been terribly ashamed of in the thirties. (Sometimes the forties bring a relapse, but that is a matter for the pathologist, not the literary critic.) Catullus at forty would probably have read "Vivamus, mea Lesbia," and "Num te leæna," and "Miser Catulle," with nauseated disgust. What could he ever have seen in that dreadful woman? And he had said that he loved her—he, the young man from the wheat belt, loved her, the grande dame of the Palatine set, as a father loves his children! Jupiter Optime Maxime! . . . He would have been less than human if he had not tried to buy up these melancholy relics and throw them in the fire—and his fame with them.

And Lesbia? Well, if she made Catullus's reputation, he made hers; but that rarely worried her. She asked him, to be sure, to stop "truces vibrare iambos," but that was when she still cared a little about him. Probably she thought his abusive poems would be forgotten along with the persons who had provoked them; but in any case she would hardly have cared. That was not the Claudian way.

For Lesbia was not only one of the first of Rome's emancipated women, discovering with the zest of a pioneer that sauce for the goose was sauce for the gander; she was also a member of the Claudian family, whose distinguishing characteristic was that it regarded its doings as nobody's business. A century later that family went out in a blaze, if not exactly of glory, at any rate of renown that has endured for two thousand years; and one is tempted to regard Lesbia and her brother Publius, the president of the Honest Ballot Association of the day, as a sort of dress rehearsal for Agrippina and Nero, in whom the Claudian house showed what it could do when it really tried.

Claudians never explained, which is a pity; for much could have been said on Lesbia's side. If she had ever been annoyed into setting it down for posterity, it would have been one of the most valuable monuments of the age, a compendium of "What a Young Man Ought to Know." More than the lost books of Livy and Tacitus, more than the perished histories of the second and third century, this is the greatest bereavement in Latin literature—the letters Lesbia never wrote to Catullus.

Lesbia's husband was a highly respectable stuffed shirt. When he went to Verona as governor of Cisalpine Gaul, and took her with him, she was much in the position of a Victorian Duchess transported to Melbourne or Cape Town, or a lady of Mrs. Astor's Four Hundred exiled, in the early nineties, to Kansas City or Denver. One had to do something in Verona; and here was this young Catullus, with something of a metropolitan manner, who could write pretty verses about one's pet sparrow, and display a devotion that might be rather sophomoric, but was none the less gratifying to a lady on the threshold of middle age. . . . Also he was a nice boy, who deserved a better training than he was likely to get from that Aufilena woman, or such impossible creatures as Ipsithilla.

An eminently practical lady, this Lesbia, about affairs of the heart. Probably her one real passion was politics,

politics as a game, the pulling of the strings which had
but lately become possible to Roman ladies. As for the
bed and board, they were equally necessities of existence, pleasant enough in their regular recurrence but
not to be sentimentalized. If this hard-boiled noble-
woman was ever genuinely shocked in her whole life, it
must have been when she discovered that Catullus had
followed her back to Rome; she must have felt almost a
religious horror when he reminded her "dicebas
quondam solum te nosse Catullum." . . . "But, my
dear boy! That was last spring. . . . Oh, of course I
said it; one does. But do you take these things literally
in Verona?"

Yet, for the time, he seems to have remained in
favor; he met all the bad young men, he spent his time
at Lesbia's house, yet not a *salax taberna* to his way of
thinking (though doubtless staid citizens had so regarded it for quite a while); and then he discovered
that Lesbia had decided that she needed a change of
diet. After all, to a lady getting on in the thirties, an
admirer who talked about "nobis cum semel occidit
brevis lux" could not have been altogether agreeable.

Catullus's subsequent behavior cannot be excused
even on the ground of youth; only as a peculiarly virulent case of one of the more violent types of insanity.
As Mr. Wright observes, he behaved like the most
jealous of husbands, which was a novelty to Lesbia.
Her husband, apparently, had always been complaisant; it was beneath the dignity of a Cæcilius Metellus
to notice anything that he was unable to stop. But
Catullus noticed everything and waved it before the
eyes of all Rome. Verona stuff, she must have reflected;

in the wheat belt they still went in for the double standard.

From her viewpoint, it was ridiculously unfair. But she was too proud—and too prudent—to reply. For when she did make a final tentative effort to mollify him he responded with some bitter remarks about "simul complexa tenet trecentos" and this parting advice:

> Nec meum respectet, ut ante, amorem
> Qui illius culpa cecidit, velut prati
> Ultimi flos, prætereunte postquam
> Tactus aratrost.

Lesbia, after all, had some literary taste; she must have seen that it was useless to argue with a man who could write himself an exit line like that.

And then he died—died at Verona, died when he was thirty; and Lesbia lived on, perhaps, through the civil wars and proscriptions that all but annihilated the Roman society she had known. In the fifties Catullus's poems had been news, town topics; in the forties, and thirties, Lesbia may have reflected that they were fading into the dark. Who cared about those things, and those people, now? They were dead and their ideas were dead; Julius Cæsar was honored by the filial piety of his grandnephew, who was making himself great by following a policy as different as possible from Cæsar's; Cicero was gone, Lesbia's husband and brother were gone, all the smart young men who were such admirable lovers and such indifferent poets were gone too. Who remembered, now, the parochial politics of the last days of the republic? Who would ever remember that a young poet from the wheat belt, who really did very well as a translator of the Alexandrians, had also written absurd lampoons on Cæsar, and had behaved quite abominably toward a woman who would no longer pretend to love him after she was tired of him?

So may have mused the white-haired old lady who had outlived her loves and her hatreds and her times. But she had failed to allow for the fact that although Catullus came to Rome, he came from Verona.

For a thousand years after Lesbia and Catullus and Cælius and Cicero were forgotten, when even Cæsar was little more than the title of a man named Palæologus in Constantinople and a man named Hapsburg in Vienna, a citizen of Verona found an ancient manuscript under a bushel basket—and spread the news to the world because it appeared, on examination, to be the work of another citizen of Verona. And Lesbia, whose only fault in this particular affair was that she fell out of love first instead of waiting till Catullus was tired of her, goes down in history as the supreme instance of a pernicious woman.

All stories should point a moral, in this moral age; and the moral of this one is that no matter how bored a lady from the metropolis may find herself when exiled to the sticks, she should never have an affair with a poet; still less with a great poet; and least of all with a poet who is highly regarded in his home town.

THE PASSING OF THE GREAT RACE

The subjoined chapter from the official "History of American Literature in the Twentieth Century," prepared by the Federal Bureau of Literary Enforcement, will not appear until April 1, 2013; but I have obtained advance proofs by an inversion of the familiar process which enables historians to interpret with confidence the state of mind of by-gone ages, even or especially in default of documentary evidence. Truth being timeless, a formula suited to reconstruction of the past is obviously quite as applicable to preconstruction of the future.

"THEY laid Henry James in his grave and John Barleycorn passed away, to rise again on the third day." So begins Leopold Nadelbier's *The Golden Decade* (New York: Merkur-Verlag, Alfred A. Knopf Nachfolger, 1953) inducting the reader into the Heroic Age of American letters, the nineteen twenties, when (the virtually unanimous voice of contemporary criticism leaves no room for doubt on this point) all novels were important and all novelists were great.

Confronted by this astounding phenomenon, the obsolescence for a dozen years of all degrees of comparison but the superlative, the thoughtful student cannot but wonder why this truly Great Race, as gifted and as mysterious as the Cro-Magnons or the Proto-Nords, should so soon have passed away. What were the hidden causes of the decline and fall of American literature from this brief apogee to its present state in the twenty-first century, when a respectable level of uninspired competence is general, but true greatness is deplorably rare? Why were our ancestors so far above us? Why this brief flowering and sudden decay?

The question cannot be answered without some consideration of the characteristics of the Golden Decade. Let no one be misled by the apparent irreverence of Nadelbier, for he lived a generation later. Of the splendors of the Golden Decade he could have had only fragmentary infantile memories; but he knew that his own generation was unsatisfactory enough, and it is impossible to escape the conclusion that his history of his parents' time was colored by an unconscious envy of those who had been old enough to be out after dark in the Golden Decade. Not till 1987, be it remembered, was the doctrine of obligatory irreverence to one's immediate ancestors superseded by Heckwelder's great biological discovery, that every Younger Generation is destined to become, in the fullness of time, an Older Generation; that in the truceless war between fathers and sons, the sons have no sooner won their foreordained victory than they throw away its fruits by becoming fathers.[1]

Moreover, the men of Nadelbier's day, perhaps suspecting that they were epigoni of a nobler race, were addicted to a defensive cynicism; they were ill-equipped

---

[1] Some adumbrations of this truth may indeed be detected in earlier writings, but there is no evidence that anyone acted as if he believed it before 1987.

to understand or appreciate the Great Romantics who flourished in the Harding, Coolidge, and Upshaw administrations.

For the Golden Decade (if one may retain the metallic metaphor) grew out of the Iron Quinquennium; it began with the simultaneous triumphant conclusions of the War to End War and the War to End Rum. It is true that neither war nor rum remained ended for any length of time, and that the principal result of the wars to end them was only a perceptible deterioration in the quality of both. None the less the Heroic Age began as a reaction against the hard realities which the world had endured from 1914 to 1919.

It had been predicted during the war that the literature of the first years of peace would be romantic, but had not been foreseen that it would be Romantic in the technical sense, Romantic as opposed to Classic—or, in more modern terminology, subjective as opposed to objective. During the war life had been intensely and uncomfortably objective; the reaction was inevitable, especially as the prosperity of America after the war fortunately relieved American authors from the continued concentration on objective realities which was necessary in Europe.

The Classic contemplates the Universe, conceding it *pro tanto* objective validity, and is concerned with the Individual only in so far as he has a place in the Universe, which is not apt to be very far. He seeks to delineate a structure, an order, with axes of reference by which each part may be fitted into place. But the

Romantic is concerned with the Universe only as it delights, or (more probably) annoys, the Individual; he is not interested in finding the Individual's place because he has a subconscious suspicion that it would not be of flattering prominence. In the Golden Decade the astronomers, the physicists, the chemists, were finding much evidence of order in the universe, even if that order was not fully discernible; but the artists rarely found it and rarely looked for it. Their eyes were turned inward, toward a spectacle of such dazzling brilliance as to pale the attraction of all others.

Even so superficially objective a writer as Sinclair Lewis is less interested in Gopher Prairie than in his own annoyance at Gopher Prairie. A Classic, confronting Gopher Prairie, would have asked not only, How do I feel about it? but What, after all, is it, and how did it get that way? Lewis approaches perilously near the Classic attitude in dealing with George F. Babbitt, which may perhaps explain not only why *Babbitt* is still read in our time when *Main Street* has gone to join *The House of Seven Gables*, but why *Main Street* sold considerably better than *Babbitt* in the Golden Decade. Mr. John dos Passos, essaying to put a complete account of New York on paper, is able to report how it affects his five senses, especially the olfactory; but when it comes to answering even the primary question of What is it? (without going behind the returns to ask Why is it?) he merely throws up his hands and answers, "It's a mess."

Even in the Heroic Age, there were cantankerous persons who were unable to accept that as a completely satisfactory explanation.

BUT with objectivity, standards of reference were also discarded. If I and My Emotions are the only objects worthy of contemplation it becomes necessary (lacking instruments of precision for the measurement of egos, which had not as yet been invented) to take every ego at its own valuation; when all authors are chanting the Song of Myself, the prize must go to the one who sings loudest. And the critics of the Heroic Age were children of their time; they were Romantics too, their souls fared adventurously in a world where all pieces were masterpieces.

The old theory that a critic was a surveyor, who plotted the position of his subject relative to certain fixed points, had gone out of style—partly because certain points, previously regarded as fixed, had perceptibly moved. From this arose the hasty inference that there were no fixed points. Anything was as good as anything else and perhaps better in a formless and perishable universe. This, it will be observed, was a form of Heracliteanism. Heraclitus, to be sure, was also a sort of Romantic reacting against stereotyped classicism; but it may be doubted if he would have approved of all these early-twentieth-century applications of his doctrine.

However, the view that a man's worth depended on his own assessment certainly effected a tremendous liberation of forces. Like the Elizabethans, the men and women of the Golden Decade confronted a new world and they reacted to it with a truly Elizabethan eagerness, even if this usually took the inverted form of a gloomy gloating over the emptiness of things. It was an Age of Great Discoveries. Novelist after novelist set forth into unknown seas and came back freighted with strange merchandise. Sherwood Anderson discovered that life is perplexing and that human relationships involve grave difficulties. Sinclair Lewis discovered that narrow-mindedness was painfully prevalent, especially among people who disagreed with him. Joseph Hergesheimer discovered that gentlemen in the later forties are apt to have an itch for sexual variety. Charles G. Norris discovered that you can't have everything and that what you have not seems more desirable than what you have. James Branch Cabell discovered that nothing amounts to much, anyway. And as no one was callous enough to inquire, "What of it?" a good time was had by all.

From novels of the time, one obtains a detailed account of what the men and women of the Heroic Age were like, or rather what they liked to think they were like. They regarded themselves as lecherous, voluble, and ineffectual. But alongside the very reading matter in which they furnish this self-portrayal, the advertising columns tell a different story. The hero of fiction talks continually and never lacks for listeners, even when (as is usual) he is talking about himself. But in real life, if we may believe the advertisements, no man could obtain a hearing at the dinner table unless he were prepared to pass lightly and gracefully from Leonardo da Vinci to the Heliolithic culture and thence to the Dawes Plan; while still more admired in society was he who played the saxophone instead of trying to talk at all.

An author who identifies himself with his hero and depicts that hero as lacking in industry and persistence rather weakens his argument by embodying it in a laborious novel of 500 closely printed pages. The heroines of fiction of the Golden Decade fairly crackled with sex appeal; but the millions of dollars spent to advertise deodorants compel the historian to the conclusion that the women of the period must have been unappetizing, to say the least, until they had undergone elaborate and costly chemical treatment.

So one must conclude that the ruthless realists of the Golden Decade in fact sentimentalized themselves heavily; the neo-Byronic movement, like its prototype a century earlier, produced plenty of Byronists but no Byrons. But, as they themselves would have been the first to admit, what they were is of less importance than what they thought they were.

For it is no fair criticism of the Golden Decade to say that little of its product has any interest for posterity. It was not written for posterity but for contemporaneity. Moreover, since Heckwelder's discovery it has been acknowledged that each generation is in its turn posterity. The writers of the Heroic Age, depicting themselves for themselves, may be excused for concluding that that portion of posterity which they themselves at the moment were, deserved no less consideration than those installments of posterity which were yet to come.

They were followers of Heraclitus; their motto was πάντα ρεῖ οὐδὲν μένει—everything is transitory, nothing is permanent. They were interested in what they were doing and few of them cared much about how they were doing it. Obviously future ages,

with no personal interest in the What, would be attracted only to such literature of the Heroic Age as
paid some attention to the How; for πάντα ρεῖ οὐδὲν
μένει passes the death-sentence on the most admired character types of the period. Future ages would
care as little about them as the people of the Golden
Decade cared about the heroes of Richard Harding
Davis (who also reflected the aspiration, if not the
reality, of his time); but with future ages as such the
Heroic Age had no concern.

But presently a disquieting fact (which had been
obvious enough to Heraclitus) became apparent to his
disciples too. The Heraclitean formula applies not
only to perceptible phenomena, but to the perceiver;
year by year the writers of the Golden Decade were
themselves moving forward into future ages, year by
year they were becoming their own posterity. They had
lived in a three-dimensional world whose points of
reference were Myself When Young, My Emotions, and
My Contemporaries; but now this compact system was
utterly deranged by the intrusion of the fourth dimen-
sion, Time, the fourth point of reference, Myself When
Older.

Conjecturally, the beginning of the decline and fall
of the Great Race may be dated from the moment when
Sinclair Lewis took his stand on a pulpit in Kansas
City and challenged God to strike him down. There
was silence in Heaven for a space considerably longer
than half an hour, and gradually the horrid suspicion
spread that Lewis's interest in God was rather more
acute than God's interest in Lewis. God's position,
whatever it may have been before the challenge, was

precisely the same thereafter. For the position of Lewis, not quite so much could be said.

But obviously no change in Lewis's standing could affect the standing of George F. Babbitt and Leora Arrowsmith; there they were and would still be. And this demonstration that a sufficiently competent product might be more durable than its producer undermined the whole metaphysical basis of the Golden Decade. No longer could it be argued that all authors were equally important because they all had egos; no longer was mere declaration of intention sufficient qualification for citizenship in the Republic of Letters. Into the primitive equalitarianism of the Heroic Age there began to creep a class distinction based on durable achievement.

ONE can imagine the dismay which must have afflicted the Great Race when it became apparent that the postwar boom was over and the period of deflation had set in. Gifted persons who had wasted their substance in riotous writing argued that the fiat currency had been in circulation so long that its demonetization would work unjustified hardship on many whose only fault had been the taking too seriously of what they read about themselves in book reviews, and would correspondingly enrich others who had laid up a store of sound money through no particular merit, but only because they were built that way. And naturally enough the authors of the United States presently followed the example of the farmers, and besought Congress for legislation which would enable them to continue to earn a return on inflated capitalization.

That they failed was not their fault; a dozen years earlier the constitutional amendment requiring that every writer should be taken as seriously as he took himself would have gone through with little opposition. It was the ill fortune of the authors to arrive too late; the country was becoming a little sick of constitutional amendments and of attempts to repeal the laws of Nature by act of Congress. And so the Golden Decade ended, American literature was reorganized on a more stable basis, and presently the overwhelming majority of the Great Race was forgotten.

It is not necessary to enumerate the works of the period which have survived the erosion of a century; they are familiar to every educated reader. But they may be generally described as the works in which the author not only threw off his auto-erotism and fell in love with his subject, but fell in love sensibly and to practical effect, like the young man who labors to give the object of his affections a suitable and worthy home. The books, in short, in which the author saw not only himself but what he was doing; and what he was doing not only in relation to himself, but in relation to things external and objective which, whatever their transitoriness, were in fact there, or at least somewhere, at the time; so that he depicted not only the Thing-in-Itself but the Thing-in-Its-Inescapable-Relation-to-Other-Things, not least of these other things being the reader who, lacking the author's innate conviction of the importance of his theme, had to be shown.

The Golden Decade was an age of impulses, unconcerned in results. After a century its impulses are forgotten, its results are all that remain to us. Hence we may underestimate it, but if we do it is the fault of those who lived then, and who cared little where they were going because it was so much fun to be on the way. We may regret that that bright dawn faded so soon, but the Passing of the Great Race was inevitable. Its members succumbed to a disease for which no remedy has yet been discovered.

They grew up.

BEDS OF IVORY

A Note on Contemporary Anti-Semitism

SOME of my Jewish friends are keenly interested in what they call the demobilization of antagonisms, specifically that long-standing antagonism between Jew and Gentile which is somewhat inexactly termed anti-Semitism. That term tells only half the story, for the correlative feeling among Jews, which might be called anti-Aryanism, is historically the older of the two; nor was it the Aryans who were its first victims, but the Semitic neighbors of the Israelites— Canaan, Edom, Moab and Ammon. Historically, also it appears quite clearly that the starting-point of this antagonism was the Jewish religion. But we have gone a long way from origins; the religious element counts for little in such antagonism as exists now.[1]

American anti-Semitism is peculiarly a problem for New Yorkers, and not merely because half the Jews of the country live in New York. A good deal that takes the form of anti-Semitism is really anti-New Yorkism. Which is the most cogent of arguments for the demo-

[1] At least in America. A gifted Austrian Jew lately argued in *Harper's* that much of current European anti-Semitism springs from hostility to Christianity, a religion invented by the Jews and sold to the Gentiles. The European of to-day, this writer contends, observing that the Jews do not use this creed of their own manufacture, cannot help regarding it as a kind of cheap goods produced purely for the export trade, like the calico and beads which the European trader unloads on the innocent natives of more savage continents.

bilization of antagonism between Jews and Gentiles in New York. The most noteworthy demobilization of an antagonism in recent history is the shoving into the background of the centuries-old hostility between France and England. What did it? Not brotherly love, on which some optimists count for the disappearance of anti-Semitism, but fear of Germany, the urgent pressure of a greater antagonism.

In the besieged city, local strifes and partisan rivalries are apt to be forgotten; it is a question of all hanging together or all hanging separately. Nearly all American Jews, and a great many American Gentiles, live in besieged cities; New York is the one most immediately threatened, but every American city of any local preëminence is or soon will be in the same predicament. The one cardinal issue, the one irrepressible conflict in American politics and American ideology to-day, is the antagonism between city and country. It appears in different forms—wet against dry, Catholic against Protestant, older immigration against newer immigration—on all of which there is room for difference of opinion. But on the fundamental issue there is no room for difference among city dwellers between Catholics, Protestants and Jews, between Mayflower Descendants and steerage descendants; not even, ultimately, between rich and poor. The farm and the small town look on the city as a reservoir of wealth to be taxed for the benefit of the back country, and as a sink of iniquity to be forcibly reformed; and thanks to gerrymanders and disproportionate representation, which are inextricably imbedded in many state constitutions, they are getting away with it. Against the

Volstead Act the cities have so far rebelled with some success; but they have been unable to get away from paying taxes, and if Messiahs of the bush like Mr. McAdoo and Senator Borah had their way even the Volstead Act would be disobeyed only at the risk of being shot. Every city man, Jew or Christian, has a direct and vital interest in resisting this crusade which is directed equally against his business and against his pleasure.

Now, in New York City, a good many long-standing antagonisms are visibly being demobilized in the face of this imminent danger. New Yorkers of all religions, races and classes have got into the habit of voting for Al Smith because they recognize that he is their powerful bulwark against the hatred of the farmer. The Republican party in New York City is dying out, so far as local elections go, because it can no longer follow the lead of the up-state Republicans. To the city man, even if he calls himself a Republican and votes the Republican ticket in presidential elections, the Tammany district leader is a good deal more congenial than a Republican from a farm or small town up-state. For the city Republican perceives that he and the Tammany leader are essentially of the same kind; while he and the up-state Republicans are of different and antagonistic kinds. If he is ever inclined to forget that, his up-state brother can be counted on to remind him, promptly and forcibly.

New Yorkers are born, not made; but they may be born anywhere. A natural New Yorker born in North Carolina and a natural New Yorker born in the Russian Pale have more in common than the Carolina New

Yorker and the folks back home in North Carolina,
when he returns for a visit after ten years in Manhattan. And when it comes to New Yorkers, whether Jew
or Christian, of western European ancestry and culture,
there are no vital difference beyond individual varia-
tions. I am no ethnologist, but I keep my eyes open
as I walk around the streets of New York, and I believe
that the Jewish race is as much of a myth as the
Nordic race. The Russian Jews strike us as alien precisely as would Russian Christians of the same economic class if they came to us in quantity. (Not that a
good many of them do not turn into perfectly good New
Yorkers, especially when they get away from the orthodoxy of the first generation.) But western European
Jews are essentially our own people. They spring in the
main from the same complex racial fusions as western
European Gentiles. Their religion, when they retain
it, differs very little from Modernist Christianity; and
when they drop it they are still less distinguishable
from Gentile rationalists or indifferentists.

THE essential New Yorker (and there are more of him,
and of her, every day) might be either Jewish or
Christian in temperament and habit of mind, and even
in appearance. Look at the faces on Broadway and see
if the local culture of Manhattan is not turning out,
before our eyes, a local racial type; anthropologists who
argue that climate and local culture build up a regional
cast of countenance can find a hundred exhibits to offer
in evidence, in any New York theater crowd. New
Englanders of the old stock rarely look like old Englanders; after three hundred years, I doubt if you will

find many New York Jews who look like Jews, though you may find Jewish traits in men whose ancestry is seven-eighths Gentile. For this climatic and cultural assimilation—assimilation of Gentile to Jew, be it remembered, as well as of Jew to Gentile—will be accelerated more and more by intermarriage as time goes on. Not too rapidly; the inclination to find a mate in one's own group is too strong. But by the third generation the melting pot is apt to be melting away rather industriously; in the arts and the demi-arts, where assimilation has gone farthest, intermarriage of Jew and Gentile is already fairly common.

Conservative Jews, of course, shudder at the idea of assimilation, but they are trying to sweep back the tide. Already it has visibly begun; and now that the inflow from the great reservoir of orthodoxy in the eastern European ghettos has been shut down to a mere trickle it will go on faster and faster. And it ought to be promoted by the feeling of solidarity which must spring up in urban Jew and urban Gentile as they stand together against the attack from the farm.

This city-country antagonism is of course an old story; it existed and made trouble, in the ancient Athenian state; it was epidemic in eastern Europe after the war. In Bulgaria, Stambulisky's farmer government treated the inhabitants of the few small cities as Kansas farmers would like to treat New York. In Hungary it gave a biting edge to political antagonisms, according to an acute Hungarian Jewish observer [2] who lays

[2] Eugene Bagger, in the chapters on Stephen Tisza and Michael Karolyi in his *Eminent Europeans*.

much of the sanguinary bitterness of revolution and counter-revolution to the antipathy between a rural aristocracy rooted for a thousand years in the soil, and the modern intellectual-industrial urban culture of Budapest, which is largely Jewish.

And a somewhat similar feeling may have promoted that regrettable failure in mutual comprehension between the Plantagenet kings and the Jews of York, representatives of different types of civilization both of which had their good points, and which have not learned to get along with each other even yet. For the Jews (with some help from the Northern Italians) virtually invented modern city life. Medieval complaints against the Jews, aside from a pious indignation against the race that crucified Christ, were in the main the same as modern rural complaints against the city. So in America to-day the anti-Semitism of the Klan would blaze as hotly, though in different phraseology, against the Gentiles of New York, if there were not a single Jew within the city limits. City Christian and city Jew look just the same to the Christian farmer, and the sooner they find it out the better.

HENRY FORD, and the godly Klansman at the head of the creek who pays Henry Ford's debts, without knowing it, when Wall Street gets Henry in a corner, may then obscurely feel that they are standing up for the primitive Aryan culture of the countryside against that abominable Jewish institution, the city. But they are not. They are following the lead of the Jew quite as much as is the urban business man. Or even more; they are following a Jewish tradition which the Jews themselves have outgrown.

For where did this peculiarly religious antipathy of the back country against the city originate, this conviction that God made the country and man made the town; that the horny-handed agriculturist, despite his addiction to roadside amours and wholesale ax murders, is none the less the guardian of all the virtues, while the scoundrelly desk man is skating along the primrose path from which he must be forcibly diverted, for the good of his own soul, by the embattled farmer? Well, that question may take us a long way back. I suspect that it originated ten or fifteen thousand years ago, when some Neolithic hunter, going into the thatched village to trade a bearskin for a new stone hatchet, ran up for the first time against the law of supply and demand. But its first appearance in history—Western history, at any rate—is plainly visible; and from that first appearance the filiation of ideas and reasoning and even vocabulary can be traced down clearly to the fire-breathing rural evangelists and country politicians of our own time. As a religious and moral issue—or, if you prefer to be candid about it, a social-economic issue presented in religious and moral language—it began with the words of Amos, who was among the herdsmen of Tekoa, which he saw concerning Israel in the days of Uzziah king of Judah, and in the days of Jeroboam the son of Joash king of Israel, two years before the earthquake.

This Amos looked around him and gathered the impression that things were going wrong in a variety of ways, as possibly they were. Amos thereupon concluded that the evils of the time could be cured only by a return to the old-time religion; by which he meant, as every prophet in every age has meant, to his personally revised concept of the old-time religion, and no other. The Jewish prophetic tradition has been the source of much of the spiritual vitality of the Western world, Jewish or Christian, but its sociology can hardly be regarded as very sound.

For consider some of the words of Amos the herdsman of Tekoa. "Woe to them that are at ease in Zion, and trust in the mountain of Samaria . . . that lie upon beds of ivory, and stretch themselves upon their couches . . . that chant to the sound of the viol, and invent to themselves instruments of music, like David; that drink wine in bowls, and anoint themselves with the chief ointments; but they are not grieved for the affliction of Joseph."

There were no beds of ivory in Tekoa. Back there in the hills they were not guilty of the moral turpitude of inventing to themselves instruments of music, and chanting to the sound of the viol. No doubt they drank wine, but they drank it from a goatskin, *more majorum*, and not from bowls. And because the abandoned denizens of the city, or some of them, had beds of ivory and liked music with their meals, Amos concluded that they were not grieved for the affliction of Joseph.

All sacred tradition agrees with him. But if you turn to profane history you must conclude that they who seemed to be at ease in Zion, and trusting in the mountain of Samaria, were just as grieved as Amos for the affliction of Joseph. Only, they were not so ready with cocksure remedies, for they knew more about it.

What was the affliction of Joseph? Well, it seems there had been some bad crop seasons. People still pray for rain in some parts of this extensive country, but even in Kansas they are no longer inclined to blame local dry spells on divine wrath inspired by the wetness of New York. Aside from this temporary hardship the affliction of Joseph consisted simply in this, that Israel was a small buffer state, occupying strategically important territory between two great powers. That this was a matter of the gravest concern at the capital of both Hebrew kingdoms, all Old Testament history attests. Israel had risen when Assyria and Egypt were both weak. In their interludes of weakness thereafter, a strong King of Israel like Omri or Jeroboam II could stand on his own feet. Otherwise there was need of diplomacy, of combinations with the Aramæans or Phœnicians, of leaning for the moment on one or the other of the great powers, playing Assyria against Egypt or Egypt against Assyria, or both ends against the middle.

Naturally the rulers of Judah and Israel made mistakes; the worst of them was the long war of Israel with the Aramæans, which weakened both nations till they were easy victims of the eventual Assyrian advance. But the major portion of the blame for that seems to lie on the kings of Damascus. Israel and Judah made other blunders, too, political and economic. But read between the lines of the biased historians, who wrote after it was all over with the advantage of the second guess, and you will see that pretty nearly all the kings who seemed to be at ease in Zion and trusting in the mountain of Samaria were anxious hard-working persons who did the best they could. To the secular historian it seems that Judah and Israel did pretty well in retaining even the shadow of independence for so long.

But all this was too deep for Amos. "I was an herdsman, and a gatherer of sycamore fruit; and the Lord took me as I followed the flock, and the Lord said unto me, Go, prophesy unto my people Israel." Amos, too, did the best he could; he blamed what seemed blameworthy by the standards of Tekoa, the only standards he knew; and two years afterward came the earthquake, and Amos stood justified before the Lord and before the people. Never since then has there failed some inspired gatherer of sycamore fruit who hears the compelling inward voice, and goes forth to preach judgment and damnation against those who lie on beds of ivory and chant to the sound of the viol, and drink wine in bowls when the goatskin is good enough for Tekoa.

THE social sciences were not highly developed in the eighth century B.C.; a rustic Hebrew zealot cannot be blamed very harshly for thinking that there was some connection between military-economic power and correctness in theology. But when one finds the same line of reasoning in statesmen of this enlightened republic one cannot help wondering just what is meant by the concept of human progress. Persons of a teleological turn of mind, who regard the Hebrew race as having been permitted to exist for the sublime purpose of bearing witness of God to all the nations, may quite reasonably approve the policy of the Hebrew prophets. It follows, then, that the fall of the Hebrew kingdoms, and the Captivity, were foreordained and necessary parts of the demonstration of what must happen to a nation whose theological views are inaccurate. If Israel had listened to the prophets and taken their advice, however, this sublime object lesson could never have taken place; so one is constrained to follow eminent theologians of later time and hold that the stubborn idolatry of Israel was foreordained too. Either way, one cannot help feeling that though it was a grand object lesson it was rather hard on the Hebrews who took part in it.

But a secular person—for instance, a king who was less interested in the teleological interpretation of history than in the happiness of his subjects—might well feel that the primary objective of foreign policy was the securing of the welfare of the kingdom and the people who lived in it; and of this class were most of the kings of Judah and Israel. There were certainly some bad characters among them, men whose public and private lives were far from ideal; but regard them, for the moment, from the viewpoint of the good or ill they did to other people, rather than their success in the care of their own souls, and you must admit that they averaged a good deal better than the prophets.

About the worst of the kings, according to the sacred narrative, was Manasseh, who reigned five and fifty years in Jerusalem. "He did that which was evil in the sight of the Lord, after the abominations of the heathen"—in other words he was tolerant, a crime which no prophet, ancient or modern, has ever been able to forgive. He had sense enough to submit himself to the Assyrians, as they went past on their way to conquer Egypt, and possibly his pliancy toward foreign religions was part of the price. Deplorable, from the large ethical point of view; but convenient for the people of Jerusalem, who might otherwise have been mishandled by the Assyrians in the ingenious and uncomfortable Assyrian way. A writer of the prophetic party, a century or two later, after the Exile, asserted that this moved God to announce, "I will cast off the remnant of mine inheritance, and deliver them into the hands of their enemies." With all reverence toward the inspired historian, one must set this down as the second guess of the grandstand manager. What Manasseh actually did, at the moment, was to deliver his people out of the hands of their enemies; his reign seems to have been a period of peace and prosperity such as the kingdom of Judah seldom had a chance to enjoy.

True, "he shed innocent blood very much, till he had filled Jerusalem from one end to the other." Whose innocent blood? That of the prophets, who could not endure the sight of a Judah peaceful, prosperous, and tolerant; who would have upset Manasseh's diplomacy that saved the nation, and would themselves have shed such blood of unbelievers as might have been necessary to enforce conformity to the old-time religion, if Manasseh had not put them out of the way. After twenty-six centuries one still feels a glow of admiration for Manasseh. If he had to shed any blood at all, he showed excellent taste in his selection of victims.

In the time of Manasseh's grandson Josiah the prophets and their party got the upper hand; they "found" the Book of Deuteronomy in the Temple, and persuaded the young king to promulgate it as a new constitution. Heretics were abolished in Judah as thoroughly as they were later abolished by Torquemada in Spain; much blood was shed in this grand pogrom, but of course it was not innocent blood, for it belonged to the adherents of false religions. Now this was perhaps no serious misfortune, for these religions promoted some reprehensible and uncomfortable practices; but when Josiah let the prophets persuade him that doctrinal soundness and an improvement in sexual morality were all that were needed to make Judah a great power, he committed what must be regarded as an error from the point of view of practical politics.

Josiah's God, through the prophets, had made him a downright promise that if he adopted and enforced these constitutional amendments, "the Lord thy God shall bless" the people; specifically, he had promised Josiah that "thou shalt be gathered to thy grave in peace." Josiah took this literally; he was unaware of the exegetic theory to be advanced in the light of later events that the covenant bound Josiah but did not bind his God. Relying on these promises, Josiah set his army in the way of the King of Egypt (who had marched past Jerusalem on his way to attack somebody else, and would in all likelihood have let Josiah alone if he had not had delusions of grandeur); and at Megiddo the Pharaoh's Greek hoplites, whose doctrinal theology was most unsound but whose armor was complete and impenetrable, scattered the Jewish army and killed King Josiah, whose God had promised him that he would be gathered to his grave in peace.

It is perhaps the greatest triumph of the Hebrew prophets and their followers that they managed to explain this away to their own satisfaction, and to that of later generations (after time had removed Josiah's contemporaries, on whom personal observation of this misadventure must have made a painful impression).

Now undoubtedly the prophets believed that by law observance and law enforcement little Judah would become the military equal of a great power; just as Amos believed that the affliction of Joseph was due to an increase in the comforts of living, rather than a permanent and irreparable inferiority in wealth and population. The necessary implication of the prophets' teachings on foreign affairs is that a man's strength is as the strength of ten, because his heart is pure; that by virtue of orthodoxy and continence a thousand Jews would be able to beat ten thousand Assyrians. It is surely not going too far to say that this doctrine has been somewhat discredited by the lessons of history.

Isaiah, certainly, was a statesman and diplomat of ability, who served his country well. But over against Isaiah set Jeremiah, a defeatist who gave aid and comfort to the enemy, and richly deserved the execution for treason which he escaped only because an irresolute king was afraid to offend his popular following; or Elisha the son of Shaphat, whose religious convictions compelled him to promote a revolution, an overthrow of the dynasty, and a general massacre of people who disagreed with him, which must have seriously weakened the nation for the Aramæan war.[3]

I would not be understood as undervaluing those

---

[3] The whole-hearted thoroughness with which King Jehu, whom Elisha put on the throne, carried out the will of God as made known to him by Elisha, grieved and horrified the prophetic party.

great and good men. Their accomplishments were
enormous and generally praiseworthy. They invented
the teleological interpretation of history, which a recent writer has described as ancient Israel's sole contribution to universal culture (he failed to add that it
is probably the most pernicious error in the history of
human thought). They showed an admirable resilience,
when the march of events had discredited their political theories, by spending the years of the Exile rewrit-
ing and editing the history of their people into one long
alibi for themselves. They composed some beautiful
rhapsodies, invented some striking figures of speech,
and laid up a treasure of literary allusions which were
very handy for the writers of later ages, until the general disuse of the practice of reading the Bible made
the allusions unintelligible; and they produced some
ethical ideas which have been of great value to subsequent generations.

But to the people of their own time, the people of
Judah and Israel among whom they lived and worked,
they were on the whole a curse, an affliction, and a disaster. One of the noblest of them, after the independent
existence of the nation had come to an end, drew that
famous and magnificent picture of Israel as the Suffering Servant of God. Historically that is broadly true;
but Deutero-Isaiah might quite as truthfully have
added that most of the sufferings were inflicted on
Israel by the prophets.

But it was generally understood that in this complicated matter the
blame for whatever was done wrong should be ascribed to the
King, whereas the credit for whatever was done right belonged
to the prophet.

ALL this is ancient history, you may say. But it is not. A large part of the population of these states, a group stronger than any other in ethical and cultural controversies, and very powerful in politics as well, still lives in the ideology of the Hebrew prophets; its members may not, as a rule, understand or believe the theological concepts underlying their philosophy of life quite as thoroughly as Elijah or Amos, but they act on them none the less. Here lies the origin of that feeling which expresses itself, now, in the holy war of rural Fundamentalists against the ideas and behavior of the city population; cigarettes, short skirts, synthetic gin, the Pope and Darwin are denounced in the spirit of Amos. If it is something we don't do in Tekoa, it is an abomination unto the Lord. But read history, and see if you do not agree that more good for more people has come out of the Samarias than out of the Tekoas.

These gentlemen are following the oldest and most respectable Hebrew tradition. If there is any anti-Semitism, in the most fundamental sense, in this present controversy, it is practiced by the Jews and Gentiles of New York, who claim no more than the privilege of living according to their own notions without submitting to the cultural dictation of the farmer. Amos's theories about the debilitating influence of urban luxury no longer seem to have much influence among his co-religionists. If the Jews have learned that he was mistaken, it seems not beyond hope that some day the generality of Christians may perceive it too.

PROLEGOMENA TO A FUTURE CHRISTOLOGY

EVERY Sunday some reverend clergyman views with alarm the revolt against religion, and quite as often some earnest atheist points to it with pride; this in an age which is the most religious since the seventeenth century. (The Great Revival of a hundred years ago seems to have been not so much an outbreak of religion as a wave of mass hysteria similar to that which was set off by the return of Charles Lindbergh.) The people who predicted that a return to religion would follow the war were right; failure to perceive that their prediction has been verified is due only to a confusion of religion with Christianity. There is certainly a revolt against Christianity; but those who are most shrilly crying it down are the devotees of a new and fanatical creed which seems likely to develop most of the faults of Christianity, and not quite so many of the virtues. If the new religion (make no mistake, that is exactly what it is) gets the upper hand, we may presently find that the little finger of Mencken is heavier than the loins of St. Paul.

For Mencken's ideas have become a body of doctrine (not very well systematized as yet, but the theologians of his flock can be depended on to attend to that in time)—the doctrine of a new religion which, lacking an official name, may as well be called Mercurianity; a creed which covers more departments of life in practice than Christianity ever attempted to control even in theory. It prescribes not only what you shall think, but the words in which you shall clothe your thought. Nine contributions out of ten to the *Mercury* are written in as near an approximation as the contributors can manage to the style of the master; and I have reason to believe that this is due to no compulsion on his part, but to the self-sacrificial devotion of his converts.

For Mr. Mencken's style, when he writes it, I have as a rule much admiration (though he is a good deal better when he writes about somebody he likes, such as Beethoven, than when he unlooses his Schrecklichkeit on an enemy); but it is like cut whisky when you get it at second hand. That, however, is a point of no importance to his worshipers; for to the Mercurian this is a matter of theology and not of esthetics. Mencken's style is only a style for Mencken; but when other people write it, as they try to do by thousands, it is the jargon of a religious cult, just as the good English of the King James translators and the so-so Latin of St. Jerome have become the hieratic languages of sects of longer standing. By these ritual phrases true believers recognize each other as surely as in the days of the Stuart Restoration or the Neronian persecution, and the mystic tongue is undoubtedly a powerful factor in promoting their cohesion.

This is certainly the most extraordinary, and possibly the most important, occurrence in America since the war—the welding of assorted disgruntlements into a new church, as thoroughly regimented as any Christian body and quite as intolerant, even though the intolerance, for the moment, must be taken out in talk. This restriction may not long endure; if Mercurianity keeps on growing it may before long be the state church of this enlightened republic. Already it is as strong in numbers, and as much stronger in influence, as was Christianity at the beginning of the reign of Constantine; and as happened with Christianity, a lot of people will join it as soon as membership becomes politically profitable. Like fourth-century Christianity it is the slick new city religion, still suspect on the farm; and like that Christianity it is a syncrasy of diverse elements, held together by a fanatical refusal to compromise with older creeds, and a bigoted conviction of its monopoly of salvation.

One wonders what Mr. Mencken himself may think of this process that has changed him from an iconoclastic Ishmael into a heresiarch, and then into the Messiah of the coming orthodoxy, with even higher honors in prospect. Quite possibly he regards it with the perplexity and dismay which one may imagine Jesus of Nazareth as feeling, if he had returned to life at any period between the ministry of St. Paul and that of Aimee MacPherson. Those who know Mr. Mencken personally tell me that he is a kindly and modest man, compact of all the Christian virtues and not at all inclined to lay claim to divine honors. No doubt, like other prophets, he set out to teach men the truth with the idea that the truth would make them free; a praiseworthy intention which failed to take into account the incurable propensities of the human race. For like all other prophets, he sees his followers falling into line and parading before him in joyful goose step, proclaiming that his truth is the sole truth, by which alone we may be saved.

Already he is identified with the Logos; before he has been dead ten years his biography will be furnished with all the paraphernalia of deity. If the citizens of Dayton, Tennessee, had so far yielded to their impulses as actually to lynch him, during the great trial of strength between Yahveh and Baal a few years ago, he would have been deified already.[1]

All of which, I imagine, is not altogether pleasant to a man of Mr. Mencken's turn of mind. But whether he likes it or not, he cannot stop it now. Nothing he might say or do could avail against the apparently inextinguishable human need for a personal savior and an anthropomorphic god.

GIVE me something to stand on, said Archimedes, and I will move the world. Most of us repeat his cry, but with much more modest ambitions; without some firm foundation we cannot maintain our equilibrium at all. If there is anything that history teaches beyond dispute, it is that so long as it can hope to find anything else to stand on, the human race will not stand on its own feet.

Well, the ancient foundation that was good enough for our fathers has been pretty badly undermined of recent years, for which the blame (or the credit, if you prefer) must be ascribed to the reverend clergy, or at any rate to that dominant faction of the clergy which has always insisted that the power of God unto salva-

[1] Mencken's flock, however, is not yet purged of Arian elements. In an article in the *Saturday Review* by one Bernard Fay, otherwise unknown to me, I find the following: "Mencken, Waldo Frank, etc., are great men." This insidious form of denigration by classification is, to say the least, unsportsmanlike.

tion would not work unless you believed in such dogmas as a flat earth and a geocentric universe, the six-day creation, the unpardonable iniquity of bobbed hair, the Sinaitic authority of the Volstead Act, and Jonah's whale. A few irreverent skeptics who conceived that the clergy might possibly be mistaken in this association of ideas managed to save a remnant of intelligent people for Christianity; but most laymen, taught to believe that the holy men knew what they were talking about, when they gave up Jonah gave up Jesus too.

The resultant dilemma of the contemporary intellectual, with or without the capital I (if there ever was an intellectual whose I was not capital) has been set forth by Mr. Lee Wilson Dodd in the early pages of *The Golden Complex*. The critical intelligence, he observes (buttressing himself on the testimony of so regular an intellectual as Mr. Joseph Wood Krutch) no longer believes in God; Man feels himself lost, and all his high purposes with him, in a Universe which has no visible purpose at all. For unfortunately the human race is incurably teleological; it must have a Purpose before it can get up steam, it must see the Goal before it can start on the journey. And few of us are either so consciously pragmatical as to be content with a goal which we know is only a mirage, or so industrious as to endure even a few more marchings weary without some assurance that we shall be gathered home.[2]

This is a fair statement of the present crisis, and a

[2] I have expounded this difficulty in more detail in a novel, *Strange Woman*, to which I refer anyone who may be interested in further examination of these matters.

very serious crisis it is. The purposeless intellectual is one of the commonest and most depressing spectacles of our time, and something ought to be done about him in mere humanity, for his own sake and that of the spectators as well. You might say, on regarding him casually, that what he needs is a swift kick; but that judgment would be hasty and unscientific. What he really needs is a Rock of Ages, and it is not surprising if he is inclined to find one in any bowlder that projects a little way above the landscape.

In all of which, of course, we only repeat the experience of the Romans eighteen centuries ago. Rural conservatism sticks to at least the forms of the old-time religion, but the urban intellectuals have pretty largely had to let it go. (It is a tribute to the merits of Christianity that it takes so much killing; Zeus and Odin could not have survived the asininities of the Christian clergy for a single century.) Well, what then? In these matters, Nature abhors a vacuum. Some few people are tough-minded enough to try to stand on their own feet, even though they feel no solid rock underfoot, but only shifting sand. But for the majority it is as true as ever that if God does not exist, He must be invented. Pallid philosophy, the balanced ration of scientific dieticians, is too flat and tasteless for the average palate; so the multitude turns to the more savory fare of mystical salvation cults. Especially the intellectual multitude, which popularized the concept of "herd consciousness," and has offered itself as an object lesson of just what that term means.

As in Rome, plenty of new religions compete for the custom of these earnest seekers after the True, the

Beautiful and the Good. Most of the intellectuals appear to regard Mr. Mencken as their substitutionary paschal lamb (if he was not slain for them, he has done their thinking for them, thereby relieving them of a penalty of original human cussedness that would have been more lingering in its agony); but a bellicose minority offers its bull on the altar of Dr. John Broadus Watson, and Mr. Dodd seems to think that Watson's proprietary creed, Behaviorism, is the next predestined manifestation of the World Spirit.

In this it is hard to follow him. Possibly, as he lives in New Haven, he was unduly impressed by the great behavioristic taurobolium that took place there a year or two ago. At the moment, Mercurianity seems to be outdistancing Behaviorism as surely as Christianity outdistanced Mithraism. The Behaviorists have that first essential of a successful religion, a hot intolerance, and they enjoy the further advantage of an elaborate systematic theology such as Mercurianity still lacks; the future may possibly be theirs. But the present certainly is Mencken's.

Herein lies the significance of *Elmer Gantry*. In portions of *Arrowsmith*, and almost all of *Babbitt*, Mr. Lewis has shown that he can be an artist, when he cares to try; but to his mind art is secondary to moral edification. If Lewis's clerical novel had been written about Frank Shallard it would probably have been a great book, and it would have interested about one-tenth as many people as have read the compilation of newspaper clippings on the crimes of the clergy which he actually produced. Lewis, enriched by a succession of best sellers, could easily have afforded to

The Show Window Of Elmer Davis, Gay and Salty

SHOW WINDOW. By Elmer Davis. New York: The John Day Company. $2.50.

Reviewed by

STARR LAWRENCE

THE essays of Elmer Davis, collected in "Show Window," are more substantial than is fashionable in a day of brilliant surface writing. They do, too, deserve that much-abused adjective "salty." For all the essays have the tang and flavor and slight bitterness of salt.

Mr. Davis' far-famed "Portrait of a Cleric," is reprinted here, and, as it did on its first appearance in Harper's, outwears the new and humorous volume with a wealth of

diatribe against H. L. Mencken, which will, no doubt, be quoted freely in the proposed "Schimpflexikon" of the much-abused editor of the American Mercury. Although in many of these essays he is as militant as the Hon. Mencken himself, Mr. Davis' literary essays are as unorthodox as they are enlightening. Thus he considers the appeal of "Sorrell and Son" and concludes that the book's wide popularity was due to its gusto. Gusto is a quality contemporary literature sadly lacks. Novels are suffering from anemia and the public is eager for a reaction. Ir Warwick Deeping's books they find what they are looking for, plus a good old-fashioned sonorous style which is anomalous in a day of clipped nervous sentences.

Certainly Elmer Davis does not share the defects of his brother writers, for "Show Window" is a vigorous

a success in the essay corresponding to that of Warwick Deeping in the fiction world.

DOWN STAIRS

Telephone RITtenhouse 1000

write a good novel for the entertainment of a few
thoughtful people; he preferred to lay it on with a
trowel so that the dullest mind, the most fanatically
reverent Fundamentalist, could not fail to see what he
was driving at. *Gantry* was very bad art and very
good theology, from the Mercurian point of view. Lewis
was writing a missionary tract against a religion which
he hated; he felt no more need of being fair to the
Christians than Fathers of the Church felt of being
fair to the heathen.

It is true that Lewis seems to regard himself as an
atheist; so do most of the Mercurians. But that is only
because the formal apotheosis of Mencken has not yet
taken place. Mencken himself would doubtless call
himself an atheist, but mere modesty prescribes that.
The early Christians, after all, seemed atheists to a
pious Greek or Roman. Whatever the Mercurians believe about the Absolute, the essence of their creed is
a fiery unshakable faith in their great Mediator. I am
told by college professors that large numbers of their
students (chiefly the "atheist" intellectuals) believe in
the literal inspiration of the *Mercury* from cover to
cover, commas and all, quite as firmly as their great-
grandfathers believed in that of the Bible.[3]

Unbelievers scoffed at the coincidence that after
Lewis dedicated his clerical novel to Mencken "in profound admiration," Mencken promptly reviewed it in
the *Mercury* as the greatest thing since Rabelais. (This
must have brought sore searchings of the heart to a

[3] My own solitary contribution to the *Mercury* was on a purely
secular theme. Pending an authoritative ruling, it need not be
regarded as canonical.

minor apostle of the new dispensation, Mr. W. E. Woodward, who went no farther back than Voltaire to find a work of equal stature. Rank Laodiceanism, Brother Woodward.) But this derision was based on a misunderstanding. The book expressed Mencken's ideas; much of it, even, was written in Mencken's style, the ritual language he has imposed on his followers. His review, accordingly, was no more than an approbation of the soundness of Lewis's theology and the correctness of his liturgical erudition.

For, as I remarked earlier, Mencken has, properly speaking, no literary taste at all; as thoroughly as the members of the Congregation of the Index he judges a book by its doctrinal soundness and by nothing else. You need only read his "literary" criticism in any large quantity to find proof of this on every page; but I think the most amusing instance of it was his change of heart about Mr. Ford Madox Ford. Mencken used to go out of his way to show his contempt for Ford, even when Ford still called himself Hueffer; but he came round with startling suddenness on *No More Parades*. Here, he observed, Ford at last had done something—and what was it? Why, in *No More Parades*, Ford had presented a very uncomplimentary picture of the British army at war with the Germans. And for Mencken Germany is not yet beaten, the war not yet over—he goes on fighting it himself, whenever he has time; as thoroughly as any unreconstructed maiden lady of Charleston or Richmond, he is devoted to the Lost Cause.

Further testimony can be found copiously in his critical writings. If a book presents a correct view of the

Universe (*Weltanschauung* I ought to say, in mere courtesy), in other words if its theology is sound, it is a good book; it is art, and big art at that. But if it implies a view of the fundamental problems of life which differs from Mencken's it is a bad book, however excellent it may seem by profane canons of esthetic merit. (All critics have a touch of this, of course, but most of them recognize that it must be kept within bounds.) Mencken has praised many excellent writers, and done much good to American literature (though I think less good than harm, a disproportion which increases every day); but this has been incidental and accidental to his main purpose of disseminating correct doctrine.

Naturally the members of his Church follow their master in this theory of criticism; like the average Church Father, they regard a hot piece of polemic as better literature than all of Virgil with Horace thrown in. (Though I observe that the classic American writers are in process of being preserved to posterity, as was Virgil in the Dark Ages, by the tendency of the devout to find allusive foreshadowings in their pages of the sublime truths of the religion now revealed.) Which is not exactly a pleasing prospect for those of us who value the privilege of variety of opinion. Christianity has at times been pretty hard on art and letters; but when the Mercurians have had things their way for a couple of generations men may look back with longing to the good old days when they had only the Inquisition to deal with.

THE argument of *Elmer Gantry* could be summed up

in a line—*Tantum religio potuit suadere malorum*. It is two thousand years since that line was written, and Lucretius who was so sure he had demonstrated to the satisfaction of all intelligent men that God Must Go might be somewhat depressed if he knew what had happened since. Even Lucretius was no genuine blown-in-the-glass atheist; he stood on the atomic theory as his Rock of Ages, and had the regard for Empedocles and Democritus that Lewis has for Mencken. But Lucretius is not the Latin author whom Lewis most resembles; that honor must be reserved for Tertullian, a worthy truly Mercurian in his lack of sweetness and light.

Well, there was some excuse (though not enough) for Tertullian's bad temper, as there is some for Lewis's. The Church, whether Catholic or Protestant, has done some rather dreadful things, and still does them in regions where it can get away with it. In so far as *Elmer Gantry* may lead the Fundamentalist parishioner to regard his pastor with a somewhat skeptical eye, and check up his practices with his professions, it can do nothing but good, though I am afraid its obvious exaggerations have to some extent defeated its purpose. What is just as badly needed is a similar critique of the Mercurians. Some efforts indeed have been made to supply this want, but they have not gone very far for two reasons—they were attempted by men of lesser gifts than Lewis's; and the Mercurians, who with a shrewd instinct for key positions are pretty well entrenched in American literary criticism, jumped on them with great promptness and put them on the Index. The faithful have been warned not to read them and they have in the main not been good enough to override this obstacle by their own merit. The sole exception is *The Plutocrat,* whose popularity suggests that the Right Wing likes exaggeration and unfairness fully as much as the Left. For Mr. Tarkington's specimens of the intelligentsia are quite as incredible as the Reverend Elmer Gantry.[4]

It was observed above that Mercurianism is open, at present, to one serious criticism—it is hard to see just what it is, beyond a general grouch at the way things have been going. On its purely destructive side there is much to be said for it, as there was for a Christianity which ended the gladiatorial games in Rome and the human sacrifices in Tenochtitlan. But affirmatively it is still rather obscure; the only positive doctrine which emerges from the sacred writings of Mr. Mencken himself is that Germany was right in the late war. However, a fluidity of theology is characteristic of the primitive apostolic period of any religion; systematization comes later, when the first rush of excitement is past. Nor does it matter, in this present honeymoon stage of the cult, just what it is; its votaries may have the haziest conception of what they are excited about, but that does not in the least interfere with their excitement, or with their conviction that any person not equally excited deserves the rack, the thumbscrew, and the stake.

But the Mercurians will have to take hold of this problem sooner or later; they cannot consolidate their

[4] Of course *The Plutocrat* is not a theological novel in the archaic sense of that word; but it deals with matters which are included in theology by the Menckenites.

conquests by a purely negative program. We have
heard a good deal, of late, about the faults of Christianity; it might be more pertinent to inquire into its
merits. It was no accident that Christianity conquered
Rome, and then Europe; nor was by any means all of
the credit due to such persuasions as the sword of
Charlemagne and the godly adders of Olaf Tryg-
vasson. For four or five centuries men had tried to
look the Universe in the eye and had discovered that
they were not yet strong enough to do it; so they gave
it up and looked around for shelter. They wanted
something that would give them a sense of personal
importance and personal salvation, a conviction that
God is interested in me individually and is going to
take care of me. A dozen religions offered that; Christianity beat the others because it was the best of the
lot—best in the material sense, offering more satisfaction, a better value. As a historical explanation of its
success the old hymn is exactly right; "it satisfies my
longings as nothing else can do."

It was of course also ethically superior to most of
its competitors; but I suspect that the parable of Lazarus and Dives was a better sales talk for Christianity
than the Good Samaritan. Every poor man will give
three cheers for a religion which tells him that in the
blessed eternity to come he will recline in cool comfort
and be privileged to watch the wicked plutocrat sizzling
on an everlasting gridiron, and calling for water in
vain. And, be it observed, Christianity was wise enough
to defer this readjustment of earthly inequalities to the
hereafter; it all occurs after the earthly shell of Lazarus has moldered away to dust; there is no danger of

his coming back and reporting that the goods were not as represented. (How literally Jesus meant all this is beside the point; his followers have taken it literally.)

Menckenism, one notes with disquiet, is rather perilously preoccupied with the Here and Now. Certainly it gives its communicants a blessed sense of superiority to the common run of humanity; but most of them are young enough to be inclined to feel that anyway, on very slight provocation. Not till it proves able to hold the loyalty of the aged and decrepit can it be regarded as safely established. A religion which slights the useful concept of the immortality of the soul and essays to deliver the goods while the customer is still alive to examine them is running a needless risk; as is proved by the case of Socialism. That was a most attractive creed, until the Russians tried it; since when it has perceptibly declined in favor. I suspect that the fugitives from its routed host account for a good many of Mencken's converts.

Mercurianism indeed satisfies a certain Nordic patriotism, for it was invented by a blond Aryan. Even before Nietzsche some few Europeans disliked the idea that their Continent had been subjected by an Oriental religion (whose competitors, that might have beaten it out if they had been good enough, were also Oriental). But Christianity conquered Europe because it was more satisfactory than any religion which the Europeans themselves were clever enough to invent. One European religion, the latest and not the least creditable, is disappearing before our eyes—the Code of the Gentleman. I am not sure whether it is its merits or its shortcomings that have killed it, but at any rate

it ceased to satisfy the popular need. It too emphasized
the Here and Now; it promised no eternity of future
bliss; and here is the gravest fault of all European
religions. Some of them have ignored the Hereafter
altogether, and those that tried to include it have never
quite been able to throw discretion to the winds and
promise everything in the generous Oriental way. This
caution may have been ethically creditable, but it is
not the way to win converts. Stoicism was probably the
most respectable religion ever evolved in Europe, but
it was about as pallid and dismal as a reform candidate for Mayor; and like a reform candidate for Mayor
it found much favor among the more dutiful aristocrats and was enthusiastically ignored by the mass of
the people. It lacked vitamines. When a little Oriental
juice was added Stoicism became Calvinism; the doctrine of election and reprobation made life as uncertain
and exciting as a roulette game; you ran a strong
chance of being completely cleaned out but there was
the dizzy possibility, however unlikely, of huge and
fabulous rewards. Stoicism was a good static religion;
it stiffened a man to dig in and hold his ground; but
it had none of the aggressive punch of Calvinism that
enabled the Scotch to rule most of the British Empire, and the New Englanders most of the United
States.

Zeno and Zeus and Odin have had their day, and
Henry Louis Mencken may profit by their example.
He is lucky in that his following, at the moment, in-
cludes a considerable Semitic element; and he had
better let them buy into the firm while there is time.
If I were Mencken I should set to work without more

delay to draw up an eschatology—a good substantial one, full of calories and well seasoned with rewards and punishments. Unless he does that he may go the way of the gods of Olympus, who made a fine appearance but lacked durability.

Who would succeed him? I do not profess to know. Perhaps John Broadus Watson, that Sol Invictus of a creed which promises to build Jerusalem in America's green and pleasant land, if it only catches its catechumens young enough; perhaps some Buddha yet unborn. . . . Conceivably, even, a revived Christianity; for though Christianity has often enough been pronounced dead by the attendant physicians, it has a habit of coming back.

At this point, I suppose, the Mercurian (if a curious tolerance which has survived his creed permits him to read so far) will say that I am only an undercover Christian propagandist. Not at all; I am one of those persons who can regard the strife of religions with entire detachment, because they know they are going to get the worst of it whichever side wins.

Mr. Chester Crowell wrote in the *Mercury* a few years ago an argument for the Fundamentalists. More power to them! he cried; for the more completely they have their way, the sooner will Christianity be thoroughly discredited. Whereas if the Modernists get the upper hand Christianity will be a reasonable and humane religion, and Heaven knows how long it may take us to get rid of it. (I reproduce his argument from memory, but I think not inaccurately.) Just so the Church Fathers felt less bitterness against Nero, who

was a bad advertisement for his creed, than against
Julian the Apostate who came dangerously near making paganism ethically respectable. Mr. Crowell wrote,
if I remember, as an infidel indifferentist; but his very
argument is proof that he is an infidel only as concerns
Christianity, that whatever he calls himself his is an
anima naturaliter Mercuriana.

An intelligent atheist ought to be whole-heartedly
on the side of the Modernists for the simple reason that
they will let him alone; when they dominate the church
there is no persecution. But unhappily a good many
atheists make atheism a religion, and a missionary religion at that; the late activities of the Freethinkers'
Society of New York suggest that if they had the
power they would be quite as dangerous to religious
liberty as the church has ever been. Here one may
borrow a distinction from the Baptist Church, which in
the early nineteenth century was divided between the
Hardshell and Missionary factions. The Hardshells
have suffered undeserved opprobrium because their
name happened to pass into the general vocabulary as
a term of abuse; but their true differentiation was not
dishonorable. They merely had more faith than their
brethren.

They believed as firmly as the Missionary Baptists
that God meant that the whole world should ultimately
become Baptist; but they were willing to trust Him to
bring this about in His own good time and His own
sufficient way, without taxing the faithful for the support of foreign missions. This doctrine was dangerously
attractive to the parsimonious; but there was something

to be said for it, especially from the point of view of the heathen.[5]

The hardshell atheist is willing to let other men believe what they choose, so long as they accord him the same privilege; but he is doomed to be ground between the upper and the nether millstones unless the Modernists get control of Christianity. And if they do get control of it one thing can be predicted—there will be a good deal more of Jesus in it, and a good deal less of Paul and Augustine; in other words, it will not be what past ages have known as Christianity.

IT's the old-time religion; it was good for Paul and Silas and it's good enough for me; it satisfies my longings as nothing else can do. . . . No one who has seen the happy life of a truly devout Christian of the old school—a good man as well as a good Christian, who fought the good fight of faith and died in sure expectation of a mansion in the skies—no one who has seen that can help feeling that here is something which, if you lose it, can never be adequately replaced. You may say that the satisfaction is as illusory as that which you get from liquor, that both are escape mechanisms; but the old-time religion was probably the most satisfying escape mechanism that was ever invented. A man who has had that, and has lost it, is apt to be

[5] I have only the highest respect for the motives of contributors to foreign missions; they believed that they had the best thing in the world and they wanted to pass it around even if they had to bear the whole cost of distribution. But unless you believe that the salvation of a single soul outweighs any amount of annoyance and disturbance, it can hardly be denied that they did more harm than good. Not quite so much can be said against the missionary atheists; or for them either.

as enviously morose as the enthusiastic drinker whom a corroded stomach has driven to the refuge of the water wagon. And just as some of the hottest prohibitionists are reformed drunkards who cannot bear to see anybody else enjoying what they cannot have any more, so the really bellicose atheist may be inspired by no nobler emotion than a reminiscent jealousy.

Nevertheless the old-time religion is ceasing to satisfy; it was implicated (sometimes accidentally but sometimes necessarily) with too many things that will not bear close inspection. Hence the spectacle, above mentioned, of the Critical Intelligence lost in the Waste Land; hence the panic rush to Mencken's salvation cult. When the old-time religion no longer satisfies our longings, most people are going to try some other religion rather than see if they cannot make shift to do without the longings. Give me something to stand on— anything but my own feet.

Well, the Modernists are trying to build a bridge over the bottomless pit into which the Critical Intelligence is in danger of falling; and one can hardly withhold admiration from their gallant endeavor. But a bridge must be strong enough to carry its load and it must be observed that the Modernists have as yet built nothing that will support any very heavy traffic. Their task, of course, is immensely more difficult than that of the Fundamentalists, whether Catholic or Protestant. However Patrick Cardinal Hayes, William New York (as I suppose Bishop Manning would like to subscribe himself), and the Reverend Doctor Bill Sunday may differ in other respects, they have this in common—if you accept any of their respective major premises, all the rest follows without argument. The answer is either yes or no; and it is not surprising that a good many timid persons say "yes" at once and then stuff cotton in their ears to shut out any murmur of disagreement.[6]

Now the great weakness of the Modernists is that they have no major premise. If the atheist lacks a goal, the Modernist seems to lack a starting-point. His intentions are excellent and so are his ethics, but his metaphysics leave a good deal to be desired. I am not widely read in Modernist theology, but I surely do the movement no injustice in taking as a fair sample of its teachers the Reverend Doctor Harry Emerson Fosdick. I have never seen or heard this gentleman, but I observe that he seems to have an extraordinary capacity for fostering and fomenting religion in very intelligent people; he is, as our ancestors would have said, filled with the Holy Spirit. Which must be due to his personality; for when you read his doctrines in cold print they are not overwhelmingly cogent. They seem, in fact, to be as plainly an escape mechanism as the gospel of the camp-meeting evangelist; the latest improved model, certainly, with all sorts of modern improvements and the more artistic dull finish; but an escape mechanism none the less.

What is Fosdick's major premise? Take it from his

---

[6] Once you put it on this plane the Catholics have of course a much more plausible argument than any Protestant. Logically all Fundamentalists ought to turn Catholic, but these matters are not regulated by logic. Besides, Catholicism is open to a fatal objection from the standpoint of the Protestant Fundamentalist clergyman —only one man can be Pope at a time.

own writings. "The root of Christianity is reverence for personality, and *the faith that God must care for the spiritual values of His universe.*" (*Adventurous Religion*, page 44; the italics are mine.) Observe that "must"; unless I utterly fail to understand what Fosdick is driving at, that is his major premise. For he says further: "Whatever else a man may obtain without God, he will still live in a world that, like a raft on the high seas, is aimlessly adrift, uncharted, unguided, and unknown." (*Ibid.*, page 150.) That is true, and no man would willingly live in that sort of world—if he could persuade himself that there is any other sort of world to live in.

Whether the soul of man is immortal or not, Fosdick rightly observes, "makes a tremendous difference." If earthly inequality and injustice is not to be redressed hereafter, one must fall back on subtler and more indirect arguments to defend any attempt to live decently. Abner Teeftallow's mountaineer friends could not see why the village infidel did not get drunk and raise hell generally. Fosdick would not put it so crudely, but all the logic of his doctrine points to that same conclusion.

So, he sums up (*Adventurous Religion,* page 198): "I cannot believe that this ascending struggle of mankind is doomed to end in a hopeless cinder heap. . . . We cannot submit to the mental confusion, the triumphant irrationality of an existence where death is finally victor over all." Well, nobody likes to submit to it; but suppose you are going to have to submit to it, whether you like it or not. I do not find in Fosdick (or anywhere else, for that matter) any evidence that we have any other choice. What his argument comes down to is that he believes in God and immortality, because otherwise the Universe would be meaningless and Fosdick would be uncomfortable. It is a popular creed, as Fosdick's following attests; but not even the religion of the Middle Ages was quite so anthropocentric as this. When Margaret Fuller accepted the Universe, Carlyle remarked that she had better. But Fosdick is not so resigned; he must have his own favorite brand of Universe and he refuses all imitations.

Here is a major premise through which you can stick your foot; but even granting it validity, there is a further and serious flaw in the logic. Surely it is conceivable that this large and intricate universe—this federation of universes, it begins to seem after the late researches of the astronomers—may have a meaning, without any necessary corollary that the residents of this planet figure very largely in that meaning. This structure seems to have a mathematical order, and may have some further order, of a nature as yet incomprehensible to the human mind; but is it implicit in the eternal scheme of things that Fosdick must be comfortable?

THE same fallacy vitiates the recent endeavor of a distinguished scientist, Dr. Robert A. Millikan, to make a peace by negotiation between science and religion. Both science and religion, he says, have been taking themselves too seriously. So they have; so has everything and everybody else; in this particular all we like sheep have gone astray. But Dr. Millikan appears to feel that one must be constructive, and unfortunately constructive persons must take themselves seriously. "This is possibly true, but it may be mistaken," is not the argument which will popularize a new religious discovery. At any rate Millikan corrects himself by presently becoming at once more constructive, and more serious, than the facts seem to justify on closer examination.

"The Fundamentalist and the atheist," he says (*Science and Religion,* page 87), "seem to me to represent much the same type of thinking. Each asserts a definite knowledge of the ultimate which he does not possess." And on the next page: "The God of science is the spirit of rational order and of orderly development. Atheism, as I understand it, is the denial of the existence of this spirit"—and he goes on to say that if you pretend that atheism means anything else you are dodging the question and trying to get away from what is coming to you. This leads up to his famous declaration that if he had to choose between Fundamentalism and atheism he would choose Fundamentalism, which gave so much joy to the faithful.

In this profession some of the more excitable unbelievers saw only an effort of a scientist to buy off the invading barbarians; but it seems to me no more (or no less) than muddy thinking. Millikan's line of reasoning is substantially this: (1) A man who is what I call an atheist is a fool; (2) An atheist is what I call him; (3) Therefore, an atheist is a fool. This may be good polemic, but it is bad logic. There are certainly atheists who assert a definite knowledge of the ultimate which they do not possess; but the name is commonly applied to others who go no farther than to confess that they see no ground for including what is ordinarily termed God—the God of religion, not the God of science—in the working hypotheses by which they must guide their conduct. I hope, for the sake of the credibility of science, that Dr. Millikan does not thus allow his anger to becloud his reasoning when he gets inside the atom.

For the God of religion and the God of science are two very different beings. There is nothing new about this God of science, this spirit of rational order and of orderly development; we know somewhat more about the order and the development than we used to, but the essence of the concept was familiar to Spinoza, to Aristotle, to the author of the Book of Job. No one has yet shown any connection between this mathematical deity and human aspirations, or the immortality of the human soul. The electrons by virtue of whose temporary agglomeration I exist may be indestructible (though science has destroyed so many of its own indestructibles, of late years, that I should be reluctant to bet money on it); they may severally be destined, in the course of the various disintegrations and redintegrations of the members of the cosmos through the next few decillions of millennia, to perform much more important and honorable functions than those in which they have been engaged since the year 1890. But I do not expect to get any personal satisfaction out of it.

You can accept Millikan's God without getting rid of Fosdick's cinder heap. The evidence points to an orderly universe; but who started it, and with what purpose? Is there any evidence that the "spirit of orderly development" is any more interested in the doings of the human race than in what is going on around Arcturus or Aldebaran, or in that far-distant island universe which can be seen through the window of Orion? Is there any reason to believe that He, or It, is even as much interested, or interested at all? So, within the framework of the thought of his time, reasoned Epicurus, and I do not see that Millikan has advanced any further. In the Modernist fashion, he regards God as a sort of corporation in which the human race owns stock; but he cannot pretend that our holdings are more than infinitesimal, nor can he give us any information as to the location of the majority interest.

J. H. Jeans is, I suppose, a scientist whom Millikan would regard with some respect; and he has lately suggested that what we call Life may be only a sort of rare degenerative disease of sidereal old age, an infection of decayed universe-tissue, obscure, infrequent and remote. You can accept Millikan's cosmology, then, and still have no reason to believe that Man is more than a corn on the toe of the cosmos—a cosmos, says Jeans, which may conceivably be devised for other and more stupendous purposes.

Millikan's God, in other words, is no other than our old friend the Absolute; and it did not take the human race long to find out that in the Absolute there was little nourishment. It would profit Dr. Millikan, for whose attainments in the more exact sciences one must feel the highest respect, to give some attention to the history of the science of thought—an inexact science certainly, but one which has at any rate caught one or two of those bits of eternal truth which, according to

Millikan, have at sundry times and in divers manners been revealed to Man. He would discover that this Absolute God has been no help at all, in finite human problems; that persons less austere than Aristotle are apt to need a sort of Assistant God, a Demiurge, a Logos, a Mediator; and that this Mediator, in a very short time, becomes the chief or only god, with the Absolute shoved into the background, even though his relegation has to be explained by some such pious expedient as the doctrine of the Trinity.

Millikan's religion is no doubt a good religion for Millikan, to which extent I give him three fraternal cheers. But when he abuses people who disagree with him he implies that he regards it as a good religion for everybody. Try to propagate this faith and you will make more Fundamentalists, as Millikan perhaps unconsciously realized. Recognize your spirit of rational order and orderly development; but if you try to find any personal consolation in it, any side door which enables you to escape the hopeless cinder heap, you will get, ultimately, no better answer than God gave Job—You don't know what it is all about, so you had better take it on faith.

So Modernism, on examination, appears just a little too pragmatic for the fastidious taste. Your Modernist, whether Jew or Christian, insists as vigorously as the Fundamentalist Christian or the Orthodox Jew that atheism is a sterile creed. Hear that distinguished Liberal rabbi, Dr. Nathan Krass, as lately reported in the New York papers: "A world without order, the product of chance, mechanistically put together and materialistically conceived, a world without moral or spiritual significance, becomes a chaos and a jungle. Life is then purposeless, without meaning, and each one becomes a law to oneself. Agnosticism is unfruitful because it leaves men irresolute, uncertain, hesitant and hence unproductive. Its moral influence is bad as there is no positive urge to goodness. Its spiritual influence is nil as it offers no vision that inspires. Religion generally and Judaism especially gives us a unified conception of the cosmos . . . it gives zest to life, courage to the despondent, hope to the downcast and a glorious goal to the strong."

Well, no one ever denied that religion is comfortable. The Modernists would be a little more persuasive, however, if they offered evidence that it is true.

It was argued in an earlier chapter that the artist ought to do precisely what the Modernists are doing—to make a selection from the data of experience and arrange them in a pattern which in one way or another should be entertaining. That is sound doctrine, for the artist; but I am not so sure of its validity for the theologian. It would seem a little safer to keep fiction and religion in separate compartments. And possibly the artist may here render some small service to religion; by providing entertainment, diversion, escape, he may hearten his customers to do without escape mechanisms during office hours, and see what they can make out of the universe not as they would like it, but as to the best of their knowledge it appears actually to be.

It must be admitted at the start that it does not appear to be very appetizing. There is order in the universe, but so vast and intricate an order that we can hardly have any considerable part in it; it may be doubted if we figure in it more than infinitesimally, if at all. If Dives gets the better of Lazarus here below, it does not seem probable that Lazarus will ever get a chance to turn the tables on him; and whatever the race at large may in the course of eons accomplish, there is visible at present no worthier ultimate destination than Fosdick's cinder heap.

This attitude toward the universe is not a commodity that can be popularized by a sales campaign; it has no such attraction for the customers as the offerings of St. Paul or Mencken or Fosdick. All that those who hold it can say is that this is the way things seem to be and we might as well try to make the best of it. We do not enjoy standing on our own feet, but finding nothing else to stand on, we prefer to try it rather than slump in a heap.

And a good many people have slumped in a heap of late years. The old rules of the game were tied up with supernatural sanctions that have lost their plausibility, so recently there has been a pretty general inclination to play the game without any rules at all. It begins to be apparent that that does not work very well; some rules there must be. And surely it is not too much to hope that we can compile some provisional code which does not pretend to be graven on tables of stone; which may be used as long as it is useful, and replaced with something else when it is no longer workable or no longer corresponds to the best picture we can make for ourselves of the way things are. As a matter of fact there have already been published several tentative gropings toward the formulation of a new rationalistic morality, which I suspect would differ from the old code mainly in that it would be somewhat more flexible and less savage. No one having authority has synthesized these endeavors, because the true rationalist (not the Menckenite, or the Watsonite) is pretty slow to concede the authority of another in such matters. But doubtless like most codes it will be widely in practice before it is ever formulated at all.

The Supernaturalists will fight that, of course; they dislike a new morality in practice but they would hate it even worse in principle. It would seem as if one could count on the Modernists to help in this formulation (being Constructive, it ought to appeal to them); and indeed Dr. Fosdick himself lately made some remarks pointing in that direction, which earned him a sound rebuke from Bishop Manning for disagreeing with Manning and God. But the Modernists, I am afraid, would be a broken reed to lean on; if they mean what they say they cannot dissociate their morality from their eschatology. Fosdick has sniffed at the "obdurate and joyless heroism" of people who try to live decently even though they are unable to subscribe to the teleological interpretation of history. "The more lucidly," he observes (*Adventurous Religion,* page 168), "a man should perceive how thus all large human hopes were illusions in essence as well as in form, the more difficult it would be for him to keep heart in the struggle."

That is true. Rationalism (if that is the proper name for a theory which recognizes Millikan's spirit of orderly development, but finds no evidence that that spirit is going to do anything to satisfy our longings) is a creed for the tough-minded, as is proved by the occasional epidemics of student suicides. But surely there is respectable religious precedent for choosing the strait gate and the narrow way, if you happen to think it is the right one.

THE test of any religion is what it can give its adherents when they are visited by the Terminator of Delights and the Separator of Companions. And here, of course, no faith ever devised can rival Fundamentalist Christianity, so long as you can persuade yourself that it is plausible. St. Paul has been one of the gravest afflictions of the human race, but he made extensive reparation by writing the fifteenth chapter of First Corinthians, which has consoled more people at the time when they most needed consolation than anything else ever written. He warped millions of characters, stultified millions of minds; but at the same time he satisfied their longings as nothing else can do.

Paul was quite as sure as Abner Teeftallow that the question of immortality makes a tremendous difference. "If after the manner of men I have fought with beasts at Ephesus, what advantageth it me, if the dead rise not? Let us eat and drink, for to-morrow we die." The obdurate and joyless heroism of the village infidel who does not get drunk and raise hell generally seems to have been quite incomprehensible to him. If the dead rise not, it is every man for himself and devil take the hindmost. Nevertheless there are and always have been people who have managed to bring themselves to fight with beasts in no hope of future reward or fear of future punishment, but merely because they felt that the beasts ought to be fought on general principles. If any concerted effort were ever made to encourage this sort of behavior, it might become more common.

One such person, I gather from his writings, was the late Dr. Charles MacLaurin of Sydney. He concluded his volume of essays on the fatal diseases of famous historical characters, entitled *Post Mortem*,[7] with some general observations on death, as it appeared to a doctor who had been viewing it for several decades in war and peace. MacLaurin was not afraid of the predestined cinder heap; he did not pretend to like it, but there it was, so far as he could see, and he saw no point in trying to persuade himself that it was an optical illusion. He faced it, and accepted it, and did not let it worry him. To MacLaurin, it was not survival after death but behavior before death that made a tremendous difference; it seemed to him that there was some advantage, both to the individual and to the race, in trying to give ourselves reason to be proud of the way we have lived, even if the dead rise not.

Whether you prefer MacLaurin's answer to Death, or St. Paul's, is a matter of taste. Paul says it is all a mistake, it is not really true; that by some divine hocus-pocus we shall all be changed, in a moment, in the twinkling of an eye, and shall live forever afterward in bliss beyond imagining—all of us, at least, who agree with the doctrinal theology of Paul. Whether that is true or not nobody knows; but pending corroboration, I submit that it is the answer of a

[7] American edition published by Doran in 1922.

child; that however firmly St. Paul may have believed that it was an objective reality, it is as much of a wish fulfillment as the story of Jack and the Beanstalk. Whereas MacLaurin's answer is worthy of a mature and civilized man.

They think they have answered a man who holds such views, observed MacLaurin, when they say that his creed is sterile. Well, possibly the human race is still in its infancy and must have its fairy stories, whether or not they correspond to the facts as we can at present see them. Even so, I do not perceive the total sterility of this endeavor to do without them. It is a creed that casteth out fear, and casts it out to stay out; for you are beyond fear when you know the worst and stand up to it. Even on purely pragmatic grounds, there is no reason to be ashamed of a faith that enables a man to look the Universe in the eye, and stand on his own feet even though he knows that presently they will be swept from under him.

REMARKS ON THE PERFECT STATE

IT came like a Voice From the Past, that gleefully vindictive drawl from the trolley seat behind me, "Yes, sir, we've got rid of the liquor and we're goin' after the tobacco next. We'll make this country fit to live in yet."

Here, I reflected, was optimism; not in several years had I heard anybody boast that we had got rid of the liquor; and the promise that tobacco would be done away with next, though heard often in 1919, reflected an optimism as to the possibility of making the citizenry perfect by statute which has rarely been met with since the honeymoon days of the Eighteenth Amendment. Yet I suppose there are still plenty of people who believe that tobacco and bobbed hair and mixed bathing can be got rid of by passing a law; that prohibition can be perfectly enforced by passing a few more laws.

Well, how has this theory of government worked? To argue from current instances would be unprofitable; the famous facts about prohibition are too much a matter of opinion. But luckily history does offer an example of what happens when the government sets out to make the citizens spotless by law. Ancient Sparta carried the practice of legislating virtue into the population to an extent that would shock even the Anti-Saloon League; so far as "Thou shalt not" can accomplish it, Sparta was the perfect state. Probably no commonwealth in the world's history has been so much admired as Sparta; Spartan virtue is proverbial. And fortunately Sparta has been extinct long enough to enable us to investigate it somewhat dispassionately and find out what those Spartan virtues really were.

Sparta owes its modern reputation—if any ancient state can be said to have a reputation in a world which is industriously trying to forget classic antiquity—to the political theorists of the eighteenth century. They admired Sparta for the same reason that they admired the Noble Savage—because they knew nothing about it. They knew that Sparta was poor, frugal, and simple (in theory); poverty, frugality, and simplicity were virtues apt to be overvalued in a world whose standards had been set by the court of Louis XIV, and few eighteenth-century philosophers took the trouble to read deeply enough to find out if the theory corresponded with the fact.

But Sparta's fame did not originate with the eighteenth century; it began with Sparta's contemporaries, with the other Greek states. Why did they admire Sparta? Because Sparta could beat them all in battle; because, when every other Hellenic state had to count on the chance of a revolution every year or two, Sparta went through centuries without a successful revolution. Sparta, in other words, was organized on an efficiency basis. Our outstanding business men favor prohibition because it will make Americans efficient; so far Sparta, where prohibition was carried to the limit, can be set down as an argument for the affirmative. The Spartans were certainly efficient; the only question is, efficient for what?

As every schoolboy used to know, the Spartan constitution was laid down by one Lycurgus, far back in the mists of antiquity. Now let us consider, first of all, who the Spartans were. They were a tribe of warlike invaders that had conquered a large and fertile country. Some of the inhabitants, the *perioikoi* as they were afterwards called (the people who lived round about) were merely conquered; they had to submit to the political control of the Spartans, to help fight their battles, but they had modified home rule. They were subjects, but the rest of the conquered population, the helots, were slaves. Slaves and subjects together outnumbered the Spartans, perhaps eight or ten to one. Obviously, then, the first business of the state was to keep down the discontented servile population—the first business and pretty nearly the last. In seven or eight hundred years of independence Sparta managed to do nothing well but that. Which must be set down to the credit of Lycurgus.

This gentleman's true nature and doings have become somewhat veiled by legend. Doubtless much that was ascribed to him was the work of later ages, but it makes little difference; the men who completed his work had been trained in his spirit. Since this article aims at moral edification, it will do no violence to historic truth to use the word "Lycurgus" as the ancients used it, denoting not so much a personality (though Lycurgus was probably a real person) as a state of mind.

At any rate, it appears that this Lycurgus was a public-spirited citizen of a type all too common to-day. He saw that the machinery of state was not running to his satisfaction and decided that he was divinely appointed to set it right, at any cost and by any means. For some reason long forgotten, Sparta had two kings, of different families, equal in power. Lycurgus was a king's brother and afterward guardian of a posthumous nephew; he could have been king himself, and his refusal to accept the throne was much admired by the ancients. All credit to his abnegation; but surely it is no great discovery that it is less onerous to be the Power Behind the Throne, who gets the glory when things go well and escapes the blame when they go badly. Who would not rather be Wayne B. Wheeler than the Assistant Secretary of the Treasury in charge of prohibition enforcement?

Lycurgus tried to be the power behind the throne, but his nephew evidently made some trouble for him. So, with a heavy heart, Lycurgus proceeded to straighten things out and reorganize the state. He had considerable support from the Delphic oracle, the Supreme Court of the time; but in all candor it must be set down that he actually persuaded the citizens to accept his new constitution by the means so successfully employed by Lenin and Pilsudski. He got his gang, armed them, and seized the state by force. Behind the constitutional laws that he laid down—and they regulated the citizen's behavior with a completeness and stringency which the most radical of our reformers would hardly dare advocate now—he got the authority of the Delphic oracle; these were not human laws but divine, they came not from Lycurgus but from Apollo; to disobey them was not merely a crime, but sin and blasphemy. Still, the fact remains that the constitution was put over, not by religious sanction, still less by popular vote, but by illegal force. Lycurgus will be excused, however, by the best ethical thought of our time; for he used illegal force for a Worthy Purpose. To the business man that argument justifies Mussolini; to the radical it justifies Lenin; to the moralist it justifies Carrie Nation and the Ku Klux Klan. Let Lycurgus, too, be counted among those who to do a great right did a little wrong.[1] Both his objective and his method will be approved by the efficiency enthusiasts of our time; for, says Xenophon (who admired the Spartan system highly), "seeing that those who wanted to practice virtue were not numerous enough to make the state powerful, Lycurgus compelled everybody in Sparta to practice all the virtues."

In one respect it must be admitted that Lycurgus was not enlightened—he did not see in liquor the root of all evil. Like other ancient worthies, he found that in the love of money. What then was to be done? The answer was obvious—prohibit money. Lycurgus pro-

---

[1] I once intended to be a historian, and the historical conscience constrains me, at this point, to inject a few weasel words. Most of the foregoing comes from Plutarch's biography of Lycurgus. I have made no study of Plutarch's sources; the manly art of *Quellenforschung* requires more scholarship than I have managed to retain. But purely from the look of the thing I surmise, subject to correction by those who know, that some of the "authorities" whom Plutarch followed were third-century writers whose histories were designed primarily as propaganda for the reforms projected by Kings Agis and Cleomenes. Especially this story of Lycurgus's coup d'état reads like an attempt to justify Agis's unsuccessful effort to do the same thing.

However, mythological and tendencious elements in the story of Lycurgus do not affect the point of my argument. The principal features of the Spartan constitution are well established; and if Lycurgus did not institute them it was somebody like him.

hibited gold and silver as rigidly as the Volstead Act prohibits liquor. Sparta was an agricultural state, pretty much self-sufficient in that simple preindustrial day; yet even in Sparta there had to be some medium of exchange for local transactions. Lycurgus accordingly permitted a sort of one half of one per cent money— bars of pig iron, which no citizen could possibly possess in sufficient quantity to be intoxicating. Naturally, this prohibition kept down foreign trade, but your Spartan was an isolationist. "What have we to do with abroad?" was a sentiment of which he thoroughly approved.

Another thing which Lycurgus found destructive of that efficiency for which states and their citizens exist was home life; but, with a moderation which modern reformers have not always been wise enough to imitate, he did not attempt to prohibit home life altogether. Here he followed the method which the British have lately adopted in handling the liquor traffic—he limited home life to certain hours and rigidly enforced the closing laws. Male citizens belonged to dining clubs— not by the exercise of free will as male citizens do now, but under constitutional command; if a man did not belong to a dining club, or could not pay his dues, he lost his civic rights. Inasmuch as most of the adult male citizen's time when he was outside of the club was taken up in athletic exercises, military drill, or the service of the state, he had little enough leisure to spend with his wife and family; there was small danger of his becoming too much attached to the comforts of home.

The control of the state over the citizen began at birth, when the magistrates looked at the baby and decided whether or not he was strong enough to keep. If he survived he was taken from home at the age of seven, and for a dozen years he went through the famous Spartan discipline, intensive and arduous beyond any known in our time. The nearest modern approach to it is the intellectual discipline which boys of the better classes had to undergo in the German Empire; in Germany, as in Sparta, many of them cracked under the strain, but Lycurgus, like Bismarck, felt that those who survived it would be tough enough to make the failure of the weaklings a cheap price to pay for the welfare of the state. And in Sparta, even more than in Prussia, the citizen was the slave of the state; private life, private thought, were nonessential industries in a nation which was always on a war basis.

For the Spartan was a soldier—that and nothing else. He existed to keep down the discontented slaves and ward off foreign enemies; he spent all his life till he was sixty years old, either getting ready for military duty or fulfilling it. He did not work; his slaves worked for him. To make sure that they worked and spent no time meditating insurrection, a secret rural police watched the whole country; any slave who began to show signs of thinking well of himself was promptly put to death. And in order that no man should incur the blood guilt of murder by these executions, the magistrates, upon their inauguration, always began by declaring war on the helots. They were *feræ naturæ,* and the whole year was the open season; a helot had no more rights in Sparta than a conservative in Russia or a pedestrian in the United States.

The system was admirably effective; in seven centuries the helots often revolted but never revolted successfully. The *perioikoi,* on the other hand, never revolted. They escaped the savage severity with which the helots were treated—and they escaped, also, the heaven-sent regulations which made of the Spartan citizen the Perfected Prohibited Man. Those laws applied to the citizens only; Lycurgus had set out to make Sparta a state fit for heroes to live in and he succeeded, for only heroes could stand it. The *perioikoi,* in the state but not of it, had to serve in the army and pay taxes, but they could engage in business and make money; they had local self-government; they could in a measure live their own lives. Why should they revolt? The most amazing feature of Spartan history is that the citizens, the beneficiaries of these purifying laws, so rarely revolted. But they rarely had spirit enough, for the state caught them young.

The boy's education began at the age of seven, and from the age of seven he was taught to obey orders and refrain from unnecessary thought. He was also exposed to every sort of hardship. To make him resourceful he was compelled to steal much of his food; if he were caught stealing he was punished, "not," says Xenophon, "for stealing, but for stealing inefficiency." (Perhaps in this respect we are approaching the blessed perfection of Sparta; the warden of Sing Sing has lately observed that under our judicial system criminals are punished not for murder or robbery, but for killing or robbing carelessly.)

Any citizen who thought that any boy was not behaving as he should could whip him; if the boy told his father, father whipped him too. This was only a foreshadowing of the system of rewards for civic virtue and punishments for civic dereliction under which the Spartans lived all their lives. In a state organized like an army every man was constantly under the watchful eye of a superior. Every now and then prohibition directors urge all to spy on one another for infractions of the prohibition laws. Sparta did better than that. Every citizen was constantly spying on his neighbors, looking for infractions of all the laws; and in ascending hierarchy there were snoopers and super-snoopers till one came to the Inner Circle, the Old Gang, the oligarchy that ruled the state.

Not the kings. Lycurgus had pretty well clipped their claws. Theoretically, all power rested with the sovereign people (meaning the adult male citizens, a tiny fraction of the entire population). But the sovereign people could only answer yes or no to questions laid before it by the Senate, and Lycurgus had added the prudent qualification that if the people seemed to the Senate to have "decided crookedly" the whole transaction could be annulled.

Actually, the state was governed by the ephors—overseers—five men whose duties are indicated by their title. They oversaw everything, especially the kings, who were inclined to show restiveness under a constitution which left them "much honor but little power," as Fustel de Coulanges succinctly puts it. It was very much as if the United States had two Presidents overseen by five Wayne B. Wheelers. The ephors were elected, and Aristotle says that "almost anybody" might get the job. But, observes Fustel de Coulanges again (the most penetrating and illuminative of modern commentators on Sparta), a man who was almost anybody—that is, almost nobody—if he were elected to this important office for the short term of one year, would be inclined to think chiefly of two things: What he could get out of his office in that short term, and how he could be reëlected.

Reëlection usually depended on the favor of the ruling oligarchy, the Senate; so an ephor was apt to stay on the reservation. Failing anything else, if he happened to be a poor man he could be bought. (How could he be bought when there was no money? Ah, we are coming to that.)

So the real power lay in the Senate. Senators were elderly men selected—prepare yourselves for a shock, readers who know the Senators of this degenerate age —selected for their preëminence in virtue. This has seemed admirable to the political theorists of all ages; what could be nobler than to have the state ruled by the most virtuous citizens? But the virtue in question was civic virtue; and the Spartan concept of civic virtue, says Xenophon, was "$\tau\grave{\alpha}\ \nu\acute{o}\mu\iota\mu\alpha\ \delta\iota\alpha\pi\sigma\nu\varepsilon\tilde{\iota}\sigma\theta\alpha\iota$" —to work hard at obeying the laws. Hard work it certainly was, for law observance in Sparta meant what law observance in the United States is only beginning to approximate—meticulous obedience to an infinity of petty rules. A man who had a silver coin in a locker was as much of a lawbreaker in Sparta as a man who has a bottle of homemade beer in his kitchen cabinet in Indiana. If he spent too much time at home the Spartan was a lawbreaker; indeed, it must have been harder to go through a specimen day in Sparta without breaking some law than it is in the most advanced states of this union.

Moreover, every Spartan was constantly under observation; if he broke the law he was apt to be caught. The man who saw him might not mention the fact at the time; he might save it up till election day, when it immediately disqualified the lawbreaker. Indeed, the laws of Lycurgus, like some of our state prohibition laws, were so severe that almost everybody was a lawbreaker; and the penalties, accordingly, were enforced only on persons who were on bad terms with the organization.

It might have been supposed that any man who lived sixty years in Sparta without breaking a law deserved a Senatorship; but the evidence indicates that a man suited to the inner organization got into the Senate no matter what he might have done—so long as he had not been publicly exposed; just as in our time a man may drink wet without moral turpitude so long as he votes dry. In fact the whole Spartan system might have been condensed into the first and great commandment, "Thou shalt not get caught"—a simplification of constitutional law which we have only approximated as yet. So this civic virtue which qualified a man for the Senatorship consisted essentially in staying regular and escaping exposure.

But I am getting away from theory to practice, always a dangerous thing in constitutional studies. Let us return to the theory, which, as any reformer will tell you, is much more important. Theoretically, Sparta was the Perfect State. A man spent his whole life at the great task of Law Observance. Moreover, the constitution not only commanded the citizens to be virtuous; it commanded them to be prosperous, under pain of ceasing to be citizens. The right to vote and hold office was restricted to those of pure citizen ancestry who had survived the terrific educational system—and who had money enough to pay their club dues. Originally the land seems to have been fairly evenly divided, and under a sort of entail; it could not be sold, given away, or willed out of the family. In theory, everybody had enough to live on (the helots, of course, doing the work). If a man were a poor manager, unable to make both ends meet, the state had no use for him. He had failed in the citizen's first duty, Efficiency; he sank into the class of *hypomeiones*— the lesser men beneath; he could carry a spear in the wars, he continued to enjoy the sublime privilege of obeying the laws, but he was a citizen no longer.

Lycurgus was not so foolish as to suppose that he had eradicated all lawless tendencies overnight, so he devised a simple method of detecting potential lawbreakers. The ephors, on coming into office each year, issued a general order to the citizens to "shave their upper lips and obey the laws." Failure to shave the upper lip might seem a trivial oversight; but Lycurgus knew that disrespect for one law means disrespect for all laws, that a citizen who refused to shave his upper lip was capable of murder and arson. The upper lip thus became a criterion of law observance; a man who grew a mustache was marked as a scofflaw and the authorities could take action accordingly.

Such was the Spartan system—at home and in peace time. But on military service, contrary to the custom of other countries, discipline was greatly relaxed. Accordingly, though the policy of the Spartan government was usually cautious and pacific, the citizens were inclined to give three cheers when war broke out; they went to the front in high spirits. They might be killed, but at least they would enjoy a brief vacation from Law Observance.

IN one respect Lycurgus seems to have fallen short of the rigorous virtue of our time; he was weak enough to allow a safety valve for the repressed emotions of the citizens, and that in a field where modern theory would most inflexibly refuse it—in the relations of the sexes. But this appears to have been largely accidental.

To the average Greek his wife was something better than his dog, a little dearer than his horse. Athens was worse than the other states in this respect; Athenian women lived a sort of harem life, restricted to the bearing of children and the management of the household; any good Athenian would have regarded a barbarian slave as his intellectual equal sooner than his wife. Naturally, women so treated were apt to be feeble, timid, and stupid; what the system made them almost seemed to justify the system. Even in Athens there were rumblings of feminist discontent; they are hinted at in the plays of Euripides and have lately been brilliantly if conjecturally restored in Mrs. Mitchison's excellent historical novel *Cloud Cuckoo Land*. But to the average Greek, women simply were not people.

In Sparta they were. To begin with, Spartan women, for purely eugenic reasons, underwent a vigorous athletic training; like Spartan boys—indeed, the boys

of any Greek state—the girls exercised and played
games, danced and paraded in public, stark naked.
Exercise made them strong, eurhythmics made them
beautiful, pitiless publicity gave them self-possession.
Willful bachelors and men who had funked their civic
responsibilities were not allowed to look on at these
undraped processions—a notable improvement over
the standards of our time, for probably these classes
would include most of the occupants of the front rows
at Earl Carroll's revues. Sparta, then, bred "fierce,
athletic girls" a good deal more attractive than the
shrinking inhabitants of the women's quarters in
Athens; they were as strong and agile as the men;
they may have been rather stupid, but there, too, they
were the men's equals. Sex equality was perfect in
Sparta except that women could not vote; but women
were as good as men only because neither men nor women had ultimately any rights at all. Male or female,
the Spartan citizen was the slave of the state.

A depressed commentator on our time has lately remarked that we are approaching the Spartans in our
"deliciously naked bi-sexual athleticism" and that this
is making us as unromantic as the Spartans. The gentleman is in error. Athletics in deshabille did not make
the Spartans unromantic; almost all the real love stories
in classic Greek history come from Sparta. These Spartan girls were desirable and they were desired; and
neither the law nor public opinion interfered—unless
any given amour seemed to run counter to the interest
of the state. Then it was stopped in short order. But
there seems to have been a good deal of friendly
promiscuity; a man might lend his wife to a friend,

with the lady's consent; and where the lady consented but not the husband, public sentiment seems always to have been with the lovers.[2]

The law also ordered the young husband to live at his club for the first year or so after marriage, visiting his wife only by such stealth as he would have had to employ in visiting some other man's wife. Apparently this too was ordained for eugenic reasons, but naturally it worked as an admirable preservative of emotional intensity. The Athenian had a choice between his dull wife and the polished but mercenary hetaira, who might be an Aspasia but was more apt to be a Lorelei Lee. The Spartan got his emotional interest from women of his own class, strong and beautiful, and at least as intelligent as he was.

But this was the one bright spot in Sparta; and, as George Moore or one of his parodists says (the distinction is not always easy to remember), "there are times when one is not thinking of girls, are there not?" Lycurgus foresaw that; he foresaw that life in Sparta would sometimes bore the Spartans, difficult as this may appear to have been. All the more would it bore them if they had a chance to contrast it with anything else. It occurred to him that a Spartan who spent any length of time abroad was not likely to come back to Sparta.

Here our time has failed lamentably to live up to Spartan standards. It is several years since we have heard anything of the dream, once cherished by the Anti-Saloon League, of keeping American citizens out

---

[2] *E.g.*, the affair between Akrotatos and Chilonis, reported in detail in Plutarch's life of Pyrrhus. The historians have preserved other instances.

of Cuba and Canada. Lycurgus was more successful; on the ground that the citizens of pure Sparta must not "acquaint themselves with the habits of ill-educated people," he virtually prohibited all foreign travel except on military service or business of the state. But there were ill-educated people even in Sparta, foreigners who lived there on business, or because political warfare had exiled them from their home towns. For fear their behavior should set an evil example of frivolity before the purified and single-minded Spartan, Lycurgus drove them out—all but one or two foreign poets who were allowed to remain on condition that they write "hymns to obedience and concord"—that is, administration propaganda.

And this practice was followed from time to time forever after. The Spartan standard of morality was admitted (by the Spartans) to be perfect; but it was feared that the citizens might not stick to it if they had a chance to hear of anything else. So every few years the ephors would hold a "foreigner drive" and purge the state.[3] We deport aliens who violate our laws

[3] As the Spartans were men of deeds, not words, the most detailed statement of the philosophy underlying these periodic ξενηλασίαι is found in no recorded pronouncement of a Lacedæmonian ephor; but, curiously enough, in the address delivered on June 22, 1927, to the Pennsylvania Bar Association, by the Honorable John Garibaldi Sargent, Attorney General of the United States. "The Attorney General went on to say," runs a news dispatch, "that many persons have come to this country from places 'having social and political systems and theories very different from ours, and so understanding us and our theories and foundations of Government but little or not at all.

" 'And we have those who would profit—would live by—preying upon these weaknesses, this ignorance, and who seek to strengthen their position, to forfend against attack by instilling into the minds of those they would victimize the idea that the law is an instru-

(or some of our laws). In Sparta only the citizens were adjudged worthy of submission to the divinely inspired constitution of Lycurgus; but every now and then all foreigners were deported for having had the bad taste to be born foreigners. In early years naturalization seems to have been easy; Sparta needed to fill up gaps in the citizen body caused by war losses. But presently, as the divine system swung into operation, naturalization ceased. No man not born a Spartan was worthy to become a Spartan. Indeed, as time passed fewer and fewer Spartans were judged worthy. Inequalities of property reduced more and more citizens, unable to pay club dues, to the rank of "the lesser men beneath"; others were degraded for breaking under the strain of the educational system or infringing on one or another of the laws of Lycurgus. Once the citizen body—that is, the adult males who had worked hard, and successfully, at obeying the laws—may have numbered anywhere from five to ten thousand. After seven centuries under the constitution of Lycurgus there were only seven hundred, out of a total population, citizen, demicitizen, subject, and slave of perhaps half a million— seven hundred simon-pure stalwarts who in a state of spies and sneaks and snoopers had managed, by virtue,

---

ment of oppression, designed and used to deprive the people of pleasures and comforts which are rightfully theirs. . . .

" 'Day by day, because someone pays for the doing of it and because the great body of law-abiding citizens is complaisant and says nothing to show its approval, flippant, jeering writers, publishers, soap-box orators and cabaret performers sow the wind and society reaps it all in whirlwinds which blast and destroy.' "

The Honorable Attorney General's English is not quite so lucid as the average Spartan's Laconian, but his idea manages to muddle through.

influence, or luck, to survive the laborious and hazardous occupation of being a Spartan.

How did it work? Well, it certainly promoted efficiency —of a kind.

Sparta lived for the art of war and nothing else. There was next to no Spartan art in historic times. Back in the dawn of history, before Lycurgus, there had been the beginnings of a native school of poetry; after Lycurgus poetry was suppressed like all other non-essentials. When the government needed a poet for propaganda purposes it hired one from abroad, who could be counted on to understand the terms of his employment and write what he was paid to write and nothing more. Other arts, too, had been making their beginning; Sparta, before Lycurgus, seems to have been human. After Lycurgus it grew human beings occasionally, despite the system, but they were usually driven into exile or died early and violent deaths at home. The Spartan was a standardized type; if any individual differed from the orthodox pattern out he went—out or down.

Sparta, in short, was the business man's dream of a state where nothing was allowed to interfere with business. Its business was war, and there it was notably successful. For three hundred years no Spartan army lost a major engagement, unless you count the stand of Leonidas and his single battalion at Thermopylæ. The system devised by, or ascribed to, Lycurgus was among the most tenacious and durable that Europe has ever seen. Other Greek states had continual and ruinous revolutions; in Sparta uprisings were few, and till the very end, when Rome was already overshadowing the horizon, they were never successful. Pericles himself confessed that other Greeks, at war with the Spartans, were only amateurs against professionals; citizen armies composed of short-term-service men had little chance against the Spartans who were making war or playing war all the time.

And this success naturally gave Sparta an enormous reputation—the sort of reputation that the United States enjoys in Europe to-day. In our time economic strength has replaced military strength as the criterion of national power; we have not been quite so single-minded as the Spartans but we have had a good deal of luck and have done well the one thing we chiefly set out to do. Accordingly, people admire us and envy us as the other Greeks admired and envied the Spartans; and even as the Spartans admired themselves, so do we.

But they are still our models; as yet we merely approach them. Bad manners and peevishness are not yet so common in American diplomacy (though visibly increasing of late years) as they were in Sparta, but we are learning. Envoys from another Greek state came to Sparta for food in a season of famine; they brought bags and, trying to emulate the famous Laconian brusqueness, they merely observed, "The bag wants bread." The Spartans told them they were too verbose; the sight of the bag would have permitted the rest to be inferred. It sounds rather like our dealings with a debt-funding commission; but nobody dared talk back to the Spartans, as nobody dares to talk back to us. Eventually the envoys got their bread, as foreign debt-funding commissions usually get their debts scaled down;

but the Spartans, like ourselves, managed to do it as ungenerously and ungraciously as possible.

But why should not the Spartans have admired themselves? Everybody had to admire them—in public; and they had to admire themselves, in public, to silence a growing private uneasiness, a feeling that all was not well. For the Perfected Prohibitions of Lycurgus had made a happy state of unhappy citizens; and so, wrote Xenophon at the height of Spartan prestige and power, "all the other Greeks admire the system, but none of them would like to adopt it."

So Europeans of to-day admire our prosperity, but few of them would like to live here.

The system worked well—too well; its own success brought about its ruin. For it depended on keeping foreigners out and keeping the Spartans at home; and after Sparta had won the Peloponnesian War and had acquired an empire both became impossible. Spartans abroad had long been notorious for their bad manners and rapacity; fortified by the self-esteem that sprang from the consciousness that they were the Chosen People, living under divine laws, they regarded themselves as above criticism (especially as they had the Spartan army behind them); but after they won the war they became insufferable.

And how they went abroad! "All the chief men," says Xenophon, "are eager to spend their entire lives as governors of the overseas possessions." Why? Because abroad they were freed from the necessity of Law Observance; and when they had put the laws of Lycurgus behind them they usually threw overboard the laws of ordinary human decency as well. Naturally enough; ordinary human decency had been ignored at Sparta because observance of the statute law comprised the whole duty of man. A Spartan governor overseas could have given points in misbehavior to the wildest American tourist in Paris.

But only the wider opportunity for misconduct was new; Spartans abroad had always been easy victims for the puniest of temptations. For the cardinal point of their system was money prohibition. At home the Spartan knew only pig-iron money, non-intoxicating in fact; when he went abroad he was willing to take anything offered him. Bribery was common enough among all the Greeks, but what distinguished the Spartans was their cheapness; a Spartan general could be completely intoxicated by an amount of gold or silver that would have no effect at all on an Athenian who had been used to taking gold and silver in moderation all his life, who could take it or leave it alone.

Show a Spartan a few drachmas and his mouth began to water. History is full of instances. King Leotychidas, commanding an expeditionary force in Thessaly—a king, commanding the most powerful army of the time—was actually bought off by a gloveful of gold, a few hundred dollars' worth. It is as if Ludendorff had agreed to give up his offensive of 1918 for a suitcase full of francs. King Cleomenes, one of Sparta's greatest generals, failed to take Argos, the ancestral enemy; he laid the blame on Apollo, who had given him a misleading oracle, but that was an old story—Apollo was blamed for a good deal in those days which was the result of mere human frailty. It seems that he had sound political reasons for spar-

ing Argos, but back home everybody believed he had
been bribed; evidently that was always the most obvious explanation. King Pleistoanax, marching on
defenseless Athens, was bought off by Pericles. He at
least got a fairly decent price, but Sparta later had a
twenty-seven years' war as a result of this display of
easy virtue.

This was not the only result of the bone-dry prohibition of money. Prince Cyrus of Persia put up the
funds which financed the latter part of the Peloponnesian War for Sparta and her allies. When the war
had been won there was a good deal of money left over,
and Lysander, the Spartan commander-in-chief, sent
it home to the government—public money belonging
to the state. It was in charge of Gylippus, a man who
had won the decisive battle of the war, who held much
the same position in the Greek world of the day as
Marshal Joffre in modern Europe. But Gylippus, when
he got his hands on those bags of money, felt and behaved like a dry agent in charge of a carload of
confiscated liquor. He unsewed every one of the sacks,
took out some of the money, and sewed the sacks up
again. . . . Unfortunately Lysander had sent an in-
voice along with the money, so Gylippus was discovered and fell from his high estate. Some people
blamed him, some blamed Lysander for trusting him;
but nobody blamed Lycurgus for writing prohibition
of money into the constitution.

This money caused another crisis in Sparta; for it
was the first money that had legally been imported in
four or five hundred years. Not that gold and silver
were unknown in Sparta, despite the constitution; there

had long been a lively bootleg trade. Foreigners from just over the border were persuaded to lend their names as dummy owners of gold and silver which somehow or other happened to be possessed and consumed on the premises by Spartans. But this was the first time that money had come in openly and in full view. A fraction of bone-dry zealots wanted to pour the vile stuff into the sea; but the rulers of Sparta were politicians and they had learned the great political lesson that so long as you respect the constitution in theory, it matters not how you behave in practice.

So they decided that money could be possessed for a public purpose, though not for private use; and before long Sparta was simply dripping with gold and silver which was all possessed for a public purpose, at least when anybody asked about it. Land could not be sold, according to the constitution; but some ingenious person tacked on an amendment to the effect that it could be given away. Before long inequalities of wealth were as great in Sparta as anywhere in Greece; the Spartans became known as the greediest and most money-loving people of their time. And this when money had been absolutely prohibited in Sparta for six hundred years, and was absolutely prohibited still.

The laws of Lycurgus were never repealed till a conquering invader ordered it when Rome was already at the door; but in the last century or two of Spartan independence the divinely inspired constitution was regarded much as Samuel Butler says the Christian religion was regarded in Victorian England: people would have been equally horrified at hearing it criticized and at seeing it practiced. Eventually there arose in the state a reformer (a king, like most Spartan reformers) who proposed that the heaven-descended laws of Lycurgus which were still theoretically in force should be enforced in practice. And the citizens, says Plutarch, "were as alarmed at the name of Lycurgus as a fugitive slave about to be returned to his master."

This rash young optimist who tried to make prohibition prohibit was promptly snuffed out. Emulating Lycurgus, he too got an oracle from Delphi; but he was up against politicians of the old organization who knew too much about oracles to take them seriously. Failing in that, he copied Lycurgus once more, got his gang, and set out to take charge of things by force; but the Spartans had been clubbed into virtue once and did not propose to let it happen again. The protagonist of strict enforcement was done away with, like everybody else who had tried to shatter the Spartan system.

But even then the constitution was not repealed. Too many vested interests had grown up under its assorted prohibitions; most of the rich men, and all of the politicians, were satisfied with things as they were. There came another reformer king who succeeded for a little while; but he was beaten in battle and with a sigh of relief Sparta went back to the old ways.

Strict enforcement had been tried—tried for centuries—and it would not work. Like Russian Communism, it could not have succeeded unless all the world had been converted to it (and quite possibly not then). So long as there survived lesser breeds without the law of Lycurgus, the Spartan's uprightness lasted only till he got across the frontier.

Sparta had done as much as any state can, more than

any other state ever tried, to change human nature. It had accomplished much. It had bred a nation in which envy and jealousy, lying and deceit were all but universal, a nation of spies and snoopers in which everybody was watching everybody. It had produced a standardized type of citizen which had no equal in Greece for dullness of mind in everything but strategy and statecraft; an unimaginative type which would have endured the laws of Lycurgus if any human being could. It had abolished the refinements and the graces; even when Spartans did a courteous act, as in the famous instance of the ambassadors to Athens rising to give their theater seat to an old man, they managed to do it ungraciously.

But apparently there are limits beyond which no education can change human nature. Sparta had not made men so unnatural as to withstand temptation abroad when they had never been exposed to temptation at home. It had not enabled them to improvise character to meet sudden exigencies; for the law had gone into infinite detail with the precise object of making character superfluous. Lycurgus had swept away previous laws, but he had not been able to repeal the law of nature that virtue and temperance and self-control are acquired only by practice, that you cannot say a man is good until he has had, and rejected, the option of being evil. So long as there was a temptation anywhere within reach, the average Spartan was sure to fall.

BUT even in the last days of decadence nobody dreamed of repealing the constitution of Lycurgus. It was a national distinction—almost the only national distinction now that Spartan armies composed of freed slaves and grumbling bankrupts had developed the habit of losing battles. Sparta's glory had faded but all the citizens still enjoyed the sense of virtue, the reputation for virtue that belonged to all who lived under the divine statutes of Lycurgus.

Spartan virtue was already proverbial; and as Rome drew nearer and nearer, thoughtful Spartans—if the educational system had left any Spartans capable of thought—must have realized that this was about all that Sparta would leave behind her when she passed into history. The Lycurgan efficiency had been entirely too efficient; whatever Sparta might have been, under his prohibition laws Sparta had actually turned out to be a state which kept down the slaves and nothing more. (A brief experiment in empire, yes; but that ended in disaster.) Politically Greece was dying; Athens, Sparta's great rival, was already as good as dead, as a political entity. But, visibly, there was something in Athens that would never die.

And Sparta? Sparta had no Parthenon; Sparta had produced no Æschylus, no Aristophanes, no Socrates; even the history of her own great age would be passed on by Athenian hands. Sparta would be remembered only as the paradise of prohibition—the state where constitutional amendments had compelled everybody to practice all the virtues. To that reputation, and the constitution to which they owed it, the Spartans clung tenaciously. It was all Lycurgus had left them; it was their one ewe lamb, and they cherished it the more tenderly because there was no need to practice the virtue so long as they had the reputation.

We are a long way yet from Spartan virtue; and it seems rather less likely than it seemed half a dozen years ago that we shall ever reach it. But there is no harm in seeing just exactly what lies at the end of the road; though it is perhaps too much to hope that citizens of this great and prosperous republic, moving on, divinely guided, toward sterilized efficiency, will be very passionately excited about the lessons of history.

HAVE FAITH IN INDIANA

MY unworthy feet have lately [1] trodden the sacred soil of the Hoosier state, where I was born and might be living yet if I had found anybody within its confines who would give me a job when I got out of college. Since the adventurous person who ultimately did give me a job lived in New York, I became a New Yorker. Years passed—quite a number of years when laid end to end as one usually finds them—and I became completely denationalized as a Hoosier; now I can eat spaghetti with one hand, but not fried chicken. Often my business took me across Indiana to Chicago, but I never went back home.

And of late years I became afraid to go back to Indiana. Strange tales came from what had once been the Earthly Paradise. (If you doubt the accuracy of that epithet, see any Indiana novel for confirmation.) The Happy Valley had been turned into a hotbed of hatred and suspicion. The moon was still fair along the Wabash, but almost everything else, according to returning voyagers, was unfair. Where once the Shawnee and Pottawattomie had terrorized the countryside, men and women now stood in dread of the Kleagle and the Kligrapp. Candle lights still gleamed through the

[1] This was written in June 1926, in a pious effort to defend the old Fatherland against unjust aspersions. The Hoosiers, however, are a peculiar people, and some of them did not like it, though it tells no more than every Prosecuting Attorney knows, and considerably less than has since been spread on the records of various courts and investigating committees.

sycamores, but their pallid flame was dimmed by the glare of the fiery cross.

Laws of fantastic ferocity had been imposed on the blameless Hoosier, whose native mildness hardly seemed to require such stringent repression; and the natural reaction had fomented wild and shameless orgies. Conservatives and intellectuals escaped from the state with the same kind of relief as other conservatives and intellectuals felt when they fled across the frontier of Soviet Russia. Worst of all, said scouts who had observed the decline and fall of Indiana, the Hoosiers had become afraid to talk. They no longer even talked politics. If this were true, then indeed the glory was departed.

Nevertheless I nerved myself last summer for a return to familiar scenes, a *recherche du temps perdu,* much in the mood of Regulus going back to Carthage. A visit to Indiana, if one could believe rumors, was an adventure fraught with bizarre perils. ("Don't drink anything in Indianapolis," a Hoosier refugee urged me as I left New York; "they have to put Coca-Cola in it to kill the taste.") But the perils, after all, could be evaded with circumspection; what could not be evaded was the arid disappointment in the return to what had once been a Garden Spot and was now little more than a Devastated District, the discovery that the old Hoosier salt had all been washed away by Coca-Cola and other beverages dear to the Anti-Saloon League, that the Hoosier gets his politics from the Dragon or the Titan instead of rolling his own.

All a mistake, friends. The decease of Indiana has been greatly exaggerated. I do not challenge the accuracy of various reporters who have brought these horrendous tales back to New York. At certain times and in certain places, no doubt all they said was true; in certain places much of it is true still. Indiana has changed in sixteen years and in some ways changed for the worse; but, so far as I could gather, it has lately changed for the better, and there is hope that the patient's improvement may be steady from now on. The organism was attacked by a violent disease, but it seems to be setting up a resistance, a reaction, that may ultimately give it immunity.

And the Hoosier essence is still there. Indiana has always been a more salient and individual commonwealth than most of its Middle-Western neighbors; it possesses what the eastern Europeans would call cultural autonomy. And that native culture seems to be, in the main, still intact. If the Hoosiers talk politics less than they used to (and I heard plenty of politics talked), it may be not so much that they are afraid of listening Klansmen as that the savage stringency of their state prohibition law has inevitably made liquor a topic of absorbing interest. "We think too much about liquor out here," an eminent Hoosier confessed to me, "and talk too much about it. It isn't that important. But when the state legislature declares that liquor or the prohibition of liquor is more than the Constitution and the ethics of a gentleman and everything else, everybody's sense of values is twisted a little out of focus."

Yet I think I heard as much talk about automobiles as about liquor, and with good reason. Walking is a lost art in Indiana; whoever has to go farther than across the road takes an automobile; if there is any Hoosier so debased that he does not own an automobile (which I doubt) he is less than the dust beneath his neighbors' chariot wheels. The foreigner, rashly proposing to walk two blocks down the street, is regarded as a dangerous person of Bolshevist tendencies, attempting to corrupt Middle-Western purity by introduction of the un-American customs of the Atlantic seaboard. The colleges of the state might well add a new event to their track meets—the hundred-yard walk, if they could find anybody hardy enough to endure the strain.

If Darwin and his allied and associated evolutionists are right (this is one of the few topics on which the Indiana legislature has not yet laid down the law), legs in Indiana will presently become vestigial, and ultimately will drop off altogether. Some few ladies may retain them for purposes of ornament—not too many, it may be hoped—but for the rest of the population legs have already been replaced by the automobile. The Hoosier of to-day talks about engine trouble and tire mileage as much as his grandfather talked about his rheumatism, and for the same reason.

So I am not much impressed by this alleged decline of political conversation. Changes there have been; but the two great cottage industries that made the state famous—literature and politics—flourish as luxuriantly as ever. While these twin pillars stand the Hoosier temple is secure.

OUTWARDLY the Indiana of to-day looks about the same as the Indiana of 1910, except a little more weather-beaten; about the only additions to the architecture of the state are a couple of hundred thousand filling stations. This gives a curious sense of timelessness to the New Yorker who is used to seeing his home town pulled down and rebuilt before his eyes every few weeks; none the less, there is something to be said for the Hoosier theory of using a serviceable house till it wears out rather than squandering all your savings on building another just a little better.

But I am told that Hoosiers do not build houses because they spend all their money for automobiles; they wear out old clothes because the money that once bought clothes now buys gasoline. It does seem that houses which have been on the premises for several decades might at least be painted once in a while; and I understand that a couple of years ago there was a general movement toward renovation. But just about that time the Florida boom came along, and the money which had been saved up to paint the house went to Florida and has not been seen since.

Carl Fisher of Indianapolis made countless millions in Florida; so did a few other Hoosiers who got in on the ground floor. But the rest of Indiana, the general sucker investor, got just about what the general sucker investor usually gets. It was a hard blow because it came at a time when the state, in common with the whole corn belt, was hard up. Many a farmer had counted on paying off the mortgage with his profit on the resale of those water-front lots in Florida; and now, as the diplomats say, he is compelled to envisage a new situation.

Relatively, if not absolutely, Indiana is less pros-

perous to-day than it was in 1910, which may have
something to do with the changes of temperament, of
interest, of emphasis which have undoubtedly occurred.
But in the main, of course, these alterations are trace-
able, directly or in reflex, to the Ku Klux Klan.

One finds it hard to imagine why the Klan has such
a hold on Indiana. What has the nervous Protestant to
be afraid of in a state which has hardly ten per cent.
of Catholics and one per cent. of Jews? Well, he finds
a good deal to be afraid of. One hears strange tales
among Hoosiers—for instance, that the lease on the
Vatican has expired, and the Pope, unable to pay the
increased rent demanded by his landlord, is now living
in disguise in Cincinnati, ready to cross the frontier
the first dark night, seize Indiana by a *coup d'état,* and
turn it into a papal satrapy. (His Holiness will find a
lot of friends in Dearborn County, the border march
adjacent to Cincinnati, which is undoubtedly a weak
point in the Hoosier *cordon sanitaire.*) Just why, out of
all the Protestant communities on this planet, the Pope
should select Indiana as the object of his wicked desires, is not apparent to the foreigner; but to the
Hoosier it is clear enough. Indiana is the most desirable
spot on earth, and any potentate might reasonably
covet it. (The *locus classicus* on this point in Hoosier
literature is Mr. Tarkington's *The Man From Home.*)
At any rate this theory seems to be widely held in the
rural districts, and the Protestants are all on guard.

The intelligent people of Indiana (and despite emi-
gration, forced and otherwise, the state is still probably well above the average in percentage of intelligent people) find it hard to understand how these

abysmal depths of ignorance and bigotry can exist in
a state which has long been noted for the excellence
of its schools, which has probably produced more
normal-school principals and professors of pedagogy
than any other commonwealth in the country.[2] But a
report on the state schools, published a few years ago,
after investigation by a local committee which could
not be suspected of alien bias, throws some light on this
topic. Indiana got its pedagogic reputation by an early
start. About 1870 its schools were the best in the world,
by the standards of 1870. They still are—by the standards of 1870; but states which give more attention to
scholarship and less to basket ball show up a little
better by the standards of 1926. (It may or may not
have been a coincidence, but the principal signer of
this report moved to Chicago shortly after its publication.)

Possibly this willingness to stand on a reputation
won long ago accounts for the spread of the Klan.
It is well known that the Klan began to take hold of
Indiana about the time it began to lose ground in
the South. Perhaps it spread because it gave to persons of no importance a sense of consequence and an
illusion of something to do. In Indiana it certainly
owed much to the organizing ability of a Grand

---

[2] It was the Hoosier schoolmaster, not the Hoosier novelist (nor
even James Whitcomb Riley) who really made the state's reputation as the modern Eden. The surplus population which the state
could not support, in the generation following the Civil War, emi-
grated to teach school, *in partibus infidelium;* teaching, among
other things, that there was no place like Indiana. Now the population is controlled and almost stationary; such emigrants as there
are go to Detroit to make cars, or to Chicago to become railroad
presidents.

Dragon who, one was told at the time, had "sold" the Klan in Indiana on the basis of love rather than hatred. That the gentleman's concept of love was somewhat violent is suggested by the fact that he was presently tried for rape and murder and is now serving a twenty-year sentence in the penitentiary; yet the argument has this much support, that the Klan in Indiana has generally refrained from the local acts of violence common in other states where it flourished. In Indiana the Klan has done its work in politics; which proves that the Hoosier Klansmen, after all, are essentially Hoosiers, expressing themselves in politics as all Hoosiers will.

The 1924 election gave the Klan control of the state. First of all the Klan, with the Anti-Saloon League, got control of the Republican party. The Republican state ticket ran far behind Coolidge that year, but Coolidge pulled it through. Possibly he does not deserve all the credit; the Republican candidate for Governor, Major Ed Jackson, and the Democratic candidate, Colonel Carleton McCulloch, were both Nordic Protestants; but McCulloch had not made Nordic Protestantism a gainful occupation and he suffered the added handicap of being an intellectual. At any rate, the Klan and the Anti-Saloon League got control of the state and proceeded to cash in on it.

The state prohibition law which they passed—the "smell law"—is a marvelous document. One hears of legislators who staggered from a whiskey-laden table to vote for the law, and back to the whiskey-laden table; but Indiana is not the only state which lives by the great principle that it matters not how a legislator drinks so long as he votes right. Certainly, the statute which they put on the books is the culmination, in one way or another, of the process that started with Magna Carta; the Nordic genius for self-government never produced anything more remarkable.

To sell, possess, or give away liquor calls for a mandatory jail sentence of thirty days to six months (for a first offense); so does the display of a cocktail shaker in a drug-store window. One who is merely intoxicated in public may escape with a fine; one who drives an automobile while intoxicated—an offense which accounts for a good many traffic killings a year, in Indiana and elsewhere—goes to jail for from thirty days to six months. But one who transports even a spoonful of liquor in an automobile—unless he transports it in his own digestive system—is guilty of a felony and goes to jail for from one to two years; possession of a distilling apparatus is *prima facie* evidence of intention of unlawful use, and the possessor is a felon who spends from one to five years in a penitentiary.

If any fluid is poured out or carried away while the premises are being searched, it shall be held to be *prima facie* intoxicating liquor intended for unlawful use or sale. Proof of the possession of empty bottles that have contained intoxicating liquor shall be admissible as evidence—and the smell of the bottle is often sufficient. Also, if a bottle is found on your premises, though a passer-by may have thrown it over the fence, it is your bottle unless you can prove the contrary.

It only remains to add that this amiable enactment provides that "any citizen, organization, or association

within this state" (which of course means the Klan
and the Anti-Saloon League) may employ an attorney
to assist the prosecutor; and that charges shall not be
dismissed unless the reason for so doing is laid before
this attorney for his inspection.

Surely this ought to enact virtue; if the citizens can
be made righteous by the power of the secular arm,
Indiana ought to be the Spotless Commonwealth. And
what is the result? Why, one result I have already
mentioned—that a young woman lately back from
Indianapolis told me that they had to use Coca-Cola
to kill the taste; and another refugee from Indianapolis
told me that they got drunk and rolled on the floor,
lost to all sense of moderation.

But I gather that both the virtue and the iniquity of
Indiana have been greatly exaggerated. (That is the
penalty of spending as many years as I spent in the
newspaper business; one discovers that everything has
been greatly exaggerated.)

I did not see, in Indiana, anybody drunk and rolling
on the floor; nor did I encounter anything the taste of
which needed to be killed by Coca-Cola. I understand
that among the lower classes, unable to pay the prices
which the better element puts up for whisky brought in
via Detroit, a favorite drink is Jamaica ginger diluted
by Coca-Cola; and the prosecuting authorities have had
much difficulty in breaking up this traffic because the
state law merely forbids intoxicating liquor "and every
other drink, mixture, or preparation of more than one
half of one per cent. of alcohol content reasonably likely
or intended to be used as a beverage." It had never

occurred to anybody that Jamaica ginger was reasonably likely to be used as a beverage.

Those whose delicacy is affronted by Jamaica ginger are said to sate their unlawful desires by dropping a tablet of aspirin into a bottle of Coca-Cola. The effect is alleged to be powerful while it lasts; it wears off in half an hour or so, but then you procure another tablet of aspirin and another bottle of Coca-Cola. Maybe so; I am a middle-aged family man with no appetite for adventure; I didn't try it. Nor does it seem that anybody with friends in Indiana would need to try it; the prohibition law is said to be effective in the country districts, where there was never much drinking anyway; but, so far as I could gather, the percentage of humidity is as high in Indianapolis as anywhere in the country, except for New York and the East Coast of Florida.

Then is this majestic statute, this super-prohibition law, ineffective? Not a bit; but one gathers that it operates only against certain people. If somebody who stands well with the authorities is arrested, the case may be shifted to a lenient court; and if he stands well enough with the authorities he is not even arrested. One hears of delegates to a Republican convention drinking their fill in rooms protected by policemen, just as it is said to be done on the wicked Atlantic seaboard. But then the Republicans are the Klan party, the Anti-Saloon League party, the party of law enforcement, and naturally their delegates are privileged.

Some people undoubtedly have had bad luck. They tell a tale in Indianapolis of a burglar who broke into a house and was discovered by the householder. Dodging about the cellar with the police closing in on him outside, he had the good luck to find a couple of bottles of homemade wine, of the kind which is perfectly legitimate under the Volstead Act but obnoxious to the higher morality of Indiana. Clutching a bottle in each hand, the burglar walked gleefully out into the arms of the police; and the householder was forthwith arrested and sent to jail, while the burglar so far as the story tells, was set free as a watchful and law-abiding citizen.

No Hoosier who has a treasured bottle anywhere around the house dares to fire his cook, or get into a dispute with the plumber. Plumbers, and carpenters, and readers of gas and electric meters, are said to look for liquor with great diligence when they enter a house; if they can reach it they take some of it; if not they reserve their information in case there is any argument about the bill. In so far as the moral leaders of the United States are laboring to make this a country of spies, of sneaks, of snoopers, and informers (which is pretty far) Indiana undoubtedly has a good running start. When an automobile driver in the rural districts of the state is arrested for speeding, his car is usually searched for liquor. The Supreme Court has held that this search is illegal, but in many counties it goes on just the same. There is a difference of opinion at present, among sheriffs and prosecutors, as to whether it is illegal to stop your car by the roadside, with all the lights on. A good many sheriffs hold that such conduct is *prima facie* evidence of immoral purposes; and when they seize a car thus stationary they

are apt to search it, in the hope that a half-empty
flask may let the occupants in for a year in the penitentiary.

All of this sounds as if Indiana were a dreadful
place to live; but as usual, things are not so bad as
they sound. Any Hoosier who has no influential friends
may find himself in trouble at any moment; but not
so many do. As with all laws whose ferocity far out-
runs public sentiment, the violence of this one is considerably mitigated in practice. Sensible prosecutors
try to discriminate between men who sell liquor and
those who possess it for their own use, between travel-
ing bootleggers merchandising from their automobiles
and tourists who happen to have brought a bottle up
from Florida in a suitcase. Judges, too, are apt to
make some effort to fit the penalty to the crime; jail
sentences are mandatory but they can be suspended,
and often are; and where judges and prosecutors fail,
juries often—though not always—do the same.

It would be pleasing to report that this is the work
of the old and famous Hoosier sense of humor, but
apparently it is not. It is, to be sure, the work of the
sense of proportion; but humor as such, so far as I can
observe, is less common in Indiana than it used to be.
At any rate, where the sense of humor fails, the sense
of self-interest comes in. Chicago automobile clubs have
advised all persons driving to Florida to dodge well
round Indiana, since Indiana is full of sheriffs who
delight in ripping apart every car that comes through
in the hope of finding a spoonful of evidence which
may send a felon away to the pen. This has resulted
in a considerable loss of trade for Indiana hotels and

filling stations; and human nature being what it is, that fact has registered on the minds of Hoosier authorities.

The prohibition law has undoubtedly promoted greater kindness to cooks and greater fraternity with plumbers; it has skilled Hoosiers in the Spartan virtues of caution and evasion; it has taught men to mistrust their friends, which, according to current American morality, is that much to the good. It has done a good deal, but I doubt if it has greatly reduced the volume of drinking, though it has certainly boosted the price of liquor. But then there is little evidence that any prohibition law is primarily intended to reduce the volume of drinking.

But even the transcendent purpose of prohibition laws, the cementing of the power of the Anti-Saloon League and its allies, seems to have been ill served by this inspired enactment. The State superintendent of the Anti-Saloon League has had things his own way for some time. Once, with a group of friends he gestured at an Anheuser-Busch sign overhead. "Ain't it dreadful, boys, that that sign should be allowed to stand?" "But, Doctor," protested one of his hearers, "that sign advertises ginger ale." "I know," said the good doctor sadly, "but the very name makes people think of beer."

Lately, however, the worthy doctor has found himself in trouble. In his annual report he imprudently accused the state Supreme Court of "wet tendencies," and was in due course cited for contempt. At this writing the question is still under debate, but the defendant's attorneys have found it advisable to set up

the defense that he was only exercising the inalienable
right of every citizen to free thought and free speech.

When the Anti-Saloon League has to come out for
free speech, it has lost its Hindenburg Line.

THE Klan, too, is apparently less powerful than it
used to be, though still powerful enough. Two years
ago it had most of the state press terrorized; the two
old-established Indianapolis papers shook speechless in
their boots, and the *Times,* which dared oppose the
Klan in politics, found that its carriers were followed
by Klansmen who stopped at every house where a
Times was left and warned the householder that he
had better stop reading the vile sheet. But of late
various papers, if not exactly coming out against the
Klan, have at least dared to admit that it is not
necessarily a felony for citizens to hold opinions dis-
approved by the ruling oligarchy.

The conviction of the late Dragon seems partly responsible for this; he managed to run the state government from jail during his trial but seems to be less
successful in running it from the remote penitentiary
near the Michigan line. His removal dislocated the
Klan leadership and, so far as the profane outsider can
gather, it even set up two discordant parties among the
sheeted paladins themselves, doubtless the pro-rape
and anti-rape factions. A Grand Titan was lately fined
for rape; and this behavior of Titans and Dragons
suggests that perhaps the Klan's enthusiasm for female
purity proceeds ultimately from a jealous cherishing
of the *droit de seigneur.*

One great effect the Klan domination is having—

the political solidification of most of the intelligent people of the state. For the Klan in Indiana is essentially a proletarian dictatorship. Like all proletarian movements, it includes a few astute individuals, themselves anything but proletarian, who control it and direct it in their own interests; but its membership is almost exclusively composed of the hill-billies, the Great Unteachables. And because the state is controlled by organized ignorance and malice, most of the intellectuals have been forced together for self-defense.

You find plenty of men and women in Indiana who tell you that they are Republicans but vote the Democratic ticket. Not that all the Klansmen are Republicans; but the majority of Democratic sentiment is against them, whereas the Republican party from Jim Watson down is only the tail to the Klan kite. In Indiana as elsewhere, the difference between Republicans and Democrats is little more than a hereditary tradition; but the tradition is still powerful.

If the Klan control of the Republican organization lasts long enough, there will be a real class distinction between the parties in Indiana. The Democrats will be the aristocrats, the party of intelligence; the Republican strength will lie in the unlettered masses and in the few rich men who find the unlettered masses useful in their business. Twenty years ago it was otherwise; the strength of Hoosier Democracy lay in the masses, the majority of the intellectuals were Republicans. But the Republicans, calling themselves the party of intelligence and morality, have visibly become in Indiana the party of ignorance and vicarious morality; there is no place for the intellectuals to go but over to the Democrats. (There are not enough intellectuals, however, to enable the Democrats to carry the state.)

This division is hardly likely to last, of course; presently the Klan will lose the Republican organization and allegiances will return to the old home. Probably it should not last; for the alignment of all the intelligence of the state on one side tends to iron out temperamental differences and local differences which contribute a good deal to the salty variety of Hoosier culture. Here again, prohibition and the fanatical violence of its supporters have erected a paramount issue which throws all difference of opinion on minor matters into the shade. But this is only a tendency; a tendency powerful just now, but by no means solidified into an enduring state. Many things have happened to Indiana, but much of the essential Hoosierism remains untouched.[3]

For—I revert to my theme—the essence of Indiana is literature and politics; and in those basic key-industries Indiana is still there.

A YEAR or two ago there was some little apprehension about the future of Indiana literature. The tall syca-

---

[3] I pass over the great eruption of charges and counter-charges, investigations and exposures and indictments, politic retirements to the hospital by eminent statesmen about to be confronted with inconvenient questionings, etc., which broke out in Indiana about the time this article had its magazine publication, and is continuing spasmodically even yet. Relevant as this may be to my topic, I omit it for three reasons: (a) it is not edifying to the soul; (b) it is not peculiar to Indiana; and (c) the majority of Hoosier voters have indicated that they regard it as a trivial matter, in no way vitiating the divine commissions of the Klan, the Anti-Saloon League, and the Grand Old Party that freed the slaves, saved the union, and sold Teapot Dome.

mores of Hoosier letters—Tarkington, Ade, Nicholson, McCutcheon—still towered above the forest, but they were beginning to be weary in well doing; and they had dominated the field for so long that they had discouraged competition. Ambitious young Hoosiers had developed the habit of going to Detroit to produce automobiles instead of settling down in Indianapolis to produce novels; and the most promising of the younger writers, Mr. Scoggins, chose to employ his talent on the alien scene of Latin America. Something had to be done in the way of planting the next crop if the romantic optimism of the Mid-Western corn belt were not to yield to the gloomy realism of the Northwestern wheat belt.

Hence the Indiana Literary Field Day, held at Culver Military Academy, one of the oldest and best-known schools of the Middle West, and promoted by a committee which hung up a series of prizes for the best essays, stories, poems, plays, and book illustrations by school and college students. The prizes included cash money, in sufficient amount to make the average student wonder if after all literature was not about as profitable as running a garage; and the conferring of the awards was made a ceremony more impressive, to the winners, than any university's bestowal of honorary LL. D.'s. In the way of literary pageantry there has been nothing to approach it since Herodotus read his history at the Olympic games, or Wolfram von Eschenbach won the poetry contest at the Wartburg.

The action takes place on a perfect spring day, on the shores of Lake Maxinkuckee, with a background of semi-military, semi-academic buildings and an over-

head canopy of maples and elms. All around are
seated the beauty and chivalry of Indianapolis and
way stations, not forgetting a considerable delegation
from Indiana's best known extramural extension, Chicago. For extra men and gentlemen of the chorus, several hundred cadets in full uniform, which is full
enough to realize any schoolgirl's dream of military
splendor.

On the platform in front of Memorial Hall are as-
sembled as many as possible—which is a good many,
Culver efficiency and Culver hospitality being equally
well known—of Indiana authors, editors, publishers,
publicists, and critics, pedestaled like the statues in
the Siegesallee, that all aspiring young literati may
have them pointed out—"This is what you too may become, if you only persevere." Leading up to this high
altar of Pallas Athene a shaded walk, lined with smartly
uniformed cadets standing at present arms; and above
everything, on the steps of the Memorial Hall, the
trooping of the colors, laureled banners of the schools
and colleges to which the prize winners belong, that
each young laureate may remember that he not only
gets some money for himself but reflects glory on alma
mater.

The prize winner's name is called; the cadet color
bearer takes the proper banner down the walk; behind
the banner the prize winner ascends to the High Place,
escorted by a cadet aide, his tall helmet surmounted
by a taller black plume, his gilt-buttoned uniform girt
with a scarlet sash and a clanking sword; and with
a roll of drums and flourish of trumpets the name and
school and achievement of the prize winner is solemnly

recited to the applauding crowd and the incipient
author is welcomed into the goodly fellowship of Indiana literati.

Why, the ceremony has as much pomp, and as profound an emotional impact, as a presidential inauguration or a pontifical high mass. The romantic youth or
day-dreaming girl who has been sniffed at by school-
fellows for always writing poems when the gang wants
to do something else, the ugly duckling of a scholastic
community whose chief interest is probably centered on
basketball, suddenly finds that he (or she) is being
saluted as one whom Indiana delighteth to honor. At
the impressionable age, the effect is terrific. If this
idea had been put into practice twenty years ago the
Younger Generation of Hoosier letters would not be
so thin as it is now. Young writers need encouragement, and many a high-school teacher who grades
themes when he would like to be writing poems, many
a ruined realtor sitting on the sandy shores of Biscayne
Bay, wondering how he can raise carfare back to
Kokomo, might have been turned in time to literature
if in his day General Gignilliat of Culver had been
playing Mæcenas as he does now, giving young writers
not only cash, but the credit which (to writers below
the age of thirty) is considerably more important.

This all-day festivity, as perfectly managed in every
detail as a dress parade of the late Prussian Guard,
ended late at night in a pageant covering most of the
history of the world's literature. The glory that was
Greece, the grandeur that was Rome, the unassuming
merit that is Indiana, were all depicted in successive
tableaux; Shakespeare, Milton, Tarkington, Ade, Riley,

Nicholson, had their turn on the stage; and then the grand climax, the one far-off divine event toward which the whole creation moves—the prize winners of the day grouped in the spotlight, the high point of literature to which Ade and Æschylus had been only guideposts pointing the way.

To what purpose? Why, to persuade these young people that Red Grange and Gloria Swanson have not monopolized all the glories of the universe; that a poet may reflect as much credit on his college as an All-Western quarterback; that merit is searched out and recognized outside the sports page—which is not such a bad thing to impress on college students. And the result? Well, such prize-winning pieces of literature as I saw were pretty good; they showed talent. Talent, perhaps, is not uncommon; but the years of unwearied practice that are needed before most writers can cash in on their talent are apt to come hard; many a writer, potentially as good as most of us who actually write, falls by the wayside and takes to selling used cars as the easiest way. None of these Culver prize winners is apt to do that; not with the feeling that Indiana has given them a slap on the back and shoved them along the right path, that the whole state is behind them, giving three cheers as they run cheerfully the race that is set before them.

To be sure, this pageant may have given the young people the idea that the life of letters is roses, roses all the way; which—*crede experto*—it is not. I could suggest certain tableaux which were omitted; an author's wife standing off the bill collector while her husband frantically telephones to the receiver of a bankrupt magazine, asking if there is any hope of getting that check two months overdue; a novelist sitting before his publisher's desk, receiving the news that the returns of copies of his latest book are in excess of sales; a scenarist learning from a film magnate that his works contain entirely too much Sex Appeal to get past Will Hays. But to have injected these into the Field Day would have been as indelicate as to put mention of married quarrels and crying children into a wedding ceremony—as indelicate and as injudicious. Indiana, like Nature, strives to trap her children into serving her purpose, and hopes that the radiant memories of the honeymoon may carry them through some of the realities to follow.

Incidentally, students from the Catholic schools of the state won about half of these prizes, which ought to reassure the Klansmen that Catholic Hoosiers are after all Hoosiers of purest ray serene. Perhaps it will; for Hoosier Catholicism contains one notable institution which never seems to have incurred the hostility that frowns upon the Pope and his other works—the Notre Dame football team. I gather that few Klansmen are so embittered that they fail to give three cheers when this organization, the state's most powerful instrument of nation-wide publicity, wins another victory. To be sure, it is whispered that most of the squad are Protestants; that under Mr. Knute Rockne the Fighting Irish have become in great measure the Fighting Scandinavians. But this, if true, is only a symptom of the recrudescence of tolerance. The good fathers of Notre Dame are not so bigoted as to reject a triple-threat man because he happens to be a Lutheran; nor do the embattled Protestants down state fail to throw their hats in the air over the only Indiana football team that ever wins any notable victories, merely because it fights under the papal banner.

AFTER literature, politics—after it only in the temporal sense, before it in metaphysical preëxistence; for politics in Indiana is alpha and omega, the beginning and the end. I went to a Democratic State Convention, and any doubts that might have survived as to the still-there-ness of Indiana were straightway dissipated. It didn't look like the state conventions I remembered from twenty years ago; among thirteen hundred delegates there were not half a dozen black frock coats and string ties, and women were as frequent on the floor as in the gallery. But they were the same old sort of people; what is more, they behaved in the same old way.

The business of the convention was the adoption of a platform, and the selection of a Senatorial candidate to oppose the Honorable and perennial James Eli Watson. There was a prospect of a fight on the floor over the platform; a belligerent faction wanted to demand the repeal of this famous state prohibition law. Now anybody knows what a Democratic national convention would have done in a situation like that—it would have fought all day and all night and gone home to vote for Coolidge. Not so in Indiana. Probably most of the delegates thought the prohibition law was outrageous, but they were not quite sure that most of the voters did; the movement to demand repeal, instead of dying with its boots on in full convention, was quietly asphyxiated in committee; and the convention unanimously adopted a platform which referred to prohibition only in opposing unlawful and unconstitutional searches and seizures. (When a Republican convention stands by the constitution it means it is for prohibition; when a Democratic convention stands by the constitution it means it is against prohibition.)

Then came the fight for the Senatorial nomination. There were half a dozen candidates between most of whom the differences were merely regional. There was to be sure one wet candidate; he stood for an issue, the paramount issue of the moment; he took his stand firmly and unequivocally on one side of that issue; he represented a Principle. Therefore, he ran sixth in a field of six on the first ballot and practically disappeared off the map on the second. Indiana knows that principles and politics don't mix.

For the rest, there was in the first place Mr. John E. Fredrick, who was supposed to have the favor of Mr. Thomas Taggart. One hears that Mr. Taggart had no favorite, but much of the old organization backed Fredrick. There was also the veteran William A. Cullop, strong in the southwestern part of the state but not much favored elsewhere; and there were three or four others, including a Mr. Stump.

Nobody knew much about this young Mr. Stump, except that he had a good war record and was much in demand as a speaker at high-school commencements. He had no strong political backing, and it did not occur to anybody (until the first ballot showed him running surprisingly well) that a high-school commencement orator makes a wide acquaintance which he can cash in on if he knows how. Mr. Stump knew how; on the second ballot he was second only to Fredrick; but on the third ballot Fredrick threw in his strength, he rose to within a few dozen votes of the six hundred and sixty necessary to a choice, it was perfectly plain that on the fourth ballot Fredrick would go over.

Then something happened. Fredrick had attacked Cullop on the ground that he was too old. Well, thought Cullop, Mr. Stump is young and looks younger; if they want a young man, let them have him. Before the result of the third ballot was announced one county after another began to change its vote, from Cullop to Stump. Cullop had only a hundred or two of votes left, but they were scattered in many counties. County by county, he threw them in—five votes here and seven there, a spoonful at a time but impressive in their cumulative effect. Well-instructed delegates began to shout; the band in the gallery began to play; a score of chairmen of county delegations clamored for the chair's attention to get a chance to change their votes.

Hasty and belated, the Fredrick managers tried to set a backfire; what little undercover strength they had left was thrown in by the same method, the changing of county votes before the result of the ballot was announced. But already they had used almost everything they had, counting on natural momentum to put them over on the next ballot; and in politics as in war the last unbroken reserve turns the tide. Cullop had it—twenty-three votes in his home county which he threw to Stump when the Fredrick managers were just beginning to get up steam. That upset the equilibrium and from that time on it was only a question of who could

get on the Stump band wagon first. In ten minutes Mr.
Fredrick had been pulled off the very steps of the
throne and tumbled into the junk room.

I have seen a good many conventions, state and national, but I never saw anything so smoothly done as
that. Military historians tell us that the Germans won
the war of 1870 because while the French were figuring
out what was the right thing to do the Germans were
doing the right thing by pure reflex action. So is it in
Indiana politics; in a crisis their muscles and their
adrenal glands do most of their thinking for them.
They have made a life work of it; they know how. But
the end of a perfect day was still to come. There appeared on the speakers' stand Captain Albert Stump,
the nominee of his convention, who forthwith addressed
those who had become his constituents.

It was a trying moment for a young and inexperi-
enced man; but evidently Mr. Stump also knew how.
Not a word that could inflame aching wounds; not a
word that did not make for peace, harmony, and optimism. What he said I do not remember; but I have a
general impression that he spoke favorably of God
and the flag, and he certainly said something agreeable
about home and mother. When he had finished thirteen
hundred Democrats went out with the comfortable
feeling that they had picked the best possible candidate; a man who was every Democrat's friend and no
Democrat's enemy, who would come as near as any
man could to enabling every county leader to carry his
county ticket. Of course he did not actually beat Jim
Watson, though he gave him a scare. But that only
proves my thesis; Indiana without Jim Watson to

represent it at Washington would not be the Indiana of song and story; he is as essential and characteristic a feature of the landscape as the sycamore or the shikepoke.

Only one thought saddened us unterrified Democrats as we left that convention hall—the memory of the glorious opportunity that had been booted away at Madison Square Garden two years before. If only the national party could acquire something of the guile of Cullop and the tact of Stump— But nobody could who was not born and raised in Indiana.

So I came home feeling that despite kleagles and smell laws and hard times, the decline and fall of Hoosier culture was a myth unsupported by the evidence. Stands Indiana where she did? She does!

PORTRAIT OF AN ELECTED PERSON

ONE morning in April of 1927 the whither-are-we-drifting boys had the time of their lives. A dreadful thing had happened: the Honorable William E. Dever, regarded by Serious Persons as the best mayor Chicago ever had, had tried for reëlection and gone down in disastrous defeat. What was worse, he had been beaten by the ex-Honorable William Hale Thompson, who in times past had proven himself (to Serious Persons) the worst mayor Chicago had ever had.

Thompson is best known to the outer world for his famous description of Chicago, just after America declared war on Germany, as "the sixth German city in the world," and for a wartime administration so anti-war that Chicago narrowly escaped being put under martial law. But at home they know more about him than that, for they had him as mayor for eight years; and if you ask Serious Persons in Chicago about him they begin to groan. Some of them have become sufficiently toughened to laugh instead, but most of them groan even yet. If they can stop groaning long enough they will tell you that he is a political accident, an ignoramus, a buffoon. His campaign of 1927 set a record, even in American municipal politics, for irrelevance and bad taste. His cardinal issue had been settled a hundred years before he was born—freedom from the British yoke. He called his Irish-Catholic opponent a tool of the King of England, and from the platform he bellowed promises to "hand King George one on the snoot" if the royal nose were ever unveiled in Chicago.

And, as observed above, he beat the best mayor Chicago had ever had by some eighty-three thousand votes; which occasioned much despairing of the Republic. There were pained inquiries as to what is the matter with Chicago, doleful analyses of the collapse of democracy. About the only positive note in the melancholy chorus was offered by an earnest young man in New York, who wrote a newspaper editorial declaring that Thompson should be exposed.

THIS article is not a response to that appeal; I am not going to try to expose William Hale Thompson. For one reason, the Chicago papers have been exposing him as hard as they could for a dozen years; but more powerfully still, he has been exposing himself. He is no shrinking violet who seeks the shade; exposure is what he lives on, and he feeds himself a good dose of it every day. Considering what he has done in that direction, I might as well try to expose the Washington Monument.

Nor shall I endeavor to expose Chicago. It seems to me that Chicago has come in for a good deal of unjust derision in connection with Big Bill Thompson. I believe he would go just as big in any other large city of the United States. Certainly New York can point no finger of scorn; New York would probably have gone on reëlecting Hylan as long as Tammany had gone on nominating him; and Thompson seems to me ten times as clever as Hylan.

Hylan and Thompson have often been bracketed

together—the Great Twin Brethren our ablest political satirist once called them. Both are professional patriots of the anti-British type, both enjoy the favor of Hearst; and they used to foregather now and then for reciprocal back-scratching, admitting in loud tones that they were the best mayors New York and Chicago had ever had. But it was an unequal partnership; Hylan had none of Thompson's originality, none of his instinctive perception of immediate advantage; moreover, Hylan believed everything he said, even if other men wrote it for him and he didn't quite know what it was all about.

Thompson impresses me as far too shrewd to swallow his own bunk; and this opinion is corroborated by men of insight, who have known him thirty years. Serious Persons in Chicago call him an ignoramus. If he is, he is an ignoramus of the type of Henry Ford. Ford is densely ignorant about ninety-eight per cent. of the field of human knowledge, but about the other two per cent. he knows more than any other man who ever lived. Thompson may be ignorant of the art of government, but he is an expert of the first rank in the art of getting elected; and in a democracy no man is going to have much chance to practice the art of government unless he has mastered the art of getting elected first.

Why do I waste good white paper on the statement of this obvious truth? Because, obvious as it may be, it commonly escapes the notice of city clubs, reform associations, and good-government leagues.

The simple and all-sufficient explanation of Thompson is the explanation of Ford as well: they are artists. The artist is not required to possess the general education that is looked for in other men; he may have it or

he may not; nobody cares—if he can do one thing sur-
passingly well, that is enough. Thompson knows what
he has to know, and knows it better than anybody else
in Chicago. Will Rogers commented on the late election with his usual insight: "They was trying to beat
Bill with the better-element vote. The trouble with Chicago is that there ain't much better element." That is
no news to William Hale Thompson; he knows what
other elements want, and he knows how to convince
them that he will give it to them.

So, if this article turns out to be an exposure of
anybody, it will be an exposure of the Better Element,
of the Serious Persons. The trouble with the Better
Element is that it habitually regards politics in the opta-
tive instead of the indicative mood; it thinks in such
phrases as "the voters should," "the people ought." Not
till the Serious Persons realize that their major premise
is "the voters do," "the people won't," are we going
to get a grade of municipal government that is anything
to brag about. Last April the Better Element of Chicago made enough mistakes to ruin a worse candidate
than Dever; with all the experience of recent decades
behind them, they still tried to jam virtue, or what was
called virtue, down the public throat. Not, of course,
that all of Dever's supporters were Serious Persons;
they included some very practical politicians, notably
one George Brennan. But Mr. Brennan, during the
campaign, seems to have been under some evil spell;
he behaved almost like a Better Element himself.

AN astute observer who has known him for many years
remarked to me that Thompson has a tabloid mind.

You might go farther and say that he is a tabloid, in his own person. Chicago has no tabloid newspaper, but the tabloid state of mind is endemic among the population, and Big Bill has filled a long-felt want.

The essence of a tabloid is that anybody can understand it; even people who cannot read ninety-six-point type can look at pictures. So with Thompson; whatever else he may not do, he never fails to make himself clear. Of late years the Irish and Germans have stirred up much agitation in the larger cities about alleged pro-British school histories. How much there is in their argument is a matter of contention, but one thing is sure—to find out whether they are right or not you must read the histories, and you must have some knowledge of the events they deal with. Not many people, in Chicago or elsewhere, care enough about the truth to do that. So Thompson simplified the issue with a stroke of genius; he denounced William Mc-Andrew, superintendent of the Chicago schools, as "King George's stool pigeon." That is as plain as the picture on the front cover of a tabloid; like the picture, it may be faked, but few of the customers are going to be curious enough to inquire into that.

This matter of schools, which played a considerable part in the late campaign, might have been supposed to be a delicate topic for Thompson. Toward the close of his second administration two dozen of his henchmen were indicted for stealing school money. One of them was Fred Lundin, the Columbus who had discovered Thompson years before (like Columbus, Lundin never dreamed what an expansive continent he was discovering, or what it was destined to do to him).

None of these gentlemen was convicted; but their indictment put the capstone on a pretty general condemnation of the Thompson administration of the schools.

Under Dever, who followed Thompson, there were new men in the Board of Education; McAndrew was brought from New York as superintendent, and the schools improved perceptibly. None of Dever's school men was indicted; but Thompson had an easy explanation for that. "The King of England wouldn't let them be indicted." Who, you may ask, would believe that? Well, a lot of Chicago voters.

Then there is the water situation. Despite considerable effort, I do not wholly understand the Chicago water situation; but I am solaced by the assurance of experts that a lot of other people do not understand it, including William Hale Thompson. None the less, the first thing Thompson did when he took office last April was to try to unsettle it.

Chicago draws water from Lake Michigan—eighty-five hundred cubic feet a second—to dilute its sewage and wash it away down the drainage canal. Other lake cities have roared a protest that their water front will be lowered by this diversion; and the War Department, which controls the lake water, threatened a couple of years ago to cut Chicago's allowance in two unless water meters were installed in the city, to reduce the amount diverted (outside of this allowance) through the city water works to what was actually needed.

Chicago at present uses more water per capita than any city in the United States; more than twice as much as New York, which passes as tolerably cleanly. To be sure Chicago needs a good deal of water; what with the unabated smoke nuisance, and the winds that bring in prairie dust gathered over a sweep of fifteen hundred miles, a Chicagoan has to wash about twice as much as a New Yorker to maintain the same outward decency. None the less, the experts seem to think that Chicago wastes water shamefully. But Thompson made a great campaign issue of repeal of the water-meter ordinance.

He argued, one is told, that water, drawn from the lake before Chicago's doors, was one of Nature's gifts; it ought to be free as air. It takes a costly plant to pump and purify and distribute that water; a plant that must be maintained somehow. But Big Bill knew that the average voter would not figure that taxes to maintain the city water works are included in his rent, any more than the average New York voter who stood by Honest John Hylan and the five-cent fare figured that the cost of subways paid for by taxes and city borrowings and increased real-estate assessments was included in his rent. It was objected that the meter ordinance was part of a bargain with the War Department, that if it were repealed the withdrawal permit might be rescinded; but Thompson replied that no President who wanted to get the vote of Chicago would permit the curtailment of Chicago's water supply. Thanks to this nefarious measure, he declared, you could go into the flats of the poor and see five children taking their bath in the same tub of water because their parents could afford no more. Now, at the water rate that prevailed before the meters were installed, five tubfuls of water, one per child, would cost about seven and a half cents.

At the new rate they would still cost less than eight cents, a difference not ruinous, even for the average slum family.

But it was a powerful argument, all the same. The water situation is complex and obscure; but there is nothing complex or obscure about Big Bill's picture of the five children bathing in the same tub; it is as plain as the front cover of a tabloid.

Like a tabloid, too, the Mayor lives from day to day, fresh every morning. What if his pet issue falls by the wayside, rejected by an obtuse Federal government, by a hostile legislature, or even—this has happened—by a referendum of the Chicago voters? That was yesterday's issue, as dead as yesterday's newspaper. To-morrow morning Big Bill will have another, and whatever you may think about its merits, you can be sure that his side of it will be as clear as plate glass. In the twelve years since his public career began he has been on both sides of practically every question—consecutively, as a rule, but in one notable instance he was on both sides simultaneously. Even his cardinal issue, the great guiding principle of his life, "America First," suffered a brief eclipse; while America was at war with Germany he was for America second. But this has done him no harm.

For he understands his people as well as Sophocles understood the Athenians. Like Sophocles, he gives them a periodic catharsis of pity and terror, and like Sophocles he finishes off with slapstick stuff that sends them home laughing. The Athenians thought so well of Sophocles' plays that they elected him admiral, and from all accounts he was about as good an admiral as

Big Bill is a mayor. The art of politics has a lot to learn from the show business, and William Hale Thompson has learned it.

It was a showman who first really put him into politics. Before that he had made some efforts to put himself into politics, but he had never got very far; though he had picked up some connections which turned out to be useful when he did get into politics.

Thompson is a millionaire and the son of a millionaire, the grandson of Chicago's first fire chief; in short, as aristocracy goes in Chicago, he is a patrician; and if, when he went into politics, he divested himself of his patriciate and applied for membership in the common people, he was only following the example of such excellent practical politicians as Julius Cæsar and Theodore Roosevelt. He grew up on the South Side of Chicago, in the Second Ward, and his father meant to send him to Yale; but long before that menace became imminent—in 1883, when he was fifteen years old—he went to Wyoming and became a cowboy. A few years later he bought a ranch in Nebraska, and he was evidently a good cattleman. He had made money—not big money for the Thompsons of Chicago, but big money for a boy just old enough to vote—before his father's death brought him back to Chicago to manage the copious estate.

There was plenty of time for other diversions, and he devoted most of it to sport. In 1896 he was captain and manager of the Chicago Athletic Association football team, which won a championship; he was one of the founders of the Illinois Athletic Association; he was and is an enthusiastic yachtsman. I surmise that he feels himself a sportsman much more than a politician; and he certainly looks it. You will not find many men of his type in the city halls of the country; but you will find plenty of them in the clubhouse at Saratoga or Churchill Downs, at the ringside at heavyweight championship fights, in the field boxes at world's series games. See him in the street, and you might not know who he was; but you could be pretty sure he was not president of the Civil Service Reform Association or the Anti-Saloon League. I believe that Thompson's appearance alone is worth thousands of votes.

He was elected alderman in 1900, and started, at Wabash Avenue and 24th Street, the first public playground in the country. Hence you will see him set down in campaign literature as the father of the public-playground movement. One hears that an obscure reporter, long since dead, first whispered the public-playground idea in his ear. Big Bill has a habit of listening to what people tell him, and this time he certainly listened to something good; but at the moment it worked no great service to his fortunes. He held one or two minor offices, and then dropped out, devoting himself to business and sports, until local politicians who thought they saw possibilities in him brought him to the attention of Fred Lundin.

This was years later—at the beginning of 1915. Chicago had a habit in those days of going Democratic in municipal elections; Carter Harrison, the incumbent Democratic Mayor, was finishing off his fifth term. But Harrison had given no help to Roger Sullivan when that elder statesman ran for the Senate in the previous fall, and Sullivan was out for his scalp, backing Sweitzer against Harrison in the Democratic primaries.

Meanwhile the Republicans were preparing to go through the motions; and the Serious Persons, the municipal reformers, the Better Element, were preparing to back the Republican candidate in a forlorn hope. Judge Harry Olson had been agreed on by most of the leaders to carry the Republican-Better-Element banner to a moral victory; but Fred Lundin had other plans.

This Lundin had first come to Chicago, years back, as a medicine man, peddling the old Indian remedy from the tail of the wagon under the gasoline flare; and in that calling he had learned the great truth which no politician and no artist should ever forget—that it does not make any difference how good an article you are selling unless you can get them to stop and listen. He had managed to put together the disjected fragments of William Lorimer's old Republican machine; and, poking around the bulrushes in search of a candidate, he had stumbled on William Hale Thompson.

For Lundin, Thompson must have seemed made to order. A millionaire sportsman, able to finance his own campaign if other sources of income failed; with a wide acquaintance, an attractive appearance, a popular personality; and (so it may have been reasoned) not so heavy in the cerebrum as to endanger Lundin's intentions of being the power behind the throne. So Thompson put on the traditional Stetson hat of the cattleman, took the name of Cowboy Bill, and started campaigning for the nomination.

Nobody but Lundin took him seriously. Harry Olson was so sure of his nomination that he spent Washington's Birthday, just before the primary, on his farm down state; Thompson spent it going around town and making speeches. He was only a so-so campaigner then; the brilliant technic which he exemplified last spring was still to be worked out; but any campaigner is better than no campaigner and Olson, at the moment, was not campaigning at all. Worse still, Olson's financial backers were asleep at the switch; on the eve of the primaries the money to pay the local workers was lacking; one by one precinct captains turned up at the Olson headquarters, found the cupboard bare, and went home to do their bit for Thompson. On primary day the bulk of the Republicans marked the Democratic ballot and helped Sweitzer beat Carter Harrison; while the regulars turned out and gave Thompson the Republican nomination, and the support of the better-element reformers which went with it.

Carter Harrison was down but he was not out; he whetted his knife, after the Chicago fashion, and set to work to help Thompson beat Sweitzer. (Even yet, after twelve years, Thompson's conglomerate retinue includes a group which calls itself the "Carter Harrison Democracy.") Other people were also out to beat Sweitzer; he was a Catholic, and the sentiment which was later to flower in the Ku Klux Klan appeared toward the end of the campaign and drove all the fanatical Protestants to vote for Thompson. Sweitzer was of German ancestry; a few days before the election leading Germans, Austrians, Magyars of Chicago got out a handbill adorned with portraits of Kaiser Wilhelm and the Emperor-King Franz Josef, urging all citizens of Central European origin to vote for Sweitzer and the Fatherland. So all the pro-Ally vote—which included the Czech vote, powerful in Chicago—went for Thompson.

And in the meantime Big Bill was getting other votes by his own endeavors. The great negro influx was not yet at its height, but already the negroes dominated Thompson's own ward, and he was shrewd enough to recognize their rising power and play up to them. In that day the Sunday closing of saloons was a hardy annual issue in every American city; Thompson promised the reformers he would close the saloons, and secretly promised the saloon-keepers he would not. So on the 6th of April, 1915, the Honorable William Hale Thompson, the wet-dry-Nordic-negro-Protestant-pro-Ally-Better-Element-Carter-Harrison candidate, beat the unhappy Sweitzer by a margin of 148,000 votes—the most sweeping victory recorded up to that time, in any municipal election ever held in the United States.

CHICKENS come home to roost, but they never roost long on Big Bill Thompson; he moves right out from under them. Before he had been in office three months the reformers came down on him, and demanded the closing of saloons on Sunday. Thereupon the saloon-keepers produced his secret pre-election promise (he had even put it in writing) not to close the saloons on Sunday. Thompson closed them all the same and became immediately the hero of the Anti-Saloon League. True, it appeared before long that a good many saloons were open on Sunday, these being saloons that had the right political connections; but that happened in every American city in those days, and Big Bill had no difficulty in being a wet-dry till something else attracted public attention.

The something else, in this case, was a street-car strike, a serious event in any city. Big Bill settled it; he brought the leaders of the strikers and the heads of the trolley companies together in his office and told them they would stay there till the strike was settled. It was settled before supper; the employees got an increase in wages and Thompson got another block of devoted supporters. The increase in wages was presently passed on to the public in the form of higher fares, but by that time the war was on and people were too busy to think about trifles.

Big Bill's war record is too well known to need lengthy exposition; its first manifestations brought such a roar of denunciation from all over the country that eventually he throttled himself down and kept within the danger line, extending only spiritual aid and comfort to the enemy. Some men who know him well say that the hatred of England which showed itself in the War as friendship for Germany is genuine. But one thing could not escape his eye; the Germans are the largest single racial group in Chicago, and by his friendliness at a time when the rest of Chicago was taking its patriotism as hysterically as Chicago takes everything he made himself solid with them for life. Last spring, eight years after the War was over, thoughtful Chicago Germans were telling their friends, "Damn him, we know he's no good, but he made life livable for us in 1918 and he gets our votes."

He needed those votes, too, for his city administration was getting nowhere in particular. Then as now, he was an inspirational person, living from moment to moment, on bright thoughts which were here to-day and gone to-morrow. He gave so many jobs to negroes when he first took office that irreverent persons called the City Hall "Uncle Tom's Cabin." The tone of the administration, for that matter, was a good deal like a Tom show, which greatly distressed the Better Element; but Thompson had been shrewd enough to perceive something which more ponderous intellects were not to discern for years, that the average voter regards politics as a show, and will generally give his vote to the candidate who best understands how to mix up the laughs and the thrills. In the municipal primaries of February, 1919, Harry Olson ran against him once more for the Republican nomination, and once more Thompson beat him. The Germans and negroes did it; by this time the negroes controlled three South Side wards and they knew who was their friend. Once more Sweitzer had the Democratic nomination, Sweitzer who four years earlier had run under the Kaiser's portrait; but this time the Germans voted for Thompson. Maclay Hoyne, an independent Democrat, drew off a good many votes from Sweitzer; the Socialists made a surprisingly strong showing; altogether the five candidates opposed to Thompson polled 150,000 more votes than he did. But he slid in over Sweitzer, the leader of the five, by a plurality of 18,000, two thirds of it in the negro wards.

It was a day of mourning for earnest patriots, but a day of joy for practical Republican politicians, who saw in this election, among other things, another symptom of the reaction against Woodrow Wilson. In an ebullient moment in 1916 Thompson had admitted that he would accept a presidential nomination. No chance for that in 1920, but he threw in with the anti-League group, working for Hiram Johnson and against his bitterest enemy, Governor Frank Lowden, who had once ordered down-state National Guardsmen into Chicago in the heated days of 1918. Lowden and Johnson both fell by the wayside, but in the election of 1920 Thompson (and Lundin) got the state administration in their hands. At the moment he looked like a coming man.

But in 1921 he began to slip.

IT would be a pleasure to report that he slipped because of the inadequacy of the government which he and Lundin had given the city, which he and Lundin and Len Small were giving the state, but he did not; he slipped because of factional quarrels.

As to the merits of his municipal administration, there are divergent opinions. He has never been personally accused of graft; but a good many of his followers, who did not have his felicity of inherited wealth, were gravely suspected, though never jailed. Read his campaign booklet entitled *Big Bill the Builder: a Chicago Epoch,* and you must feel that his reign was a little better than the millennium; read the files of the Chicago papers (except the Hearst papers, which have pretty consistently backed him) and you will get a different idea. Thompson used to hit back at his critics with libel suits; without having added up the figures, I believe he has filed more than any other public man of our time. Only one, so far as newspaper records go, came to trial; that dragged on till one of the jurors went insane from listening to the evidence, and then everybody gave it up.

His prize performance, however, was the filing of libel suits in the name of the city of Chicago against the *Tribune* and the *Daily News,* for ten million dollars apiece. These were tried; the lower court decided for the newspapers, and the Supreme Court backed it up, holding that when the *Tribune* and *Daily News* said that Thompson's administration had bankrupted the city they were only exercising "the right of every citizen to criticize the government and its administrators."

It would serve no purpose to go into these old, unhappy, far-off things; but certainly "bankruptcy" was a bit strong. On at least one occasion the voters had to authorize a bond issue to meet current municipal running expenses, yet somehow Chicago continued to get by. Great things were done in Thompson's two administrations, and he claimed the credit; great things went on being done after he went out of office, and he claimed the credit for them too.

Most especially, the Michigan Avenue bridge was built. The wicked say it cost enough to build two bridges, still it was built, and there resulted the tremendous development of the nearer North Side. Other mighty deeds were done; Thompson says he did them, his enemies say they were done over his prostrate form. Generally speaking, these achievements are part of the slow but implacable working out of Burnham's Chicago Plan, which goes on, now rapidly, now slowly, from administration to administration. Chicago, so long imprisoned in the Loop, has broken out at last, overflowing on the lake front, the river front, the North Side. Much of that took place while Thompson was Mayor. His enemies say that for him to take the credit is as if whoever might have been Mayor of Chicago at the end of the Glacial Age had taken the credit for the melting of the ice.

But almost any Mayor of almost any city would have claimed the credit for all this, whether he deserved it or not. Thompson's original contribution was the tabloid touch, the assumption of a new title—"Big Bill the Builder." In this last election his campaign handbook was adorned with photographs of about all the public improvements of his administrations and of Dever's too; and your well-read voter, when he looks at any large new building in Chicago, will find that phrase flashing into his mind—"Big Bill the Builder." He may not believe it, but he can't forget it.

So, toward the end of 1922, our hero set out, full of confidence, to get himself a third term. He had lost minor elections, he had experienced numerous defeats, but he still had his cardinal issue—"America First." His great forerunner Lorimer had adopted Abraham Lincoln as his spiritual ancestor; Thompson went him one better and took George Washington. "The principles laid down by Washington and reaffirmed by the twenty-six presidents who followed him" up to Wilson (you have to count Cleveland twice to make it come out right) were Big Bill's principles too, and he nearly had them copyrighted, in Chicago.

But a month before the primaries he withdrew from the campaign, "overcome," he said, "by the forces of grasping wealth and aggrandizement." A little later he offered another explanation, "My friends have crucified me."

The friend who is said to have been busiest in crucifying Big Bill was State's Attorney Robert E. Crowe.

CHICAGO politics is chaotic and incomprehensible to the outsider, but in general it may be said that it is like war in China, an exercise in changing sides. (Especially Republican politics; George Brennan has built up a tolerably stable Democratic organization, though God knows how long anything will stay stable in Chicago.) But Republican Chicago, like China, is divided into factions, personal and regional, controlled by local war lords—literal war lords, in many cases, with their retinues of machine gunners who kill more men than fall in Chinese battles. They combine, and split, and recombine, with no more stability in their arrangement than you find in a deck of cards reshuffled for each hand.

I know Chicago only from casual visits two or three times a year; but if an outsider's opinion is worth anything, I should say that what Chicago most needs —more than subways or smoke consumption or combined railroad terminals or anything else—is a Tammany Hall. It would be a godsend to the city if these double-crossing and throat-cutting factions were replaced by an integrated organization in which power and responsibility could be centralized, which would give as good government as the majority of voters are willing to tolerate.

But to return to Mr. Crowe. He was, and is, one of the most powerful of Chicago's war lords. The busi-

ness of the State's Attorney's office is the war against
crime, and luckily there is no lack of crime to war
against. So subtle are the relationships of these matters,
in Chicago, that they may best be expressed by a
theological formula—where crime abounded, there the
State's Attorney's office did much more abound. In
the pre-primary campaign of 1922-23 Crowe's faction
turned against Thompson and was strong enough to
thrust him out. Arthur C. Lueder got the Republican
nomination for mayor, while the Democrats put up
Judge William E. Dever.

Where was William Hale Thompson while the battle
of that year's election was being fought out? Don't
worry, friends; he was there. In the three negro wards
Thompson's lieutenants kept the negro voters at home
on election day, and the scattering white residents who
went to the polls carried those wards for Dever. It
was a warning that in Chicago it is easier to nail a
man to the cross than to keep him there.

Dever was elected, and straightway engaged in the
hazardous occupation of being the best mayor Chicago ever had. I take that designation on the word of
the Better Element; to the foreign eye there appear
some flaws in this perfection. But Dever undoubtedly
had some tough problems to handle, one of them being
the transit situation.

The Chicago surface lines, owned by several companies, were running under franchises which would expire in February 1927. On a seven-cent fare they were
making some money, and part of their earnings was
being turned into the city treasury as a nest egg, from
which optimists hoped that the first of the badly needed

subways might be hatched. The elevateds, on a basic ten-cent fare, were making money under long franchises; but since something would have to be done about the surface lines this was an obvious chance to unify the whole transportation system.

Big Bill the Builder had faced this problem from a distance and found a fine issue—the five-cent fare. But to restore this legislation was needed, which the state legislature refused to give him; so Big Bill, after posing for the obvious photograph—People's Friend Crucified By Interests—went on to something else. But Dever had to tackle it because the trolley franchises would expire before he went out of office; and eventually, in 1925, he submitted to popular referendum a plan for unification of surface and elevated lines, under a modified form of municipal ownership and control. It was undoubtedly better thought out than any of Thompson's ideas on the transit question; but it was not well enough thought out to get by. It offered too much municipal control for some people, not enough for others; so it was voted down. A miss is as good as a mile in politics; from the practical standpoint, this is Count One against the best administration Chicago ever had.

But worse was to come. If you want to see the man who more than anyone else is responsible for Thompson's return to power, gaze on the austere countenance of the Honorable Andrew J. Volstead. Dever essayed to enforce the prohibition laws, and while that optimistic enterprise was still in its infancy Judge Gary introduced him, at a dinner of prohibitionists in New

York, as "the man who showed Chicago that the law was going to be enforced."

This was about as accurate as most of Judge Gary's pronouncements outside of his own special field. Dever, in fact, was the man who showed Chicago that if you entrust the police with the enforcement or non-enforcement of the prohibition laws, the police will waste little time on anything else, least of all on the onerous, perilous, and unprofitable business of suppressing crime. Chicago was never a notably peaceable or law-abiding city, but the great outburst of robbery, homicide, and machine-gunning came after Thompson went out of office. It came under the best mayor Chicago ever had.

Homicide, of course, is not much of a crime in the eyes of the professional prohibitionist; but many Chicago homicides are only incidental to what the prohibitionist regards as graver offenses. For while the ladies who kill their husbands, or their lovers, may get most of the newspaper space, most of the killing done in Chicago results from private feuds in the underworld. And most underworld feuds of late years have sprung from disputes over bootlegging privileges, in the city whose standard of law enforcement aroused the admiration of Judge Gary.

I have never heard of a time, since the Volstead Act and the state search-and-seizure went into effect, when it was very hard to get a drink in Chicago. One hears that in the early days the privilege of violating the liquor laws was in the hands of ward and precinct politicians, who passed it around where they thought it

would do the most good. When Dever transferred it
to the police (for as the power to tax is the power to
destroy, so the power to suppress is the power to tolerate) he simultaneously demoralized the police and
alienated the politicians. Which is one reason why reform mayors are not re-elected.

Mr. Dever, being an intelligent as well as an honest
man, was not long blind to this; in 1926 he told the
American Bar Association that "the liquor question is
not yet settled," and intimated a belief that it never
could be settled, in the cities, on the present line of
attack. Immediately the drys damned him as a traitor;
the wets, of course, were against him already. Yet he
went stubbornly and dutifully on, trying to enforce a
law which he had virtually admitted was unenforceable.
Which is another reason why reform mayors are not
reëlected.

Meanwhile, where was Big Bill the Builder? He
was coming back from Elba, preceded by several brass
bands.

IT will be recalled that when a well-known politician
retired from office some twenty years ago, leaving his
successor well supplied with rope to hang himself,
he whiled away the requisite interval by going to Africa
to hunt big game. Thompson got a somewhat similar
idea in the spring of 1924.

Somebody had told him—and, as before stated, Big
Bill usually listens to people who tell him something—
that in Borneo there was a fish that climbed trees;
and straightway the ex-Mayor reverted to the status
of a sportsman-scientist and set out to find it. He

bet a friend twenty-five thousand dollars that he would bring back that fish, or at least motion pictures of its tree-climbing; he organized the South Seas Research Association for scientific inquiry; and he constructed a vessel which was duly christened the *Big Bill* and ornamented with a wooden statue of the Builder by way of figurehead. In that ship he was going to sail to Borneo and bring back the tree-climbing fish; and on the way he would go down the river to New Orleans, spreading propaganda for the Illinois Lakes-to-Gulf Waterway, which is one of the enterprises that he takes up and boosts whenever there is no other immediate material for boosting.

Of course the scoffers, the knockers—Big Bill despises knockers—got to work at once. They alleged that his tree-climbing fish was no novelty; that it had been described and depicted in magazines sixty years ago; that an American scientific expedition had lately brought back the motion pictures which Thompson was about to seek; that, in fact, several mounted specimens could be seen in Chicago, at the Field Museum.

None of which worried Big Bill; he went right on with his well-advertised expedition, and seventy-five thousand people saw his ship start out on her voyage to Borneo via the Chicago Drainage Canal. Something happened every day—something that got into the papers; one day, even, a newspaperman from Zion City (the village that voted the earth was flat) fell overboard and was properly rescued, by none other than William Hale Thompson.

So the *Big Bill* proceeded on its watery way—not all

water, at that—as far as New Orleans. There Thompson was compelled to leave it; business recalled him to Chicago. His friends left, too, or so many of them as had not fallen away on the trip down the river; and the unhappy captain, who apparently had supposed all the time that they were really going to Borneo, was left with his schooner on his hands and was last heard of hiring her out to fishing parties in the Bay of Panama. As for the twenty-five-thousand-dollar bet, what happened to that is not recorded.

They laugh at Big Bill even yet for that enterprise, but I fail to see why. At a time when he was out of politics it got him about a kilometer of newspaper space; it kept him in the public eye, no matter how; it reminded the public that here was a man who Did Things, or at any rate started to do them. And how many people notice what happens to any high adventure after it leaves the front page?

Our hero's tower of refuge in those days was the Fish Fans Club, that ornate and bedizened galley, resembling the Bucentaur in which the Doges of Venice used to fare forth for the symbolic marriage with the Adriatic, which is familiar to all visitors to Chicago who have ridden up into Lincoln Park and seen it anchored just off the shore. (Possibly this aquatic stronghold was intended as a reminder that Chicago's future lies on the water, as well as on land and in the air.) The Fish Fans Club itself has a history, of which only the high points can be touched here. The hull of this stately craft was originally only a humble barge; it was purchased and reconstructed by the club members, but malicious persons allege that all the work of preparing the anchorage was done by Park employees on the taxpayers' time.

However this may be, the Fish Fans Club has the name of being a pleasant retreat for persons wearied by the cares of state. Two or three years ago, while Thompson was in private life, Federal prohibition officers raided the gallant craft and found an immense quantity of liquor; but it turned out that this was the private property of a caretaker resident aboard so no harm was done to any person of consequence. But on election night of 1927 the club was almost the scene of an appalling catastrophe.

Thompson was receiving returns there that night and naturally all his friends were eager to crowd in and congratulate him. As many as the galley was built to accommodate were soon aboard, and then as many more; and still they came. Now the barge which was the substructure of this brave vessel had been caulked up to a few feet above the normal water line, able to take care of any load that was reasonably to be expected; but such a crowd had swarmed aboard this night that it was borne down until the water rose high on its sides, rose to a level where the seams were open. At once the vessel sprang a hundred leaks; and presently the engineer rushed up to the president of the club and whispered hoarsely—"Captain, the ship is sinking! All hands ashore!"

Well, by that time the boys and girls were all busy celebrating the famous victory; no mere president of a club could have made himself heard. To get this mob ashore along a narrow gang plank would be difficult enough; but harder yet would it be to get them started.

In this perilous crisis only one man could impose silence, only one voice would be heard with respect; the president of the club hastily informed the chosen favorite of the people and the Honorable William Hale Thompson essayed to deliver the warning in time.

Thompson got a hearing; he told his guests that the Fish Fans Club had sprung a leak; he advised all present to walk (not run) to the nearest exit. Whereupon they all looked at each other mirthfully and said, "Ha, ha! Bill will have his little joke." So they stayed aboard, and the ship went on sinking; but happily when it had sunk about two feet it struck the bottom of the lake, and rested there, somewhat precariously, until the visitors had gone and it could be pumped out the next day.

But Thompson did not spend all his time out of office at the Fish Fans Club; like David at Adullam, he raided out whenever he saw a chance to accomplish anything, returning only to rest and refit. He was temporarily out but he still had his factional organization and his personal following, and neither could be left out of account. He was out of favor, for a time, with the dominant group in the national Republican organization; but on one issue he guessed right when they guessed wrong. When the Republican National platform of 1924 spoke favorably of the World Court, Thompson exploded that "our foreign policy has been dictated by the King of England." Where is that World Court now? Smothered in its sleep, like Desdemona, and Big Bill made some slight contribution toward smothering it, incidentally and simultaneously making a larger contribution toward the return of Big Bill.

In 1926 that missionary bishop of the mavericks, William E. Borah, was going the rounds making speeches against senators who had voted for the World Court. When he came to Chicago Big Bill took charge of the meeting and ran away with it; Borah and George Washington were only secondary figures. Last fall Thompson put an anti-World Court candidate, Colonel Frank Smith, into the Senate. Smith had been chairman of the Utilities Commission, and his campaign fund had received heavy contributions from Samuel Insull, who owns most of the utilities around Chicago. A Senatorial committee, you will remember, asked about this; among other people, they asked Big Bill Thompson. What was his explanation of this curious behavior of his candidate? Why, that "I have tried to carry out the policies of George Washington and the twenty-six presidents who followed him." America First.

By this time, you will observe, he had already retraced most of the journey from Elba. Unsuccessful indictments of Thompson's friends Lundin and Len Small had reacted in his favor; and Dever's policemen were breaking into houses and arresting home brewers who had failed to provide themselves with the proper moral support, while machine guns sputtered merrily around the corner. But before Thompson could get back in the City Hall he must get the Republican nomination; and he got it with the help of the man who had crucified him four years earlier, the Honorable Robert E. Crowe.

Mr. Crowe, they say, had had delusions of grandeur, but by this time he had got over them; he had discovered that he and Big Bill might be reciprocally useful. There was room for a great ally in Thompson's camp, for by this time he had broken with his friend and discoverer, Lundin. He had said harsh words about Crowe four years earlier, had said that if he ever shook Crowe's hand again you could set him down as a crook. But remarks like that are rarely taken too seriously by working politicians. Righteousness and peace kissed each other, Crowe and Thompson came together, with three cheers for George Washington; Thompson helped Crowe elect his county ticket last fall, having first pledged them to America First and no World Court; then Crowe helped Thompson to the mayoralty nomination, and they set out to beat the best mayor Chicago had ever had.

SAY what you like about the taste of that campaign, it was a theatrical masterpiece. Lundin, for instance, had set up an independent candidate, Dr. John Dill Robertson. Thompson proclaimed that Lundin was a rat and Robertson was a rat, and he brought two caged rats up on the platform as visual reminder. Tabloid stuff—picture on the front cover, story inside, if you care to look for it. And I surmise that King George, whose involuntary appearance in the campaign aroused so much ridicule and disgust, played just about the same part as these caged rats. He was a tabloid picture too.

For every time Thompson said "King George" every German in Chicago had his whole 1917 complex recalled to his attention; the Germans might have remembered anyway who had been their friend when they needed a friend, but Thompson took no chances. But King George was worth more than that. The great offense of King George's stool pigeon McAndrew (that is, the great ostensible offence; I suspect a competent administration of the schools was one of the real counts against him) dealt with certain textbooks. These were not school books; they were used only in teachers' training courses which McAndrew had recommended; but they were a good talking point. For these books, it appears, shamefully distort Revolutionary history, as follows:

(1) They speak of the Scotch-Irish in Washington's army, when as every Irishman knows these were South Irish. (There are a good many thousand Irish voters in Chicago.)

(2) They pay insufficient attention to the deeds of the Polish Revolutionary heroes, Pulaski and Kosciuszko. (There are a hundred thousand Polish voters in Chicago.)

(3) They fail to mention the exploits of Steuben and the immense number of German soldiers in Washington's army. (There are two hundred thousand German voters in Chicago.)

Why no protest was made against the undoubted belittling of the achievements of the negro soldiers in Washington's army I do not know. Probably Thompson was sure of the negroes without that.

So much for King George. But, as observed above, it was not King George but Volstead, and the downstate legislators who had passed the search-and-seizure law, that really ruined Dever. Thompson could count on the Germans and the negroes, but most of the hundred thousand Polish voters in Chicago are normally Democratic. They are also normally wet, or abnormally wet, if you like. Anyhow, when Thompson strode up and down the platform promising to send the police back to their old job of fighting the crooks, and declaring that "I'll fire any cop who walks into a man's house without a warrant and fans the mattress for a pint flask," he got most of the Polish vote, and he got a good many other votes too. Chicago, brethren of the dry cause, is joined to its idols; it still contains a good many people who regard murder as a more serious matter than taking a drink.

If you doubt the accuracy of this diagnosis, consider this: In November George Brennan, running for Senator as a wet against the dry Frank Smith, carried Chicago by 83,000. Five months later Brennan's candidate Dever, running as a dry against the wet Thompson, lost Chicago by 83,000.

Apologists for Chicago point out that more than 50,-000 of Thompson's 83,000 plurality was rolled up in the three negro wards; but he got a lot of white votes too, and the above observations may explain where he got them. And the tactics of the opposition helped him powerfully.

In the first place, the title of "the best mayor Chicago ever had" was a millstone around Dever's neck; is there an instance in American municipal politics of the reëlection of any mayor who was stigmatized by the Better Element as the best the city had ever had? Another millstone was the infelicitous slogan, "Dever and Decency." As a veteran of many municipal campaigns dolefully observed after the election, "Who the hell is attracted by decency?"

How much Thompson's grotesque denunciations of King George affected the campaign is a matter of doubt; possibly not much, aside from recalling to the Germans the situation of 1917. But Thompson played it so hard that the opposition decided to reduce it to absurdity; they dressed up a negro as Paul Revere and sent him galloping down Michigan Avenue, crying, "The British are coming!" This, apparently, had no effect at all; Thompson's King-George campaign was already so absurd that it could be reduced no farther; of those who saw the Afro-American Revere a few doubtless thought that the British *were* coming, and that only Big Bill could keep them out; and the rest, discarding Paul Revere and King George, held fast to their determination to vote for Thompson and save that pint flask under the mattress.

But the culminating blunder was committed by no less a person than George Brennan himself, when in a peevish moment he remarked that "all the hoodlums are for Thompson." Big Bill seized on that with a whoop of joy; he stigmatized the Democrats as aristocrats; he paraded the platform bellowing a merry appeal—"Hoodlums, come out and vote, and bring another hoodlum with you." (Al Jolson, just after the election, gave Big Bill a bulldog which the donor had named "Big Boy," but Thompson had a better inspiration than that; he gave the dog a new name and put it on his collar for all the world to see—"Hoodlum—Mayor's Office—Chicago.") Showman stuff? Yes, and good showman stuff; it made votes. And behind that he had the solid support of the Germans and negroes, he had the scattering—but considerable—support of the people who thought that the police might better be trying to prevent homicide than fanning mattresses for pint flasks.

Is there any mystery, now, about that election? Well, one mystery, perhaps—in spite of everything, 430,000 people voted for Dever.

WELL, now that Big Bill has got it, what is he going to do with it?

Prophecy is perilous, in politics. I have already remarked on the fact that the spiritual advisers of the ancient Hebrews, so prompt and so infallible in interpreting the purposes of God, were singularly infelicitous in predicting the course of mundane affairs. Professor Julius Bewer, in his *Literature of the Old Testament,* calls attention to the solitary and trebly praiseworthy exception—the watchman on Mount Seir (Isaiah xxi: 11-12), who alone among the inspired seers of Judah and of Israel frankly admitted that he did not know what was going to happen, and advised his followers to wait and see. His example might be followed with profit by all who attempt political prognostication. I speak advisedly, having made some bad guesses myself.

But Thompson, at this writing, has been in office two months and a half, and already some things have happened, while some other things may be predicted with reasonable confidence. In spite of all temptations to belong to other nations, he will be for America First (unless there is another war with Germany; or with Poland, or Czechoslovakia, or Africa). And he will have plenty of issues; they may not last long, but he will let go of them before they die on his hands. For like most artists he lives by inspiration, not by reason, and he seldom rides an inspiration till it gives out. He can always get another one, just as good.

For example. On the day after he took office he started on another trip to New Orleans to boost the Illinois Lakes-to-Gulf Waterway. The great Mississippi floods had then just begun, and that morning the *Tribune,* which has always fought Thompson, carried a cartoon of his steamboat traversing the flooded regions while farmers marooned on the housetops cried out for help. Big Bill looked at that and wired to his vassal Governor Len Small at Springfield to entrain a speedboat which Thompson happened to know the state possessed, and send it down to meet the Mayoral expedition at Cairo. "We *will* rescue somebody," he vowed, "and I'll be at the wheel of the speedboat myself."

I believe that hope was disappointed; Big Bill's triumphal progress down the river was as majestically slow as that of the crest of the flood, so everybody had been rescued before he got there. But this trip was not in vain; when a conference of statesmen, publicists, experts and others was presently convened to discuss the problem of flood relief and flood control, it met, not in New Orleans or Memphis or St. Louis, which had seen and felt the flood, but in Chicago; it was another jewel in the crown of William Hale Thompson.

On the first lap of this voyage, moreover, Big Bill delivered himself of another happy thought. Power was going to waste, he discovered, at city pumping stations; why could it not be used to operate ice machines, so that free ice could be given to the poor at no added cost to the municipality? (Where he would find the money to build the ice plants, he did not say.) And if delivery proved impracticable, could not the ice be laid out on platforms, for the poor to gather up and take home at their convenience? I should be astonished beyond measure if anything more were heard of this enterprise; yet some few voters may keep it in mind, and reflect that Big Bill must have been balked in his beneficent purpose by the Interests.

"Make Chicago Hum" is the slogan of the new administration; on which a skeptical evening paper commented, "Hum like a humbug." Yet I have heard shrewd observers suggest that there is a possibility—and this is a notion to which the beginnings of his administration have given some color—that he may spend his third term being the Best Mayor Chicago Ever Had.

On the morning after he took office he told me, "Last night thirteen people called me up to tell me they'd seen a cop patrolling a beat." That is a tabloid picture of an issue, perhaps, but this picture is not faked. There has been a considerable decrease in crimes of violence in Chicago since Thompson came back to power; and old-fashioned persons still hold that the prevention of crimes of violence is at least as important a function of government as improving the private morals of the citizenry.

"They've been stealing half a million dollars a day in this town," he exploded as he took office. "I'll stop that; I'll run the crooks and thieves and lawbreakers out of Chicago in ninety days—and then the reformers will try to get my Chief of Police indicted." Well, they can't indict him without the assent of State's Attorney Crowe, and as this is written Thompson and Crowe are like David and Jonathan. Before long they may be gunning for each other; life is like that, especially in Chicago. Certainly the number and the activity of crooks, thieves and lawbreakers was promptly and noticeably diminished after Thompson took hold; but I suspect that you might go out to Chicago and find that some few of them are still on the premises. But if you do find them, don't run to Big Bill with your story; he will have another issue by that time.

One of his campaign promises was repeal of the state search-and-seizure law. Toward making good on that he did all he could; a bill providing for a state-wide referendum on repeal passed the lower house of the legislature but was beaten in the state Senate. Virtually all the Chicago legislators supported it, but they were overwhelmed by the down-state farming interests, eager as farmers always are to annoy the wicked city fellers. Here was another moral victory for Thompson, for it is understood that the search-and-seizure law is not going to annoy Chicago very violently so long as he is Mayor; and where is the voter so blind as not to see Big Bill as his powerful bulwark of protection against agrarian oppression?

By the time you read this the water-meter question may be ancient history; but there is one issue that will stay there till it is settled—the transit question. "I will give the solution of this problem my best thought and energy," the Mayor promised in his inaugural. But some other people were already giving it their best thought and energy; among them Mr. Samuel Insull, owner of Chicago's gas and electric companies, heavily interested in the elevateds, and Mæcenas, by a curious coincidence, of Colonel Frank Smith, chairman of the State Utilities Commission. Shortly after Thompson came back a batch of bills were introduced in the state legislature to pave the way for unification of the transit lines and a resettlement of the whole question. Opponents of the bills asserted that they were drawn by Insull's lawyers, of which Mr. Insull's protest that they were drafted "at the instance of all the surface and elevated lines acting jointly" was no very effective denial. For it was noted that all relocation of gas mains and electric conduits necessitated by subway construction or alteration in the surface lines was to be paid for by the city, out of its traction fund; an expense which, but for this happy provision, must have been borne by Mr. Insull. The city was to be reimbursed, eventually, from the revenues of the traction lines; in other words, out of the fares of the straphangers.

There were other provisions of these bills which, whether laudable or otherwise, aroused the violent opposition of the *Tribune,* the City Club, the Municipal Ownership League, and others whom Mr. Insull unkindly termed "perennial objectors." Professor Charles E. Merriam, political philosopher, reform legislator, and occasional candidate for mayor, declared that these were "terms submitted to a conquered nation," worse than the Treaty of Versailles. But whatever the weight of the forces against them, among those persons

outspokenly in favor of the bills was the Honorable
William Hale Thompson. (Rates of fare were not mentioned in the bills; they were to be settled otherwise
and later. But it was observed during the campaign
that little was being said about his old dogma of the
five-cent fare.) Thompson himself spoke for the bills
before the state Senate; Thompson's deputations in the
legislature voted for them.

As I write this, the legislature is still wrangling over
this plan for the solution of the transit problem, and
it would be reckless to make predictions as to its fate.
But I venture, none the less, this one prophecy—if it
fails, it was Insull's plan. If it succeeds, it is Thompson's.

So with other things that are going on in Chicago.
The town needs a new and stupendous civic audito-
rium to take care of great conventions. That would
probably be built in the next four years, no matter
who was mayor; but Big Bill is behind it and it will
go into the next campaign booklet too. Chicago is moving ahead, working out the Chicago Plan; in fact about
all that any mayor need do to be a good mayor, from
the civic point of view, is to stand still and let the
Chicago Plan flow on around him. Whatever your esti-
mate of Big Bill's past contribution toward the working
out of that plan, he is not likely to squat in the way
and dam its flow.

There are new faces in the City Hall, and some old
faces. Many of Thompson's old gang are gone; of
those who survive, some are trusted and some are not.
Of the new men, some look trustworthy and some do
not. But if Big Bill runs out some of the crooks, leaves

the Volstead Act to the Federal prohibition agents, and lets subtler minds take hold of some of the more intricate problems of Chicago, he may go down in histories more impartial than campaign textbooks as Big Bill the Builder.

There is, to be sure, the overshadowing figure of Mr. Crowe, who is believed to have intentions of being the power behind the throne. Well, Fred Lundin was the power behind the throne once; but he has retired into the shadows and Big Bill is still in the spotlight. One thing is certain—the people who hate Thompson, or most of them, hate Crowe worse; the people who distrust Thompson distrust Crowe more profoundly. If it came to a fight between them Thompson would probably have most of the Better Element with him. But that need not worry him; he had the Better Element with him once before, and lived it down.

And whatever else happens in the next four years, you can be sure there will always be a good show at the City Hall, always a fresh picture on the front cover of the tabloid every morning. Big Bill learned from Lundin, if he did not already know it by instinct, that you have to make them stop and listen, in the light of the gasoline flare, before you can sell them the old Indian remedy.

PORTRAIT OF A CLERIC

O N Morningside Heights in the city of New York
a great Gothic church is rising, the Cathedral of
St. John the Divine. It was begun as long ago as 1892;
but in a whole generation the exertions of the pious—
the prosperous and pious, for this is an Episcopalian
cathedral—sufficed only to complete the choir and
crossing. For years this fragment towered magnificent
but incomplete, the product of an effort that seemed
to have spent itself.

But now the nave is building, the transepts are in
prospect, there is more than a hope that before long the
whole immense edifice will be completed, clear up to
the cross that tops the spire—five hundred feet above
the pavement, the cathedral boosters will tell you, six
hundred and fifty feet above tidewater [1]—one of the
three largest cathedrals in the world. Inevitably, it will
be a monument, a monument to the bishop who
achieved in a few weeks of driving effort what three
previous bishops had failed to accomplish in three decades. And he achieved it in accordance with the best of
precedent—the twelfth-century precedent of the great
age of cathedral building, when the whole community
was united in one grand endeavor; the Scriptural precedent of the man who, when his invited guests failed to
arrive, sent out into the byways and hedges and dragged
everybody in.

[1] Lately they have changed the design again, and this aspiration
to outdo the Tower of Babel has apparently been abandoned.

This was the great inspiration of the Right Reverend William Thomas Manning, Episcopal Bishop of New York—to sweep the whole twentieth-century community of New York, Catholic, Protestant, Jewish, and about one per cent Episcopalian, into a great twelfth-century crusade for the building of "a house of prayer for all people." It was—or is so far—the crowning achievement of a brilliant career. Bishop Manning, after all, is more than a cathedral builder. He is the champion of orthodoxy, defender of the faith, doughty upholder of the Virgin Birth, supporter of the Volstead Act, corrector of dogma and morals, extirpator of heresy; and withal an ecclesiastical statesman, if not in the thirteenth-century tradition, at least in that of the seventeenth. Bishop of the most opulent diocese in the most elegant of churches, he is still young as bishops go, and brighter glories may lie beyond. Enthusiastic after-dinner speakers have called him the First Citizen of New York, the First Churchman of America; without eliciting his visible disapproval, they have suggested him for the as yet non-existent office of Archbishop of the American Episcopal Church.

Upon what meat doth this our Bishop feed, that he hath grown so great? I reveal no guarded secrets, nor am I a psychographer to uncover the hidden springs of action; I merely study the public record open to all. But from this record one or two rather curious conclusions emerge. Notoriously the right reverend bishop owes his episcopal rank to that right irreverend layman, Mr. William Randolph Hearst. Moreover, Doctor Manning regards his church (when it is politic so to regard it) as "part of the ancient historic Catholic

Church"; and certainly it was in a Catholic spirit that
he drew all New York into the building of a cathedral
which is alleged to embody the community's spiritual
aspiration. But for the method which made the cathedral possible he is indebted to that notable Protestant
sectary, the Reverend Doctor Billy Sunday.

DOCTOR MANNING is presumably cognizant and ap-
proving of his biography as it appears in *Who's Who*.
In the American version of that volume the place of
his birth is not mentioned; in the English *Who's Who*
it is set down that he was born in Northampton, England. Tradition says that he came to this country with
his parents in boyhood and lived in Nebraska and
California before going for his secular and theological
education to the University of the South at Sewanee,
Tennessee. Hagiography has neglected those early
years, though there is a legend that the future bishop
once sold groceries. But it seems curious and ungrateful
that the English birthplace should have been omitted
from the American *Who's Who;* curious, since Doctor
Manning has never made any secret of his Anglophile
sympathies; ungrateful, since if he had not been born
in England he would not now be Bishop of New York.

In 1903 he came from Nashville to New York, as
vicar of one of the chapels of Trinity Parish, a small,
slight man, with no particularly impressive pulpit elo-
quence to overcome the handicap of his stature, but a
man with a good record, sound in theology from the
conservative point of view, endowed by marriage with
the modest wealth which a metropolitan clergyman
always finds useful. Within a year he was made assist-

ant rector of Trinity Parish, whose burdens lay heavy on the aged Dr. Morgan Dix; in 1908, upon Doctor Dix's death, he succeeded in due course to the rectorate.

Now Trinity is the wealthiest and most important parish in the country; its rector is the most powerful vassal of the Bishop of New York; with the vicars of his nine chapels bound to him by subinfeudation, he is a bigger man than many provincial bishops. Years before, the mere prospect of this succession had led Doctor Manning to refuse bishoprics in the comparative wilds. But he happened to inherit his fief at a moment when Trinity was feeling the claws of the muckrake. By ancient grants the corporation held much property in downtown New York, which the growth of the city had turned into slums. A tradition of two centuries held that Trinity's business was nobody else's business, and now magazines and newspapers were making a great noise about these private matters, alleging that Trinity's tenements were unfit to live in and that some of the tenants were persons quite unsuitable as residents on ecclesiastical property. In short, Trinity real estate had become a scandal.

Manning cleaned it up—without noise; indeed, with a pious pretense (in deference to the memory of his predecessors) that there was no need to clean up at all. Nevertheless, he did clean up; he ended the secrecy of centuries; he took away a reproach. And, incidentally, he left no doubt of his admirable feeling for etymology. A rector was a ruler, and the new rector of Trinity was going to rule.

It was different when he spoke on matters outside of Trinity Parish, with the prestige, little less than episcopal, which his position conferred. He became a leader of the Anglo-Catholic party which wanted to change the name of the Protestant Episcopal Church to the American Catholic Church. His defense of the "historical and unbroken continuity" of Catholic tradition made the Low Churchmen his enemies; and they beat him, at the diocesan convention of 1915, for delegate to the next year's General Convention—the first time in all history that a rector of Trinity had been defeated for an elective office. It was predicted, then, that the defeat would make him a bishop. But as matters turned out it took a good deal more than that to make him a bishop.

For in the next few years there rose the question of the Congregational Concordat—an arrangement by which Congregational preachers, having received Episcopal ordination, might minister to Episcopalians. To the Protestant mind there seems nothing so very terrible about this, since the Congregationalists had to become a sort of sub-caliber Episcopalians before they could be trusted with these ministrations; but it roused the ire of Anglo-Catholics—all but Manning. He was beginning to be deeply interested in ecclesiastical unity, and to his Catholic brethren it seemed that he was forgetting the ancient principle that ecclesiastical unity could be attained only by everybody becoming Catholic. When Manning came out for the Concordat, his Anglo-Catholic friends whetted their knives for the lost leader.

In 1919 Bishop Greer died and the rector of Trinity

was nominated for his seat. So was Doctor Stires of
St. Thomas's, the Low-Church candidate; so also was
Suffragan Bishop Burch. Burch was the long shot,
for all that he had been Greer's assistant; he had come
late to the priesthood, having spent his early life in
the godless occupation of editing a newspaper. None
the less Burch was elected—partly by the votes of the
rural clergy who rather distrusted that urban potentate, the rector of Trinity, but partly by the votes of
High Churchmen, who deserted Manning because they
felt that his Catholicity was not to be trusted whenever
a visible advantage appeared to lie in flirting with
Protestantism.

Also, by this time Manning had mai y enemies, within
and without the Church. Some of th em, outside especially, were highly to his credit. From the beginning
of the war he had been outspokenly pro-Ally and pro-
English. Many people dislike his war record; but unless you hold that the Germans were right, or that a
clergyman has no right to support any war, it is hard
to find much fault with it. If he was anti-Bolshevist,
it has yet to be proved that conservatism is a crime.
If he had an opinion, for publication, always on tap, so
did all men prominent enough to get their opinions
published. If he was infected by war hysteria, so was
everybody else during the war—not least the radicals
and pacifists who invented the term as a reproach for
their enemies. Most of them are war-hysterical still.

He served as volunteer chaplain at Camp Upton
and apparently would have gone to France if the age
limit had not barred him; and if he was rather ubiquitous around town in his khaki uniform, why, a good

many men were ubiquitous in uniform on the internal front who were kept out of the trenches through no fault of their own. Yet Manning made enemies—perhaps because he seemed just a little too virulent for a man of God, but partly because he was English-born and honestly believed that England was on the right side.

Now granted the fact, whether you like it or not, that foreign-born Americans are apt to retain some fondness for the Old Country, it does not appear why a privilege conceded to an American born in Italy or Ireland or Germany should be withheld from an American born in England. But New York is a peculiar city with peculiar institutions. Every New Yorker has, if he is wise, two fatherlands, his own and Ireland. Manning, the most prominent Anglo-American, inevitably incurred the hatred of the Irish and the abuse of the Hearst newspapers; but it took a grotesque episode just after the war to seal and ratify the enmity that was to be the making of his fortune.

THE war had ended in integral victory, and in that month before the Peace Conference met integral victory seemed to promise an integrated world. The one far-off divine event toward which the whole creation moved seemed visibly at hand; in that millennial dawn our returning army, victors at Armageddon, must be welcomed as triumphant crusaders. Accordingly Mayor Hylan appointed a Committee of Welcome which included about all the prominent citizens of New York; which included among others, and in no obscure position, Mr. William Randolph Hearst.

If it had been meant as a joke it would have marked Hylan as a greater man than Aristophanes; but, like all Hylan's humor, it was unintentional. He saw no reason why Hearst who had made Hylan did not deserve a chief place on any of Hylan's committees. But other citizens saw much reason why Hearst, with his familiar war record, was out of place on this particular committee. They resigned, one after another, with roars of disapproval; Doctor Manning resigned, roaring if anything louder than the rest. Those who resigned got up a rival organization, the Citizens' Committee of Welcome, on which Manning was in the foreground; and they proclaimed a mass meeting in Madison Square Garden to speak out the public reprobation of the iniquitous Hearst appointment.

That meeting turned out to be a grander jest than the appointment itself, the first forewarning of the great political discovery of 1919, that the millennium had been indefinitely postponed. Three or four thousand indignant patriots rattled around in the great open spaces of the Garden, their fiery fulminations interrupted by raucous shouts of "Hurrah for Hoist, de woikingman's friend." For Mr. Hearst's astute lieutenants had not only brought in several hundred deep-lunged civilians to offer a minority report; they even had on hand a detachment of the returning heroes who had caused all the hullabaloo, soldiers and sailors in uniform. And when an exasperated chairman demanded that all who sympathized with Hearst leave the hall, the heroes in uniform led the recessional. They may have come only from near-by training camps, they may have marched out to be fed at Hearst's expense; none the less they marched out, the meeting fell flat, and the Citizens' Committee of Welcome fell with it, never to rise again.

But from its ruins there was to spring, in the fullness of time, a Bishop of New York.

Bishop Burch died suddenly, little more than a year after his elevation. Again the diocesan delegates must elect a bishop, and again Manning was a candidate. Having failed through too much Protestantism, he had lately been very Catholic. Dr. Percy Stickney Grant of the Church of the Ascension—a radical, a pacifist, a Low Churchman, everything that Manning hated— had preached a sermon on divorce; and Manning had replied with a denunciation of Grant's views as no better than approval of free love. Grant was more or less of a maverick; but among Low Churchmen there was an uneasy feeling that Manning was already a little too episcopal in his pronouncements for one who was still a mere rector (if the rector of Trinity can be called a mere rector). On the other hand, High Church- men welcomed the returning prodigal. Doctor Carsten- sen, very high, observed that the diocese needed a bishop who would ride some of the straying brethren "with a curb bit." Everybody knew he meant Grant as the wild horse and Manning as the bronco buster.

At this moment some malignant spirit inspired the unhappy Grant, who knew well enough what was in store for him if Manning were made bishop, to warn the diocese against electing any but a native American. There may have been some echo of that feeling but, coming from Grant, the suggestion would probably have been laughed off. Fortunately for the Man of

Destiny, on the day of election it was no longer a suggestion from Grant but an order from Hearst.

That day the Hearst papers carried a huge black editorial headed: "Is An English Bishop Necessary? Why? Is There No Fit American?" It was illustrated with a picture of benighted African heathen rolling over and slapping their thighs to welcome a British explorer, and the Episcopalians of New York were asked if they meant to roll over and slap their thighs before Manning. In all solemnity, they were warned that this election would decide whether they were an American Church "or only an institution for pro-British propaganda." To make sure that the message reached the delegates, it had been telegraphed to every one of them; for good measure, newsboys were stationed at the door of the Synod House to give papers to all who entered. It was Hearst's reply to the Garden meeting, and a reply in kind; the meeting had been a flop, and so was the editorial.

This was a heated election; Catholic and Protestant factions in the church were ready for a fight. Chief among the Protestants was Dr. Leighton Parks of St. Bartholomew's, who denounced Catholicism of all sorts and asked if America was to remain America or become "a Roman Catholic Irish republic." The question had some point in those days, but it is rather hard to follow the line of thought that connected Ireland and Manning. At any rate, one of Manning's supporters countered by reading the Hearst pastoral from the platform, and from that time on the only question was whether the Low Churchmen feared Manning more than they hated Hearst.

The Protestant vote was divided between Slattery of Grace Church and Stires of St. Thomas's; on the second ballot Manning, supported by the High Churchmen, had a long lead. To unify the Protestant forces Stires withdrew, and then came the break. That Hearst editorial still rankled; some of Stires's supporters felt that it was not that they hated Catholicism less, but Hearst more; on the third ballot, Manning was elected. As surely as any Ghibelline nominee of a medieval emperor, he owed his see to a secular potentate. But one doubts if Mr. Hearst got much satisfaction out of it.

ONCE a Bishop, Doctor Manning began to behave very episcopally. He had opinions, and though he has never pretended to such omniscience as Dr. S. Parkes Cadman, he has this advantage over Cadman, that his opinions can be enforced by acts—when it seems expedient. The qualification is important.

For while our Bishop can be strict, he knows how to temper justice with mercy, or at least with caution. Perhaps, indeed, he is not by nature authoritarian at all. A psychographer might explain his tendencies toward autocracy in terms of his small physical stature, the compensating gesture of a man who has to stand on a box in a group photograph to look sufficiently impressive. If Napoleon had been six feet tall, Europe might have enjoyed unbroken peace after the Treaty of Amiens. But I am no psychographer; I can only report what our Bishop has done and said.

He supports the Volstead Act as zealously as any Methodist, but with the un-Methodist qualification that he does not regard temperate drinking as a sin. He is against it, but for social reasons. But go back a decade, and one finds evidence that he is a prohibitionist for other reasons as well.

In the diocesan convention of 1916, when Doctor Manning was still rector of Trinity, there appeared a resolution pledging the clergy to personal abstinence, support of existing excise laws, and work for local option in New York. (The Eighteenth Amendment, then, was only a millennial dream.) This proposal was the work of the Reverend James V. Chalmers, rector of a poor parish on the upper East Side, the most active of the few prohibitionists in the diocese. Chalmers was used to introducing his resolution, vainly, at every convention. Once more he introduced it, and supported it with a speech about the evils of drink among the poor; but obviously without much hope of its adoption.

Then up rose the powerful rector of Trinity, unknown as yet to the public as an outspoken dry, pleading for the resolution as a stroke of ecclesiastical statesmanship, to put the church in line with a moral movement. (Yes, the dry cause was still so regarded, in 1916.) "We have been asked," he said, "to do this for the poor; but I say we must do it for the Church and the power of the Church."

They did it. One recusant who dared to mention the miracle at Cana of Galilee was literally howled down. These Episcopalians had no such convenient dogma as comforts the evangelical sects, that the wine made at Cana was unfermented grape juice of the kind Mr. Bryan used to serve at diplomatic dinners; for all they knew on authority it was real wine. Nevertheless, the man who mentioned it was howled down and the resolution adopted by acclamation. It was Chalmers' resolution but Manning's victory; they had done it, not for the poor, but for the power of the Church. Manning had had the foresight to recognize that the water wagon was a band wagon, and he had swung the Church aboard.

On divorce, he has always held the Catholic position —that there is no such thing. A few years ago he appealed to Congress for a Federal divorce law, with a pretty strong intimation that his idea of the proper law was no divorce at all. But a little later he was urging the churches to unite against divorce, and recently he has so far weakened as to advocate love and forbearance in the home as the best remedy. One cannot help wondering if our Bishop, reflecting on the history of prohibition, is beginning to lose his faith in the efficacy of the secular arm.

But where his own arm can enforce obedience that arm is powerful, as none learned better than his old enemy, the luckless Grant. In 1921 Doctor Grant's engagement was announced to a lady who had two ex-husbands living. The Episcopal canon permits remarriage to the innocent party in a divorce for adultery, but Doctor Grant's fiancée had secured her second divorce on the unhallowed ground of desertion. Naturally, Bishop Manning forbade the clergy of his diocese to perform the marriage. There was much sympathy for the pair held apart by sacerdotal authority, especially as they were not so forgetful of the proprieties as to go on and get married by a city clerk or a

Presbyterian. After years of vain waiting for the Bishop to relent, the engagement was broken.

Meanwhile the martyred Grant was in more trouble. He preached a sermon which seemed to cast doubt on the divinity of Christ. Bishop Manning promptly ordered him to recant, resign, or be tried for heresy. Liberals of all faiths and of no faith at all rallied around the menaced Grant, champion of religious freedom against dogmatic intolerance and episcopal tyranny; they were all set for a fight but their hero ran out on them. He replied to the Bishop in a long letter which sounded as if it had been written by a highly competent lawyer. Expert theologians read it through and remained in doubt whether Grant had recanted. The one thing sure was that he had not resigned.

Well, then—a heresy trial? In that excited period, men said it would split the Church. Would the Bishop risk it? The Bishop announced that he would—against any clergyman whose denial of the divinity of Christ was "clear, courageous, and unambiguous." This was hint enough for the prudent Grant, whose further utterances could not possibly be described by these adjectives; and the equally prudent Bishop, having enforced what Mayor Gaynor used to call outward order and decency, did not see fit to search the underbrush for latent heresy. In due time Grant resigned on the plea of ill health, and Doctor Manning was left in the serenity of one who has seen four-and-twenty leaders of revolts.

The iron hand in the velvet glove caressed, about this same time, Dr. William Norman Guthrie, of St.

Mark's in the Bouwerie, who had taken to adorning his services with eurhythmic dances and picturesque bits of assorted symbolism. One Sunday, when barefoot girls danced in his edifice, the police reserves had to be called out to handle the crowd. The Bishop ordered him to desist from these pagan practices, and when he was stubborn, withdrew episcopal ministration from his parish. St. Mark's threatened to secede from the Church; once more excited liberals rallied round the persecuted victim; but once more they had picked a poor hero. Guthrie's dances, however satisfactory to the religious sense of Aztecs and Hindus, seemed a little inappropriate, even to Unitarians, in a Christian church. Presently the vestry of St. Mark's came down like Davy Crockett's coon, and the offending Guthrie came down with them.

Meantime another issue had been met with Christian tolerance and diplomacy. Doctor Manning has always been a Fundamentalist and frank about it. Proclaiming that there is no conflict between faith and science, no harm in evolution, he has still declared that "Christianity stands or falls with the facts about Jesus Christ, His supernatural birth, His bodily resurrection, His ascension into Heaven. If these things did not happen, the Christian gospel ceases to have reality or meaning; the whole truth of the New Testament disappears."

In 1923 the bishops uttered a pastoral letter laying down these basic dogmas, and pointed the declaration by threatening to try for heresy an obscure Texas rector who was suspect on the Virgin Birth. Thereupon Manning's ancient foe, Dr. Leighton Parks, told his flock of St. Bartholomew's that the bishops had no

authority to fix dogmas, that there was Scriptural justification for denial of the Virgin Birth, and (most un-
kindest cut of all) that if he wanted to know about
this much-talked-of Catholic tradition he would ask
no Episcopal bishop, but Cardinal Hayes.

Was Doctor Parks tried for heresy? He was not.
He had frankly told his flock one reason why he would
not be tried—that Bishop Manning's delicacy would
restrain him from proceeding against an old antagonist.
Perhaps this explains the immunity which Doctor
Parks actually enjoyed, but bishops were stayed by no
such personal scruples in the great age of the Church.
St. Bartholomew's is a great and rich parish, where
heresy might be supposed to be more dangerous than in
Texas. But Doctor Parks had not personally and ex-
plicitly denied the Virgin Birth; and Doctor Manning
was getting ready to build a cathedral.

THROUGH the war years it had been understood that
whoever was bishop after the war would have to do
something about the cathedral. But great and good
men had been trying to do something about it for thirty
years, with no noteworthy result. There was plenty of
Episcopalian money in New York but most of it was
still *in situ;* it was not flowing into the cathedral.
What was to be done? Well, there was Scriptural precedent, when the chosen people had shown themselves
unworthy of everlasting life, for turning unto the
Gentiles.

How was it to be done? The Reverend Doctor Billy
Sunday had shown the way. When that powerful vessel

of the Spirit preached in New York in 1917 he had
had only partial support from the Episcopalians. Doctor Manning was one of many who had held aloof—
quite reasonably, for he did not believe in that kind of
religion; quite honorably, for he merely remained silent,
offering no obstacle to the good work, if any. But no
thoughtful man could overlook the lessons of the Sunday campaign as it actually worked out.

It was known that many evangelical clergymen held
about the same opinion of Doctor Sunday's kind of
religion as did the rector of Trinity but, not being the
rector of Trinity, they did not dare stand aside. They
had to go with the crowd, and shout louder than anybody to avert suspicion. In other words, the evangelical
clergy could be stampeded; they dared not stay off any
band wagon which proclaimed itself the vehicle of the
Good Cause.

Quite as important, the newspapers could be stampeded. Few New York editors and publishers felt any
sympathy, temperamental or intellectual, with the Sunday evangel; but they knew that many of their readers
did, so the newspapers ran before the great wind of
that revival. What was possible to Billy Sunday ought
to be easy for the Bishop of New York; and it was.

It remained to find a formula, and the Bishop found
it in a phrase in the constitution of his cathedral—"a
house of prayer for all people." What did that mean?
In the twelfth century, the great age of cathedral
building, it could be taken literally; for all people,
then, were loyal to the One Church; a whole community could be united in a great common endeavor to

build a Gothic cathedral, because a Gothic cathedral
in those days expressed the highest aspirations of all
men.

But twentieth-century New York is not Gothic;
twentieth-century New York is split up among a hundred religions, and only about one per cent of its
inhabitants belong to Doctor Manning's church. The
other ninety-nine per cent. had to be dragged in somehow. The Catholics could not be counted on for much
more than benevolent neutrality, but then Catholics as
a rule are not wealthy. There is much Protestant money
in New York and more Jewish money; and Jews could
be flattered, Protestants could be coerced—if it could
be made to appear that it was not Manning's cathedral,
not an Episcopalian cathedral, but everybody's cathedral, "a house of prayer for all people."

It was an act of faith to believe that a twelfth-century campaign was possible in twentieth-century New
York; but it was an act of genius to put it over, and
put it over by sheer assertion.

No one could doubt our Bishop's Americanism after
observing his truly American approach to this problem.
He began to talk about the size of his cathedral, five
hundred feet above the street, six hundred and fifty
feet above tidewater, one of the two or three biggest
cathedrals in the world. "New York," he said, "needs
and must have a building to represent religion on a
scale equal to the structures which represent the other
great interests of our life, business, educational, social."

After Bigness, Organization. The job of raising the
money was entrusted to a firm of professionals, willing
to raise money for any good cause for a fair fee, plus

expenses. The whole town was organized, committees in every parish, in every sect, in every industry, rival committees which were to meet and report each day at a pep luncheon while the drive went on. The evangelical clergy lined up for the good cause; the newspapers took it all at face value. Non-Episcopalians, unfellow-shipped in "the ancient historic Catholic church," were allowed to take the lead; Elihu Root, a Presbyterian, headed the general committee. For this is not our cathedral, it is your cathedral, everybody's cathedral, a house of prayer for all people.

In the enthusiasm of getting started, nobody asked what that meant. It would have been indelicate and at times hazardous. For while Episcopalians are not numerous, even in New York, they are rich and power-ful, not to be lightly offended; and the example of Billy Sunday had been followed with such success that every-body was climbing on the band wagon. This time, at last, it was Manning's own band wagon.

The drive started with a great mass meeting in Madison Square Garden. The lesson of that anti-Hearst meeting had been taken to heart; no danger, this time, of an empty house; thirteen thousand tickets had been distributed among the Episcopal parishes (another idea borrowed from Billy Sunday.) The theme announced by the brazen trumpet of episcopal declaration was taken up by the muted strings of a hundred minor pulpits and the dulcet woodwind of sob stories con-tributed by an able press agent; it thundered in the battery of every newspaper editorial page—"a home for the spiritually homeless," "a great common church expressing the aspiration of all New York."

It went over with a whoop, a community crusade in the best twelfth-century manner. There were even—take it on the authority of New York's most sober newspaper—miracles, two or three of them. Whether they too were provided by the press service of the drive, or appeared to the pious eye of the feature writer, I do not know; but if you believe what you see in the papers, miracles there certainly were.[2] Whether everybody swallowed the miracles may be doubted, but everybody who counted swallowed the cathedral.

Nothing in the way of a donation, said Doctor Manning, would be declined; and with one exception, to be noted presently, nothing ever was. But each could contribute his tithe in kind. For the cathedral, comedians capered on the stage and hockey players performed in the Garden; Paavo Nurmi and Willie Ritola broke records *ad majorem Dei gloriam;* and President Coolidge contributed good wishes, framed in these well-chosen words: "I trust that the efforts being made for this purpose will meet with the success its importance warrants."

From each his own offering, to each his own reward. The funds raised by hockey games and track meets, for instance, were attributed to the Sports Bay, a great pictorial window expressing the joyful labors of amateur athletes. Humanitarian protests have forced a change in the design, the excision of a picture of a sportsman shooting a live pigeon; but it does not

[2] The man who got these miracles into the newspapers—a most competent man he is, too—is now working for the firm of money raisers who put over the campaign. Whether his miracles are repeaters I do not know.

appear that the money, if any, contributed by pigeon shooters has been declined.

Then there is a Journalism Bay, to be honored with the name of the late Frank A. Munsey. Considering the esteem in which Mr. Munsey was and is generally held by newspapermen, this is about as tactful as dedicating a hypothetical Bill of Rights Bay to Wayne B. Wheeler, or the actual Women's Transept to Bluebeard. But Mr. Munsey left a heavy contribution to the Journalism Bay.

Money was being raised by the million; not much from Catholics, though there were well-advertised contributions from Catholics holding elective office, but Jews and evangelical Protestants fell over one another to reach the table which waited in vain for most of the invited guests. Indeed, some three weeks after the drive started, George W. Wickersham, Vice Chairman of the Citizens' Committee, himself an Episcopalian and addressing other Episcopalians, saw fit to observe, "I have been wondering sometimes of late if we are going to let our Presbyterian and Methodist friends build the cathedral."

Other people had been wondering that too, as the campaign went on, but this was the first time it had ever been said by a member of the organization. The first time, and the last; for whatever reason, Mr. Wickersham made no further public appearance in the cathedral drive.

BUT where was the *advocatus diaboli?* He was there, but for a long time his discordant squawk was drowned in the chorus of praise.

The first protests dealt with an apparent triviality. Gothic architecture was the natural flowering of the twelfth-century, the great cathedral age; it expressed, then, the highest ideal, an ideal actually common to all. But captious persons complained that in twentieth-century New York, with a diversity of religions and an adequately significant native architecture, a Gothic cathedral was at best an anachronism.[3]

And at worst it was something very dubious indeed. For Gothic architecture expressed twelfth-century religion, the religion of that "ancient historic Catholic Church" that Bishop Manning used to talk about. That kind of religion was meaningless or abhorrent to the Jews and evangelical Protestants who were contributing so heavily to the Cathedral of St. John the Divine; it was alien, even, to Low-Church Episcopalians. If this was really our great common church, its form ought to express such ideals as our time holds with measurable approach to unanimity; if it meant what it seemed to mean, how could it be a house of prayer for all people? (Especially as the architect in charge was that belligerent synthetic Goth, Mr. Ralph Adams Cram, himself so twelfth-century-Catholic that he makes even Manning look like a Baptist.)

These observations were made, however, by unchurched infidels, echoed by the lately chastised Guthrie of St. Mark's in the Bouwerie, who put in a feeble plea for "American architecture." But there was on record

[3] These objections, of course, apply *a fortiori* to the Gothic church now being built in Riverside Drive for Dr. Fosdick's congregation of Modernist Baptists. So far as architectural relevance goes, that church might as well be a replica of the Parthenon or the Temple of Karnak.

Doctor Manning's denunciation of a proposal for a sky-scraper cathedral in Chicago ("a poor imitation of the Woolworth Building with a cathedral concealed some-where inside"); and, more powerfully, there was the fact that the Cathedral of St. John the Divine, a quarter finished, was already Gothic. Once, painfully, it had been altered from Romanesque; it could hardly be altered again. And meanwhile another issue had come up.

A fortnight after the campaign started Bishop Manning published the news of the princely gift of half a million dollars from John D. Rockefeller, Jr., a Baptist. The next day Mr. Rockefeller published something the Bishop had forgotten, the correspondence preced-ing the gift. It is amazingly interesting; its most inter-esting passage, however, escaped public comment, though without doubt certain Anglo-Catholic clergy-men kept it, and pondered it in their hearts. Doctor Manning, once the apostle of Anglo-Catholicism, had called his cathedral "the common center and rallying point of Protestant Christianity."

Protestant Christianity! This is the Manning who had said, "The word Protestant reflects the contro-versial spirit of a bygone age; we have progressed be-yond it." But evidently we can retrogress back to it when it is a question of half a million Baptist dollars. Is there not high authority for making friends with the Mammon of Unrighteousness?

Concession to Mammon, however, has its limits, as the correspondence disclosed. Mr. Rockefeller had been "deeply impressed" by what the Bishop had said and written to him (Doctor Manning, evidently, had worked for that donation) "about the broad purpose of the cathedral." In furtherance of that catholic (with a small c) purpose, Mr. Rockefeller suggested: "Since a large minority of the funds which have already gone into the cathedral has come from members of other churches, it would seem but fitting that this large outside friendly interest should be represented by the election of a small number of laymen of sister churches to the Board of Trustees." Mr. Rockefeller desired to express the hope that this might be done, "if not now, in the near future." But he did not make that a condition of his gift.

Bishop Manning, replying, said that "we may certainly hope, and we should also pray and believe," for church unity; but "the time has not yet arrived," and "any attempt prematurely to force such an arrangement would retard the cause of unity rather than aid it." Now Rockefeller had said nothing about church unity; he had talked only about minority representation of other churches among the trustees of the cathedral. But Manning, after knocking down the straw man, came back to the point. "The clause" (expressing Rockefeller's pious hope) "that you add to your gift imposes no obligation, legal or moral, on the trustees. This being the case, we accept the more gratefully your generous pledge of $500,000."

If that formula of acceptance is not law-proof, then there are no good lawyers in the Episcopal Church.

None the less, Rockefeller had taken off the lid. The newspapers, which hitherto had refused to print criticisms of the cathedral, had to admit them now; especially as just after accepting Rockefeller's five hundred thousand Doctor Manning sent back a modest contribution of five hundred from the offending Guthrie —the only contribution, so far as recorded, that he ever refused. The contrast was a little too pointed; and Rockefeller had given respectability to those who were beginning to wonder just what was meant by his sonorous phrase, "a house of prayer for all people."

Low-Church clergymen and magazines supported his argument; they cited the fact that the Episcopal Cathedral in Washington had actually had trustees of other faiths. One of their organs, asking what a house of prayer for all people really meant, pointed out that if it meant only that anyone who felt the need could go in and pray, that function was performed by every church of every faith in the country. In vain did Bishop Manning declare that "the true and fine meaning of the phrase is understood by all." The inveterate Parks, disclosing the fact that he was not whooping up the cathedral drive in his parish, declared flatly that "this is not a house of prayer for all people." As the discussion became acrimonious, the forthright Carstensen —he who had once demanded the curb bit for Percy Grant, and not in vain—was goaded into blurting out, "It is not for all kinds of prayer or all kinds of people." In other words, it was for all people who were willing to pray like Episcopalians.

Now no one could have objected if the Episcopalians had said, "We want to build ourselves a cathedral and should gratefully receive any contributions that brethren of other faiths might care to offer." But when they said, "It is not our cathedral, it is your cathedral," when in fact it was and remained their cathedral—

why, if the merchandiser had been any but a Bishop, offering holy wares, this would have seemed perilously like misrepresentation of the quality of the goods.

But what of the secular press, that informed guide of public opinion? The secular press, with one exception, ducked the argument, aside from a few pious platitudes about sympathy and understanding. The exception was the *World*, New York's great moral newspaper, so pathetically eager to support all worthy causes, and so recklessly precipitate in picking them out. Just as the *World* later recanted its support of the turpitudinous Vera Cathcart, in whose behalf it had printed chapters from the New Testament as editorials, so now it came out valorously with the editorial second thought, "Bishop Manning Should Reconsider."

In response, presumably, to this warning (the etiology can doubtless be verified in the *World Almanac*) the Bishop did indeed unbend. Not to the point of admitting trustees of other faiths; gently he asked if anyone would wish to see the cathedral change its statutes "of immemorial standing" (fifty years) in connection with the acceptance of a large sum of money. To which obviously the answer was, Not if it can get the money otherwise. But he preached at the Fifth Avenue Presbyterian Church, declaring that "the time has come for a new synthesis of the deep religious values represented by all Christian communions" (though not for minority representation on the cathedral board). In May, when the intensive campaign was over, when ten million dollars had been raised and more was in sight, new trustees were to be chosen. Low Churchmen proposed that Rockefeller, a

Baptist, and Root and Arthur Curtiss James, Presbyterians, should be elected. But all the vacancies were filled by Episcopalians. Rockefeller had the best of the argument and Manning had the money; presumably, each was content.

It must not be supposed, however, that the contributory evangelicals got nothing. Doctor Manning actually held three interdenominational services, inviting evangelical clergymen, mere godly laymen according to Episcopal doctrine, to preach in the house of prayer for all people. By pure accident of ritual, it chanced that their unordained feet did not tread the holy ground of the sanctuary; but they preached from the pulpit. After that who could doubt that it was everybody's cathedral, even if the Episcopalians did continue to own and operate it? "The discussion," said the Bishop, "has cleared the air; let us hope it will stay clear." By way of further clarification a *Times* editorial added, "Those who do not wish to contribute may with propriety keep quiet."

So the cathedral is rising, expressing the common ideals of our great city (though now that the intensive campaign is over, nobody seems to know just what they are). There have been no interdenominational services lately, but it is a safe bet that there will be, if, as, and when required. For money is still needed for the cathedral, and Jews and evangelical Protestants still have it.

Meanwhile our Bishop (now that Grant is dead and Guthrie in eclipse) beams with brotherly love. Whether, in the view of a High-Church bishop, Jews can be saved, is a question I am not competent to consider;

but at least they have their reward here below. The gloomy Dean Inge, when in New York lately, asked why the Jews should want to rebuild Zion; let them rather, he suggested, build a new Temple of Solomon in New York. With laudable promptitude Doctor Manning came to the defense of the persecuted people; "the broadmindedness and public spirit of the Jews of this city have been conspicuously shown"—how? You have guessed it. "By their generous gifts to the Cathedral of St. John the Divine." Doctor Manning even went so far as to risk the charge of platitudinarianism; "many," he added, "of my best friends are Jews."

And for a compliment on the other side, one may refer to the Reverend Doctor Billy Sunday, who has spoken with approval of the cathedral—"a big church" —and of its builder. "Bishop Manning is one of the finest fellows going. He is true blue, foursquare on God and the Bible."

One pious hope has not been realized; before the drive started Doctor Manning declared that "the building of the cathedral will not in any way lessen the support given to other good causes, but will have the opposite effect." In fact, the cathedral campaign practically sank, for months, the ten-million-dollar drive for the Presbyterian Hospital, since salvaged from the depths by great effort; and most ironically that campaign was in the hands of the same firm of money raisers who got their due profit out of the Cathedral of St. John the Divine. But the cathedral is the house of God; the hospital, serving only man, could well be compelled to wait. Man, indeed, does not seem to count

for much in the Bishop's view of the universe. There
are wide green lawns in the cathedral close, and in the
old days, before Doctor Manning was in charge, babies
from the near-by apartment houses were allowed to
play there. Now they are kept out—put out by the care-
takers, if by some mischance they get in anyway;
which might seem a little hard to reconcile with a well-
known utterance of Jesus. But Jesus, of course, was
not a Bishop.

Meanwhile the cathedral rises, a monument to the
man of vision who got contributions from all people for
a house of prayer owned by only one per cent of the
people, who put religion over in a big way. It will be a
beautiful building, if you like Gothic architecture; an
impressive building, if you do not require architecture
that expresses something of the life around it. Beyond
doubt, the hopes and prayers and sacrifices of thousands of humble Christians, the true salt of the earth,
have gone into it; people who know what their
cathedral means to them and have never read the legal
tortuosities of the Bishop's reply to Rockefeller. And
beyond doubt some spiritual uplift has been felt by
evangelical clergymen who hug to their bosoms the con-
descension of those three interdenominational services,
by Jews who reflect that the bishop counts them among
his best friends.

In the fullness of time our Bishop (he may be an
Archbishop by then) will be gathered to his reward;
but the cathedral will remain. Perhaps his monument
may be more enduring than his brass.